# THE GOOD

UNLEASHED

# THE BAD &THE

# RUGBY

# THE GOOD

UNLEASHED

# THE BAD & THE

# RUGBY

**ALEX PAYNE**

**JAMES HASKELL**

**MIKE TINDALL**

HarperCollins*Publishers*

HarperCollins*Publishers*
1 London Bridge Street
London SE1 9GF

www.harpercollins.co.uk

HarperCollins*Publishers*
Macken House, 39/40 Mayor Street Upper
Dublin 1, D01 C9W8, Ireland

First published by HarperCollins*Publishers* 2024
This edition published 2025

1 3 5 7 9 10 8 6 4 2

Halo, horns and rugby ball graphics (title page, part
and chapter openers): Shutterstock.com

A catalogue record of this book is
available from the British Library

ISBN 978-0-00-871272-3

Printed and bound in the UK using 100%
renewable electricity at CPI Group (UK) Ltd

MIX
Paper | Supporting
responsible forestry
FSC™ C007454
FSC
www.fsc.org

This book contains FSC™ certified paper and other controlled sources to
ensure responsible forest management.

For more information visit: www.harpercollins.co.uk/green

**AP:** To my darling wife Corks, and my four kids – Martha, Harry, Mike and James. Thank you for keeping me centred – the pick-me-ups, the put-downs, the side-swipes, the bring-arounds and, most importantly, the hugs. You all know who does what. It's never boring, in either camp. May that forever be the case.

**JH:** To my daughter Bodhi.

**MT:** I would like to dedicate this book to the loyal fans of the show and the incredible *GBR* production team. Six years ago we had no idea where this journey would take us. It has been a wild rollercoaster with so many highs, but its fair share of lows; however, due to both our amazing listeners and the ninja team behind the scenes, we have managed to stay on the tracks and create something that we are all really proud of. So it's a huge thank you from me and, of course, a massive thank you to my family – mainly for putting up with the other two and allowing us to create this mad and crazy thing!

# CONTENTS

## THE GOOD

## THE BAD

## THE RUGBY

# THE GOOD

# 1

# IN THE BEGINNING

**Alex Payne:** I had a mental spreadsheet mapping out my life until I was 65: I'd turn up every Saturday and present rugby; I'd say, 'Hello, how are you?', ask the guests a few questions, then throw to the game; and after the game, I'd say, 'Thanks for watching, see you next week, goodbye …'

So when Sky nudged me out of the door in 2018, it absolutely skittled me. I'd spent 20 years very much working for 'the man'. I was literally branded. My Twitter handle was @skysportsalexp and my parents would call me 'Sky Sports' Alex Payne', insinuating that not only was that job my whole identity, but also that I'd grown too big for my boots. But now when I walked into a room, I was no longer that guy who had the supposedly dream job presenting on Sky. I had no idea who or what I was meant to be anymore.

I was steeped in rugby and had got to know quite a few people in the game, but nothing new had come up, rugby-wise, in the couple of months after I left. I was starting to think, 'What am I gonna do?' Then I got a call that would lead to my life being turned on its head.

The call was from an Irish digital company called Joe Media, who wanted me to be part of a rugby podcast they were planning to set up. When I met them, their idea was still just a sketch, but they were very keen and open to ideas. So when they started going through the kinds of people they were after for the podcast – all great players who were coming towards the ends of their careers, but not the sort of big personalities who could carry a weekly show – I raised an eyebrow and said, 'I'd get James Haskell, because he's the noisiest person in the sport, leads a mad life, knows everyone, tells very funny stories and takes his work seriously. He will take you to places those other people can't reach.'

The other person I had in mind was Mike Tindall, who ticked a lot of boxes. Not only was he a bona fide legend of the sport, having won the World Cup with England in 2003 (when I was still a work experience kid at Sky), but he also led an extraordinary life and knew lots of famous and interesting people, having married into the royal family in 2011. We'd also worked together at Sky, and we had a couple of mutual friends, so he made a lot of sense.

It goes without saying that 'Hask' and 'Tins' are competitive, because they've played rugby at the very highest level, but I also had a burning desire to succeed, in my own quiet way. Sky Sports has evolved over the years, so that nowadays there are more personality-led productions. But when I started at Sky over 20 years ago, most of their presenters were fairly identikit. We were all dressed the same, in Sky branded gear, and they trained us to be heard (although not too much) and not really seen. Our opinions counted for nothing; we were there to ask questions and bring the best out of everybody else.

Podcasts had been around a while at this stage, although they were nowhere near as big as they are now. But if I was going to do this podcast, I wanted it to be the best in the business. And I didn't think that would be the case unless Hask and Tins came on board with me.

While Tins was still thinking about whether he wanted to be involved or not, Joe Media suddenly decided they wanted to record the first show, in autumn 2018. So the first ever *House of Rugby*, as it was called then, was me, Hask and former England sevens captain Rob Vickerman, who also had a career as a pundit and commentator. Former England lock Nick Kennedy was the third man in episode two, before Tins made his first appearance in episode four.

Tins had lots of other things going on, including waving from palace balconies, so didn't really need the podcast, but I think he was looking for something regular to get stuck into. And while Tins and Hask weren't great mates, they obviously knew and had a huge amount of respect for each other. They were two alpha males, so I think there was an element of eyeing each other up and thinking, 'Yeah, I reckon the two of us could make this work.'

There was a bit of chopping and changing in those early days, but once Tins realised how much fun it was to work with Hask, he went all-in. It wasn't just the two hours' recording the podcast that was fun, it was the preamble, which is still the case today. The other day, we recorded an episode of our spin-off show *The Lock-In*. While Tins and I were waiting for Hask to turn up, we engaged in the usual idle chat about our week – wives, kids, other work. But when Hask finally came bundling into the studio, drama ensued. He'd come straight from jury service in north London, where he'd fought with the parking attendant, fought with the clerk of the court and been sworn at by a pensioner who thought he was trying to hog proceedings. In one morning, he'd hoovered up more ridiculous stories than most of us accrue in a year.

I'm sure people wonder why Tins would want to get mixed up with such a dramatic character, given his royal connections. But you have to remember that members of the royal family are accustomed to dealing with drama on a grand scale, and Tins has dug his own grave on a few occasions. So while Tins is naturally quite laid-back, and he might occasionally roll his eyes at Hask's antics, he can empathise with Hask more than most. People say you shouldn't play with fire – but playing with fire, while potentially disastrous, can be quite a lot of fun.

Hask had to get a car down from Northampton to London and record for two hours, before heading straight back up again. He wouldn't do it now, not for love nor money, but he was coming towards the end of his playing career and wanting to put some foundations in place before hanging up his boots.

There wasn't much money involved in the beginning, but Hask is savvier than most sportspeople. Others would have looked at the cash on offer and said no immediately, especially if it meant two hours' travel each way on a Monday, but Hask took a long-term view. He knew that if he turned his nose up at the opportunity, it might not present itself again in retirement. He also realised that he had a big enough personality to make the podcast a roaring success, which would mean more money coming in eventually.

Hask has taken a lot of crap down the years, since being dubbed 'Brand Haskell' by the media and Sir Ian McGeechan way back when, but rugby doesn't set people up for life. As such, it's far better to try other things and risk being mocked for it than doing nothing and getting lost in retirement.

**James Haskell:** When my agents (I forget who they were, I've had more than the FBI) told me about this podcast, I was still playing for and living in Northampton. It would have meant travelling to London and back every Monday, when I should have been resting up after a game, and I didn't feel like I was able to speak about stuff as openly as perhaps I would have wanted. I didn't want to criticise my fellow players or cause trouble of any kind. But the money was decent, so my agents kept negotiating.

What piqued my interest was when they told me that 'Payno' – or Alex Payne, respected journalist for Sky TV as he was known back then – was going to be involved. I'd been aware of Payno since I was a teenager coming through the England age groups and was always blown away by how professional he was. I'd even ask him for advice if I had any media stuff coming up.

As for the third person, a few names were being bandied around, including Mike Tindall. I played with Tins and went to his wedding, but I wasn't that close to him; we were mates but nothing like we are now. We always got on well, but he had quite a stark Yorkshire exterior, and I could never really tell what he thought of me. So when his name came up, I didn't leap up and say, 'Oh wow, that would be great!' Plus, while I knew Tins had lots of good stories, and told them well, I wondered if he'd be happy telling the more bawdy ones in public, given his royal connections. And how comfortable would he be sitting next to me while I was gobbing off?

My agents had negotiated a car to drive me to and from London every week, so I eventually signed up to do something like six months. But I didn't really know what I was getting myself into. I'd done other people's podcasts, but this was completely new. When I turned up to the studio, they'd built a set, which I think was meant to be my front room (as in *House of Rugby*). I soon realised that I'd blocked the producer Simon, an old BBC hack, on Twitter, presumably because of something he'd said about me. I liked Simon in person, and he was an excellent producer, but we weren't obvious bedfellows. Politically, he was slightly left of Lenin – in another life, he'd have probably tried to purge me – but we recorded the first show with Rob Vickerman on board and went from there.

I agreed to do the podcast because it offered consistency, both in terms of routine and money, but it was a slog in the early days. I was struggling with injury and not always playing as well as I'd like, and sometimes I'd go to bed on a Sunday night thinking, 'I really can't be bothered going down to London tomorrow.' But once Tins started appearing regularly and the present line-up established itself, I started to really enjoy it. I felt comfortable with the two of them and I realised we were doing something different. Yes, we were primarily a rugby podcast for rugby people, but it wasn't nausey, it was light-hearted and funny. And while we were honest, we weren't chucking people under buses.

**Mike Tindall:** Having retired from rugby in 2014, I moved on to the coaching staff at Gloucester. But when the head coach got sacked, I knew the new guy would bring in a whole new team, so I decided to take a year off. I started doing ambassadorial stuff for various companies and organising charity events, and at the end of that year, I realised I didn't need or want a full-time coaching job. Coaching pays terribly, and I was quite happy doing things away from rugby.

The podcast was only one day a week, and I was doing bits and pieces in London anyway. It was an evening record, so getting back to Gloucestershire would be a bit of a ball-ache, but I happened to be quite free at the time. And while the money wasn't great, Payno said it would be 40 shows a year, which meant regular income.

I was over my retirement by then. In fact, my playing days already seemed like a distant memory. I missed the occasion of big match days, the changing room fun and the routine, but the game already felt very different to when I played it.

However, I still loved watching and talking about the game, and the podcast would be an opportunity to do that while making a few quid.

People think that every England World Cup winner retired from the game is loaded, but it's a complete fallacy. When I married into the royal family in 2011, people thought I was doubly loaded, but that was simply not the case.

England's World Cup winners had a 20-year reunion in 2023, and not everyone in that room was in the same boat. A few of the guys were struggling financially, one or two were struggling with their health, quite a few had been forgotten by the public. That's why I regard myself as one of the lucky ones.

I was a bit lost for about six months after retiring. No longer being in a work environment where there was structure and support, and I was always told what to do, was strangely hard to deal with. Coming out of the sport I felt like one of the lucky ones, having achieved what I had in rugby and then I married an amazing person, who happened to be a world-class athlete too. Obviously she is a member of the royal family, which kept me in the public eye more than most ex-rugby players, but I also worked hard to build and maintain work opportunities I had created in the last few years of my career, which helped hugely.

I'd heard lots of stories about Hask long before I first played with him for England. He arrived at a time when players who were a bit different were viewed with suspicion, so when that stuff came out about his dad trying to turn him into 'Brand Haskell', the papers had a field day. Ironically, Hask was professionalism personified. No one worked harder than him and he took looking after your body to a whole new level. And when I first met him, I quickly realised that underneath all the bombast was a really good guy, as well as an insecure and sensitive one. He wore his heart on his sleeve and was very opinionated, but comments from the other lads could hurt him – he'd bristle or suddenly go quiet – and he cared deeply about doing right by the team.

I never clashed with Hask at club level (although I always remind him about how I stopped him scoring what would have been the try of his life at Gloucester), and we always got on well in an England environment, but we were never close friends. All the same, I could see that we were similar in some ways. I was a people pleaser when I was younger, desperate to be liked, and I could see that in Hask. We'd both been bashed by the tabloids and people in social media, which had made us more streetwise and cynical. We worked out that the stuff that gets written in papers and on Twitter isn't important. You can't please everyone, it's not possible, so you've got to have the attitude, 'What do the important people in my life think of me? If they're saying the same as people in the papers and on social media, then maybe I need to change. But if they're not, then I'm probably doing okay.'

On a more basic level, Hask was an enormous personality and always very funny. So when Payno said he was after Hask for the podcast as well, I decided to get on board. Nothing was ever going to replace playing rugby with your mates every day, but there were worse ways to spend a Monday evening.

# 2

# THE SECRET SAUCE

**AP:** *House of Rugby*'s sponsor was Guinness, which is about as chunky as sponsors come, and we'd achieved the metrics they'd set for us (downloads, audience engagement, followers, chart position etc.) for 40 shows after just a month. The show was unscripted and raw, but mostly in those early days we stuck to who had done what in such and such a game. It was a rugby podcast, first and foremost. Then one week, we all got quite pissed on Guinness and the show, as it is now, revealed itself for the first time: three friends with a love of rugby talking about anything and everything.

A few months into 2019, what you might call the classic line-up of me, Tins and Hask became set in stone. The chemistry between the three of us mirrored what rugby is all about. It's a sport you play with mates of all different types, with whom you go through highs and lows, on the pitch and off it. So while the podcast continued to deal with the big games and the big stories, it wasn't necessarily for the rugby purist. You didn't hear too many statistics, and we didn't apologise for that. It wasn't a place for numbers, it was a place to celebrate rugby's unique spirit and personality.

Hask brings so much energy, noise and fun that you can't help wanting to attach yourself to it and see where the journey takes you. Having said that, the production company found him pretty hard to handle. They were a small entity and he wanted cars to and from London and a dressing room rider. He wasn't quite Van Halen, who once requested bowls of M&Ms with the brown ones removed, but they were probably thinking, 'We're a two-bob operation with a balsa wood set; cars and dressing room riders aren't really our vibe.'

The sponsorship came with all sorts of Ts & Cs as to what we could and couldn't do. Hask would sink a pint in the opening 10 seconds, which would send certain people into a panic. We'd then spend the first 10 minutes talking about anything but rugby, which would make them panic even more.

Hask is an extraordinary presence. He sits outside most people's norms and is constantly pushing the boundaries of what is acceptable, at least to most people. He'll call someone every name under the sun within 10 seconds of meeting them, but only if he's decided he likes them. Hask is actually a very good judge of character and can work someone out in a very short space of time and isn't afraid of telling people exactly what he thinks. Combine that bluntness with his perfectionism, his demanding nature and the fact that he's never been wrong about anything, and you have to be pretty resilient to work with him. The reason he gets away with it is because he's also very charismatic.

We recently spent 10 days together in Australia and Hong Kong, and I can hand on heart say that I've never laughed so much in my life. When Hask finds his flow, which he does a lot, he is one of the funniest people on the planet, and anyone who's ever played rugby with or against him says the same.

Lots of people who have never met Hask thinks he's a dickhead, which is partly because he's built this caricature of himself. But that's not who he is, which makes for some very curious interactions. I'll watch people approach him, expecting him to be some overbearing rugby neanderthal, and walk away with a quizzical look on their faces, because he's just normal, civil and bright.

There is a lot going on in that enormous head of his. Hask reads a lot, which means he knows a considerable amount about a lot of different things. He has an extraordinary memory for film and sitcom quotes, including knowing the *Alan Partridge* and *Blackadder* scripts back to front. But he can also have knowledgeable and earnest conversations about current affairs.

Everyone who knows Hask properly loves him, and I think he's actually changed quite a lot in recent years. He's probably more defiant than ever, but he's more sensible and sensitive than most people give him credit for. He's been an extremely good friend to me and is the reason lots of people come on the show. For example, when we had England head coach Steve Borthwick on, my first question to him was, 'This must be painful for you, like having an injection. Why are you here?' And Steve replied, 'Because of Hask.'

On the cover of one of his books is the quote, 'James is a walking, talking contradiction', and that's him down to a T. He's very polarising, by his own admission, and I think there are times he probably wishes his life was simpler than it is. But he'd be very lost if he wasn't negotiating his way through that everyday chaos.

I'm the complete opposite to him in so many ways. I come from a very steady broadcasting background, where I was encouraged to keep out of the way. So I found stepping into this rough and ready world of podcasting quite uncomfortable at first. At the same time, it was utterly exhilarating. The shackles were off, and I think people quite enjoyed seeing these two reprobates corrupt a sensible company man who had spent his life in a suit and tie, brandishing a clipboard and knowing exactly what was coming next. As I noted in a previous Haskell book, they set about destroying my once respected broadcasting career – and it was ridiculous fun letting them do it.

**JH:** I hadn't gone into it hoping to change people's opinion of me, but it did, which was a bonus. People would come up to me and say, 'Mate, I've got to tell you something – I used to think you were a dickhead, but now I think you're alright.' It happened so often that I started interrupting them halfway through. 'Listen,' I'd say, 'I know exactly what you're going to tell me – you used to think I was a dickhead, then you started listening to the podcast, and now you think I'm alright.' And they'd always say, 'Yeah, you're right …'

The environment Payno worked in at Sky was very structured. On my last appearance, it was 30 seconds from me, 30 seconds from a suited and booted Clive Woodward, and that was pretty much that. I couldn't help thinking that it wasn't what rugby needed. It needed longer formats, it needed character and it needed somebody like Payno asking the right questions of people.

Payno is very polished, and he knows what to ask at the right times. That comes from his journalistic training and experience, which Tins and I don't have. I know people think I'm arrogant, and there are times when I create something good and I get a bit carried away, but I'm perfectly aware of the role I play on that podcast. Chloe said to me very early on, 'Don't ever think that you and Tins could do it without him, because you couldn't. None of you is more important than the other two.' And she was absolutely right.

Payno often says, 'Hask, we all know you're the star of the show.' (I am aware of how like David Brent that quote sounds: 'Haskell mused, was he the star of the show or just a chilled-out entertainer trying to help the world be a better place through laughter?')

I say to Payno in response, 'Not really, because it wouldn't work without you.' I could go off and do something on my own, but it would be pretty short-lived. And if I did it wouldn't have the journalistic rigour and polish that Payno brings, and it wouldn't have the rugby detail that Tins brings, as well as his stardust as a World Cup winner.

In the early days of the podcast, Tins and I got paid a bit more than Payno (not that any of us was making a fortune). But now whenever we do anything, it's split evenly three ways. If Tins can't do something, he'll suggest he shouldn't get paid, but I'll insist he still gets his cut. Yes, Payno does most of the admin and organising, but Tins has rugby bona fides coming out of his ears, and his little black book is more like the latest edition of *Who's Who*. And while I sometimes roll my eyes when we start discussing rugby minutiae, I can do it too, as well as bringing the ebullience that might otherwise be missing.

Payno has become our unofficial leader, mainly because he is seen as the only adult in the room. Besides, no one can ever get hold of Tins as he is either suckling at the royal teat, shooting or on the golf course. I would have put my hand up to lead but I am seen as a big child and a grenade with the pin pulled out that no one wants to handle, so for that reason most things fall at Payno's door. Then they get passed on to Tins and if they think it's worth me knowing and they have no fear of me blowing anything up, I will get to know. I am the office equivalent of a mushroom: kept in the dark and fed on shit.

Payno doesn't want to be front of house, or so he makes out. It's like that Brian Clough quote about his assistant Peter Taylor, who was really an equal partner: 'I'm not equipped to manage successfully without him. I'm the shop window and he's the goods in the back.' All that being said, Payno has become a character in his own right, which he doesn't always understand. He is no longer just steering the conversation, he IS the conversation, and his views are warranted and wanted. As I have said, he does protest a bit too much about wanting to just be in the shadows. He is a natural performer and has stolen the show more than once, especially when we are required to act for some of the hero content we film. Honestly, at times it's like watching a young Laurence Olivier.

People are always asking me how Payno is wherever I go, and when I do a DJ set, they hold up signs or writing on their phones that say, 'Where's Payno?' But it's not just Payno who gets recognised for the podcast, it's me and Tins as well. Despite all the other things I've done, I would say by far and away the biggest and most popular thing I do at the moment is the podcast. It doesn't matter where in the world I am, someone will come up and say, 'Just to let you know I am a big fan of the pod.' That's how much of an impact it's had. It also helps that Simon was a fantastic producer and editor, so the podcast looked and sounded professional. As a result, we were pulling in big numbers.

**MT:** People sometimes ask me if I had any worries about doing a podcast with Hask, given my royal connections and his reputation for controversy. The answer to that is no. I obviously need to consider how anything I'm involved in is going to be perceived, but there's no one telling me what I can or can't do, it's always my call. And I don't have to feign respect for the royal family, because I genuinely respect it as an institution.

There are people who think that some of the things I do demean the royal family, such as when I appeared on *I'm a Celebrity* in 2022. But I didn't take that decision lightly; they'd been asking me for years. And I eventually cracked because they made me an offer I simply couldn't refuse. The money I got from *I'm a Celebrity* helped fill the gap left by Covid, among other things. I wasn't interested in the 'challenge' of being in the jungle, or increasing my fame, it was purely a financial consideration.

Hask was on *I'm a Celebrity* a couple of years before me and had a mixed bag of an appearance – the editors may have played their part a little bit in his being branded at times a bully, which wasn't true – but I wasn't particularly worried about being misrepresented because I never go as close to the edge as him. I'll give you an example of how we're different. The other day, Hask thought someone was videoing him in a bar. I said to him, 'But you can't prove it', and he replied, 'I can …' He walked straight up to the guy and asked him, the guy denied it, and Hask asked if he could check his phone. The guy gave him his phone, proved he hadn't been videoing him, and that was that. Now, I wouldn't have done that in a million years, but Hask managed to pull it off because he was so polite about it. I thought it was the right thing to do, because we'd been sat there for an hour, talking unguardedly, and if that guy had been videoing us, he could have sent it to anyone. But I'm sure some people watching that exchange would have concluded that Hask was out of order.

Before I went into the jungle, Hask gave me a few pointers: if anyone pisses you off, just walk away; if an argument kicks off in camp, stay out of it and maybe even hide in the toilet; don't get involved in conversations about religion and politics; and definitely don't get involved in conversations about gender. It was good of him to give me that advice, but it wasn't really necessary because I'm not the sort of bloke to have heated arguments about those kinds of subjects anyway. I was more worried about the boredom and hunger, both of which must have been hellish for Hask, because he's miles bigger than me and has ADHD. As it was, I managed to come through it unscathed. I did all my bushtucker trials without complaint, and the closest I got to controversy was repeatedly taking down former health secretary Matt Hancock's T-shirts off the line when he was trying to promote his number for votes.

Payno had interviewed me plenty of times while working for Sky, but I didn't really know anything about him, other than he was an Old Etonian. Add in Hask, who went to Wellington College, and me, and it wasn't the most diverse threesome. The fact that I was from up north and still had a bit of a Yorkshire accent was about the only box we ticked.

I seem to remember discussing our lack of diversity right at the outset. Yes, we were three middle-class white men. Yes, Payno and Hask attended two of the most expensive schools in the country. Yes, I had married into royalty. But we were still quite different characters with different opinions on rugby, not all of them positive.

But as the podcast evolved, we knew we had to reflect what rugby looked like now. We had to get people involved who looked different, came from different backgrounds, went to different schools and saw the game through fresher eyes. And we had to get them to tell their stories, rather than just give their views on the latest games. Rugby isn't the most interesting thing, but the characters who play it are.

The chemistry was there from the very first show we did together, but it was when we started getting stuck into the Guinness that the podcast really started to take form. Back then, we had a producer called Si, who'd prepare a script and we'd maybe follow it for the first five minutes before ignoring it completely. The poor guy would be trying to create a decent show and we would be going off on side quests or necking pints. Payno would then say, 'Producer Si wants us to move on', and we would respond 'Fuck Si', and then carry on (we came quite close to printing T-shirts with 'FUCK SI' written on them). Si would sometimes come on set and try to cajole us to do stuff, and he would get the same tongue-in-cheek response. At the same time, that attitude came to define the podcast: we didn't really care what anyone else wanted us to do, we were going to talk about whatever we fancied, like three blokes chatting down the pub. With Si and the three of us we had a great team that worked well.

Hask wasn't just a loud bloke blasting out jokes and funny stories, he revealed previously hidden depths. Hask is like an onion: when you peel back a few layers, you'll find a lot of emotion, sensitivity and insecurity. This was a guy who employed a psychologist long before that was considered normal in rugby and was quite open about doing so. He'd also been attacked by the media and fans for doing things differently throughout his rugby career, which made him a very sympathetic, empathetic presence.

Sky was mad to let Payno go, but he was better off out of it because it had become quite a sterile place. He was a very experienced broadcaster by the time we started the podcast and he quickly slipped into his role as puppeteer, pulling the strings, teeing us up with all the right questions and making sure the ship was heading in the right direction, whatever chaos Hask and I were causing. He worked out where we stood on various issues, what we were passionate about, what pissed us off, what we weren't interested in, and it soon became clear that he was the most important cog in the machine.

When it came to guests, Payno was always one step ahead. And because he's a very nice man who puts people at ease, he was very good at prising interesting stuff out of people and latching on to surprising twists. He's the ultimate pro; I honestly don't think there's anyone better than he is.

**AP:** Any successful show has light and shade, and if the podcast consisted of three Hasks on the microphones, that would be a lot to take in and I'm not sure it would do much for anybody. As it is, there's something for everyone, whether you're a fan of Hask's giant personality and ridiculous stories, or you're a hardcore rugby fan and really want to know what Tins thinks about what's happening in the game, or you're a passer-by who just wants to dip in, which you can do through the lens I offer.

Hask and Tins have been there and done it and I'm just trying to hold things together. I'd describe my role as the cement between two very robust bricks; or a cross between Mrs Doubtfire and a parole officer, nannying them through the bits they don't want to do and telling them the bits they really need to do.

As well as trying to keep them on the straight and narrow, usually by feathering the brakes every now and again, it's part of my role to step back when they're going at a hundred miles an hour and try to articulate what most of the audience is thinking. That, in turn, helps the audience feel closer to the action.

Over time, we've became exaggerated versions of ourselves (maybe exaggerated versions of how we view each other is more accurate). I don't think any of my friends would describe me as an alpha male, yet I'm usually right in the middle of things when anything is going on. But when I'm with Tins and Hask, I'm quite happy to stay in the background. I also have friends who are quite arty and academic. In contrast, whenever I see a picture of Hask and his mates from outside rugby, they're all carbon copies of each other – always with their shirts off, tanned, ridiculously muscly, covered in tattoos. Tins, meanwhile, has quite a mix of friends from old school pals through to royalty. It's almost like we exist in three separate solar systems, but we work well together. And it's extraordinary the number of people who say they love the podcast because of the chemistry between us, rather than the rugby.

We even get people who say, 'I don't know anything about the game, I just like listening to the three of you.' I also think people like our authenticity. To use the vernacular of the day, we're pale, male and stale – which is quite a unique proposition for 2024 – but we're unapologetic about it. We do exactly what it says on the tin, we don't try to be anything we're not. We're quite comfortable doing what we're doing in our little corner.

We're three outsiders in a weird way. I used to be part of the mainstream media; Tins could be working for the mainstream media; Hask could be doing any number of things other than the podcast but wants to do it anyway. And we're all of the same opinion: if what we do sounds like your kind of thing, we'd love for you to tune in; if you don't, never mind. Don't shout at us for not being to your taste (that's like shouting at *Peppa Pig* for not being *Newsnight*), go and listen to something that does float your boat instead.

You might call it the 'Jeremy Clarkson approach', which is just getting on with being who you are, and letting other people worry about you not being what they'd like you to be. I happily admit that I'm not a trailblazer, but I do find the fact that we've done things our own way, and not how others would have wanted us to do it, quite rewarding. After all, the podcast isn't just us three anyway, it's us three plus guests, and we've given people of all sorts of backgrounds the opportunity to tell their stories.

# 3

# THE BUSINESS

**MT:** Thank God for Payno, because the podcast is a proper business now, even though he calls it a hobby. Somebody needs to have their finger constantly on the pulse, and that somebody is him. I simply don't have the time to keep on top of things, while Hask just isn't interested in the minutiae of the podcast.

Without Payno and the team we have built at *The Good, The Bad & The Rugby*, the whole thing would fall apart. While Hask and I are constantly out and about, Payno is almost always in his office, running his other businesses. He's always on hand, and very good at picking up the phone and general admin, which is a skillset you don't learn as a rugby player.

I'm usually the next point of contact, while Hask is at the bottom of the list. To be fair, the ages of our respective kids also play a part: my three are 10 and younger, which means mornings and after school are hectic; Hask's daughter is now a toddler, which spells mayhem; meanwhile, Payno's kids are old enough to sort themselves out.

I suppose it's not quite a case of 'Don't tell Hask', it's more a case of knowing what Hask cares about and what he doesn't. He's never going to sit in front of a laptop all day, looking at accounts and rotas and what not, his head would blow up if he had to do that, especially if he had to combine it with childcare.

When we were in Australia recently, we did this thing where we had to draw what was important to us on an egg. Payno did this beautiful design with rolling hills, the sea, his wife, his kids, the three of us and his lucky number. I drew this symbol that encompassed loyalty, love, friendship, honesty and fun, everything that I felt about my family and the three of us. Hask drew his daughter Bodhi, some DJ decks and a wallaby. When I asked him about the wallaby, he replied, 'I won man of the series in Australia in 2016.' Payno and I pretended to be put out that he hadn't mentioned us on his egg, but we weren't really because we know exactly how Hask is.

Hask seems to think that he could accomplish in a single afternoon what the rest of the team would take a month to do, despite having no real clue what goes on with the podcast business-wise (if he really wanted a full-time office job, we'd make him head of HR, because all the complaints are about him anyway).

Hask is always looking for the next thing, whether it's a new book to write or a fitness app, but he still has strong views on how the business should be run. He'll come into a board meeting like a tornado and say, 'We're definitely not doing that, that's not happening either, why are we doing this?' and while they're often valid points, Payno and I will be thinking, 'Mate, you can't start shouting the odds when you haven't had any input for the last however many months.'

I do get irritated with Hask, but it's never long-term irritation. I just wish he would stick to two or three things – the DJing, the podcast, his daughter – fit everything in around that and not get too involved in anything else, but that's not how his mind works. And while I'm not sure Hask is going to blow the whole thing up one day, he does get us in the papers quite regularly, not always for the right reasons. But that's just how he lives his life.

He'll say, 'I hate being in the papers', and I'll say, 'Well, if you didn't say anything, you wouldn't be.' The two of us were driving to a live show recently when Chloe rang. She said to Hask, 'Can you try not to say anything that will get us in the papers tomorrow', and he replied, 'I'll try not to, but you know I say whatever comes into my head ...'

All joking aside, Hask is very intelligent and astute. And while he projects this very powerful, confident image, he's actually quite fragile. He'll say to me and Payno, 'Give me direct feedback, even if it's bad, I can deal with that.' But if we give him some bad feedback, he'll get very defensive like a kid and start having a go at us about something one of us did last year. He's got an amazing memory; sometimes he'll be arguing something that none of us can remember, probably because it happened two years ago!

AP: When we have board meetings, there's only one real grown-up out of the three of us. Tins and Hask will be on their phones, like a couple of teenagers. Tins is incapable of writing a list and actioning it at a later date, he has to do everything in real time. For example, if you say to him at a meeting, 'You need to get hold of X, Y and Z', he'll have to take himself off and do it there and then. And when he returns, we'll have moved on to something else.

We do keep Hask out of the picture deliberately, not that it always goes down very well. He'll leave some shitty voice notes on everyone's phones, referring to things he wants done (none of them interesting or relevant) before disappearing for three weeks. And when he returns, he'll leave some more shitty voice notes, asking why nothing he asked us to do had been done. I'll reply saying, 'It simply wasn't required. You're miles behind the curve.'

Hask is often right about things, but he's unable to operate in an everyday work environment. In fact, if he ever worked in an office, he'd be an HR nightmare, which is why he spends most of his time on Planet Hask.

He's brilliant at what he does, which is bringing huge energy and sprinkling stardust (and, to be fair, putting on a show for our sponsors), but we have to keep him out of the loop when it comes to the day-to-day running of the business. That's not being mean to Hask, that's just playing to our strengths.

You can't have a business that blindly cracks on, thinking everything is fine when it's not. That's why I get very impatient when it comes to directions. I'll say to them, 'The restaurant is this way', and they'll ignore me and wander off in another direction. Nine times out of ten I'm right, but they absolutely love it when I get it wrong. That's when they start calling me headstrong. But I have to be headstrong because I'm dealing with two absolute knuckleheads. If I didn't have that stubborn streak, I wouldn't get heard. And if I didn't get heard, we'd be having pitfalls every second week.

**JH:** Payno was talking about taking the podcast in different directions from quite early on, but my response was always, 'Don't worry about trying to build something else until we're doing the rugby podcast as well as we possibly can.'

I try to demand excellence and won't accept mediocrity, and my mind works in a very rational and commonsense way. I always try to look at myself first and foremost on how I can improve, and is my side of the street clean. If the answer to that is no, then it's on me to sort things out. I work very hard and expect others to do the same, whether that's late nights, weekends or on holiday. This whole 'I am out of office and won't be checking my emails' is bullshit. If I can't solve a problem, I have no problem asking for help from someone doing the job I want doing better than me. We can always all do better and be better. I also have a massive issue with excuses, the culture of excuses and accepting things just because it's too much hassle to change things.

One day in the summer of 2022, we got a message from our MD, Nic, asking if everyone was happy coming to work. It was one of the hottest days ever, pushing 40°C in London, but my immediate response was, 'Yes, everyone is happy coming to work, we've got work to do!' Nic said that he was worried about people having to travel on the Tube, and I replied, 'It's always pushing 40°C in places like Dubai and Bahrain, and they still manage to work. So unless it starts raining fire, we're all going to work!'

Give people a chance and they will find an excuse not to do things or do things that make no sense, and I'm not afraid to let people know about it. That's why raising awareness of every issue and going at the pace of the slowest person in any team or group means that everyone takes the piss, and no one can be held accountable by those in charge, because God forbid you get it wrong and call bullshit on someone's excuse or attitude, you are in for a world of pain, and risk cancellation, or worse, legal action if it turns out what they were saying was true. These people always find some kind of excuse. For example, 'I need a mental health day because my cat died', or 'I can't attend the dinner as there aren't enough vegan options'.

I wouldn't want people to get the wrong idea about me. I'm not some tyrant, slamming tables and screaming in colleagues' faces. I'm actually very personable and treat everybody exactly the same. I try to be polite, kind and respectful as these are non-negotiables for me personally. However, I do have a more traditional approach to work than most of the staff we employ:

if it's good it's good, if it's shit it's shit. Life and business are not about taking part; taking part is for singalongs and bake-offs. It comes from my background as a sportsperson, where all that matters is that you work hard, are a good team person and perform when needed. Race, gender, diet or religion don't come into my world. All I see is the person and performance. If you play well and are a good team person, you are in. If you are shit, but your nan died, I'm sorry for your loss but at the end of the day you are still shit and no amount of padding or excuses is going to change that.

If I can do 101 things in one day, I expect the same of my colleagues, but that's not really how they roll. They get over-whelmed, need days off, need a lie down, switch off their phones at weekends, can't do this, don't want to do that. It can be maddening, and I sometimes have to remind myself that nobody cares as much about your work as you care about your work. I know the lads say that I don't attend all the meet-ings, jump on all the calls or just rant and rave, but I always follow up with detailed emails and make my points clear. The issue is, I don't have the time to follow up and just expect it to get done. They tolerate me being like this as most of the points I raise are valid, and because we split everything, I always get my say. So, everyone can get busy, but nothing gets done unless we all agree on it.

Since I was 17, I have been working. I have been through most of these things, tried most of them as businesses or on behalf of others, messed them up, had successes and seen all the jack the lad men, who come and offer you the world only to give you a miniature globe.

Payno, Tins and I recently did some filming for an airline campaign, which involved dressing us up in different national costumes. First, we were dressed as Scotsmen, in kilts and tam o'shanters with orange wigs attached to them. But when I started doing a shit Scottish accent, they panicked: 'No, no, no, you can't do that.' I said to them, 'Sorry, what? Me doing a Scottish accent is offensive but me dressed in a kilt and a joke shop tam o'shanter isn't? How does that make sense? Have a think about what you're asking us to do.'

Ten minutes later, I was dressed in a beret and a stripey jumper, with bulbs of garlic strung around my neck. But when I started doing a stupid French accent, they panicked again. Their cognitive dissonance was off the scale: on the one hand, they didn't see anything wrong with presenting us as ludicrously outdated cultural stereotypes; on the other, they thought that me doing comedy foreign accents was completely unacceptable. Payno kept telling me to be nice (he does that a lot) but I just couldn't deal with the madness of it all, with everyone looking at me as if I was the off-piste lunatic for not towing the party line, when I was arguing that without the element of humour, it looked like we were just taking the piss out of Scotland and France.

I know it's not our staff or what they personally think, they are just doing their jobs, and it's more a case of them enacting what brands want, but you can just imagine the conversations with these brands on conference calls that they all insist on having during the ideas phase, where no one points any of this out. It's the first thing I would have flagged. It's very odd that we now seem to have humour by committee, which means you are all things to all men and women and get nowhere. I would argue that you should never be afraid to offend people or worry about a negative reaction, if you can hand on heart say it's clearly a joke.

Be rest assured though, if it didn't go well or someone commented on our social media, *GBR* would get the public and corporate kicking. So why not do it our way instead of pandering?

I demand a lot of people, but only because I expect the same of myself. I always think things can be done better, and my forthrightness can make others very uncomfortable. So while Tins has stepped up considerably since the court case and the stress it caused, particularly to Payno (which we'll describe in more detail later in the book), I'm always going to be the third wheel, the bloke they keep things from, lest I start smashing the place up. Even though I have yet to do that. In fact the last person who lost his head was actually Payno. The issue is when he gets angry it's like a very posh elderly lady having a fit. It all gets very high-pitched and there are demands for satisfaction, questions of soundness and talk of honour. Payno makes out he is all tough, but he is like a chocolate truffle – soft-centred.

When I say Tins has stepped up, what I mean is he dials in for the calls, with either kids screaming and climbing the walls, or the sound of 'Pull!' then gunfire, or the whack of golf balls in the background, before the call gets cut off due to lack of signal. But my point is, at least he is on the call to help Payno. I have either not been told about it or I am up to my chin in dancing girls and dance music in Ibiza – which would be slightly quieter than the background of some of Tins' calls. So I don't jump on all of them as it's not conducive to good business.

Let me paint a picture of a typical podcast planning meeting. Payno will wander in, look wistfully into the distance and ask out loud, to no one in particular, what appears on the surface to be an abstract question such as, 'What would you do if somebody did such and such?' I look around thinking, 'Who the fuck is he talking to?' and then I twig that it's not an abstract question at all and that they actually wanted to gauge my reaction before revealing the complete truth. So, if I respond, 'Well, they can fuck off, we are not doing that', or

'That's bullshit', Payno will then say, 'Yes, exactly my thoughts', and move on. If I say something reasonable then Payno and Tins will go outside and whisper for a couple of minutes, then they'll return and say, 'We thought it best not to tell you, but such and such has happened …' I'll then either be reasonable or fly off the handle, ask them why they didn't tell me, and they'll reply, 'Because we knew you'd react in exactly this way …' What they have yet to figure out is, they always have to tell me a version of the story, even if the horse has bolted and there is nothing to be done.

What I find most frustrating is that I'm quite a good judge of character and will often warn Payno and Tins about what somebody is going to do. That leads to exchanges along the lines of:

'I fucking told you he was going to do that! I've seen it all before!'

'I know, I know, you were right all along …'

I'm a rationaliser, which is sometimes my biggest downfall. In my relationship with Chloe, she was very emotional, while I was very practical, which meant I'd always go straight to trying to fix things instead of just listening. Sometimes I would listen, but too often I wouldn't. I have actually done a lot of work on that now, but it takes time for it to become a habit. Sometimes saying nothing is the most powerful tool. You take action through inaction.

People's inability to think rationally and critically upsets me. If I'm sitting in a meeting and somebody starts talking nonsense, especially if I suspect they don't really believe what they're saying, I have to call it out. 'I'm sorry, I can't let that go. Are you being serious? Surely nobody else believes that?'

For example, if somebody suggests that women's sport isn't on an equal footing with men's sport because of some kind of male conspiracy to keep females in their place, I'll pick them up on it. The main reason women's sport isn't on an equal footing with men's sport is because far fewer women are interested in sport, either playing it or watching it. If there were tens of millions of female football fans in England, as there are tens of millions of male football fans, women's football would never be off the TV and women players would earn as much as the men. But most women prefer to do other things than watch sport, and when people deny that's the case, I get irritated with the dishonesty.

It's the same when people say they have no problem with trans women playing sport against women. Whether you think trans women are actually women is kind of irrelevant, the fact is they have biological advantages, which makes them competing in women's sport completely unfair. I know science is a dirty word these days as feelings are more important than facts, but it's been proven that even if you were a man (having gone through puberty) and are now a woman, if you take testosterone blockers or inhibitors it will have no real effect or only a small one. Imagine what would happen if I changed sex, took T-blockers, got some boobs and took up a combat sport against women. It would not be fair or end well. Luckily, rugby for once made the right decision and stopped transgender athletes from competing, otherwise a comeback for me could have been on the cards. I am joking of course – mind you, with a divorce pending and the need for some income, perhaps not.

When it comes to the podcast, that ability to think rationally and critically is a benefit. For example, in the early days of Steve Borthwick's stint as England head coach, most people thought he was shit and wrote him off. But Steve had suddenly inherited a team that wasn't his. He couldn't play the way he wanted to play because there was a World Cup on the horizon and finding a way to win games any which way was more important. I was able to see this, as was Tins, because of that ability to think rationally and critically. We knew what was going on, so we weren't going to start slagging anybody off, like some of the guys in the media. And since the World Cup, which didn't go too badly anyway, Borthers' England have started playing some good rugby.

# 4

# TAKING THE STAGE

**AP:** The first time I walked on stage with Hask and Tins, I thought, 'What the hell am I doing here?' I was so used to hovering on the periphery, being heard every now and again but barely seen, and now I was appearing at the London Palladium, where Bing Crosby, Frank Sinatra, Judy Garland, Sammy Davis Jr, the Beatles, and Keith Harris and Orville had previously performed.

It's been fascinating to watch a man as charismatic and bombastic as Hask – a born performer – and I've learned an awful lot from him, as well as Tins, who was catapulted into the spotlight after his marriage to Zara.

To get to the top in sport, and stay there for a long period of time, you need to have incredible self-belief, especially in the social media age, when literally millions of people are critiquing your every cough and spit. And through close contact with two champion athletes over a lengthy period of time, I've learned not to worry about the stuff you can't influence and enjoy the stuff you can.

Tins can tell a brilliant story, but he understands that part of his role is to keep us anchored in rugby, while Hask does his thing. Not only does Hask love performing, but he's also very good at it. He's a naturally very funny bloke, but people don't realise that he works very hard at it as well. It's that elite sportsperson's attitude – when he does something, he doesn't mess around, he's all-in, because he wants to be the best he can possibly be.

Hask has done stand-up, which takes balls of steel and a lot of preparation. He listens to and watches a lot of comedy, he's encyclopaedic about comedians, so when he starts telling one of his stories on stage, he's probably spent ages crafting it. It's great fun watching him build a story over a period of time. He'll try different things on different nights, seeing what gets laughs and what doesn't, and by the end, he'll have it honed to perfection.

He tells a story titled 'From Wakefield to Windsor', which begins with Tins' childhood on the bleak streets of Wakefield (which are obviously far bleaker than they really were in the twisted mind of Haskell) and finishes with him returning from Australia with a World Cup winner's medal and a princess. As soon as he starts telling it, I can just sit back and relax for a couple of minutes, because I know it's going to go down a storm with the audience.

My role is to keep a handle on the tiller and make sure Hask doesn't go off like a firework in a shop and alienate anyone. He doesn't always read the room, such as when we do corporate events. I'll say to him, 'Right, Hask, nice and easy. Just go out there, tell a few gentle jokes, nothing controversial.' And a few minutes later, Hask will open with one of the most outrageous stories in his locker. I'll be thinking, 'I'm not sure this is what HSBC were looking for …'

If that happens, my job is to try to repair the relationship between Hask and the audience, and we've worked out a very efficient way of getting him back on track without losing face: I get up and walk off stage, so that everyone knows that I'm as shocked as the audience about what Hask has just said. And if people are still upset, I might try to repair the damage by promising to send them a bottle of Blackeye Gin (which the three of us recently founded – £1.50 from each bottle sold goes into supporting players past and present, the first beneficiary being former England Red Roses head coach Gary Street, who recently suffered a life-changing stroke).

Even when it's an actual show, rather than a corporate event, I'll give an aside to the audience, to let them know that I'm one of them and find him just as ridiculous as they do. I suppose that's a key role of a straight man in double acts, and, ironically, it allows Hask and Tins to be even more outrageous.

But having spent my broadcasting career trying to get the best out of everyone else, finally being under the spotlight dragged a bit of the performer out of me. My primary role is to be neat and tidy and coax good things from Hask and Tins, which involves teeing up their stories (we've probably got 50 good rugby tales, and we might do 10 in one night) and connecting them up to form a vaguely coherent narrative. You might say that I create the flow. But I'm also able to ride on their coat-tails, chuck in the odd one-liner (usually at Hask's expense) and follow them to all sorts of weird and wonderful places.

The climax of our final live show of 2023 consisted of the three of us, plus guests, singing 'The Twelve Days of Christmas' in fancy dress, and I imagined my old Sky colleagues finding out about it and thinking, 'Bloody hell, what happened to Alex? The boy's lost it.' But we've got to evolve or die, even if it means morphing into Christopher Biggins during panto season.

The odd Christmas singalong aside, the bread and butter of our live tours is anecdotes, because that's what rugby fans crave. Professional rugby is very different to football, at least in its modern form. Whereas footballers nowadays are very guarded, rugby players are still happy to share stories of drunken debauchery and all the other nonsense that goes on in their sport. That's why fans can relate to them, because the drunken sessions, pranks and all the other nonsense isn't much different at their local rugby club.

Because we don't have a script, we never really know where we're going when we walk out on stage. We work on bits occasionally, but predominantly it's a chat between three mates, plus guests, that can spin off in all sorts of directions. A good example is a show we did at the Palladium in 2023.

The day before, Hask's separation from Chloe had made the papers, and unbeknown to us (which was very naive), there were tabloid journalists in the audience. Hask spoke about running out of cash and his daughter not having any clothes or an education – the sort of dark gags a mate would make down the pub after separating from his wife – and the journalists had a field day, making everything Hask said with tongue firmly in cheek sound as if he really meant it.

The day of the Palladium show, Hask decided to go out for a long alcoholic lunch, which is an understandable response to having your laundry aired in the paper, but everyone else involved with the podcast was very nervous. When he rocked up to the theatre with his best mate Dozzer (Paul Doran-Jones) the first thing he said was, 'I'm fucking going for it tonight.' To which I replied, 'Erm, yes, but we've got all our sponsors here, it's the big one, so please don't blow things up. Let's just have a nice, easy show. You can still be at your brilliant best without offending or upsetting anyone ...' Hask didn't want to hear any of that and walked on stage looking really quite cross, which had me right on the edge.

However, after we'd done our introductions, the first thing I said was, 'Look, we'd normally start with a gag, but tonight I'm going to kick things off by asking Hask how he is ...' Hask did 20 minutes on what it's like to have the press outside your house and writing shit about you, and it was absolutely brilliant, and really quite emotional. For me, those 20 minutes summed up why the podcast is so successful. No, we don't tick many, if any, diversity boxes, but we are still three different characters, and there are lots of people out there who can relate to us. And while they do want anecdotes, and of course some rugby, they also want that chemistry and authenticity.

I'm not sure it's a case of me *accidentally* finding out who and what I really am, but I've certainly become a different version of me because of significant turbulence in my life, even though it wasn't welcome at the time.

I sometimes look at former Sky football presenter Richard Keys and think of what might have been for me. He was sacked by Sky 13 years ago and has been at beIN Sports for 11 years, but whatever the latest Keys-based debacle, the media still refers to him as 'the former Sky Sports presenter'.

My profile is many times what it was when I was on television, which tells you a lot about how the media landscape has changed. And nobody wants to hear about my stint at Sky, they only want to hear about the podcast. Every week, people come up to me and say, 'Love the pod!' or, 'Where's Tins?' or, 'Is Hask a dickhead?' Even when I was working in Dallas, this American guy came running up to me and said, 'Payno! Payno! Love the pod!'

Only the other day, my wife saw a photograph of me when I was still at Sky, in which I was very clean-shaven, had a neat side-parting, polished teeth and a very sharp suit and tie. She looked at me, with my five-day beard, my hair all over the place, my crumpled sweatshirt, and said, 'Wow, you've changed so much.' She's right, I'm almost a different person.

**MT:** I enjoy making people laugh, and I particularly enjoy doing it off the cuff on stage. We do sit down and plan things, but which direction we go in, and what stories get told, largely depends on who we have on as a guest. So while I do get slightly nervous beforehand, mainly about whether the audience is going to enjoy it, I'm always quite relaxed once we get into our stride and I hear people laughing.

We do a meet and greet at every show, which Hask finds a bit tiresome – 'Why do I have to speak to all these nauses? Why can't I stand over there behind the velvet rope?' – but I quite enjoy it. We sometimes meet random characters we've spoken to before, and they'll often have a funny story about the show they went to or will tell us about the time Hask made them cry.

Payno gets very modest and never wants to be in the photos. I'll say to him, 'This is about the podcast and you're a part of it', and he'll reply, 'Yeah, but no one needs to see me.' He genuinely doesn't realise how important he is to the group, and that he's far more famous now than he ever was, even though he worked for Sky for years. I know he sees himself as the straight man of the group, but he's funny in his own right, especially when he starts playing on the fact that he's an Old Etonian. Hask tries to riff on that as well, even though his old school, Wellington College, is almost as expensive.

The live show with Scott Quinnell in Cardiff was interesting because Hask doesn't appreciate people walking in the same space as him. I know Scotty Q really well and Payno did loads of Lions stuff with him at Sky, so we didn't anticipate doing much that night. It was fascinating watching things unfold. Scott has so many good stories and tells them brilliantly, in his booming Welsh voice that fills the room. And because the audience were largely 'his' people, Hask had his work cut out to get a single story in. So while me, Payno and the audience were having fun, I'm not sure Hask was.

**JH:** I don't think I ever played against Scott, but he's a player I admired growing up and we've always got on well. However, when it came to appearing together in Cardiff, I had no choice but to rein it in a bit: you can't really have two centres of attention on a stage, and if I'd attempted to go head-to-head with Scott in his own backyard, there was only going to be one winner.

The lads said to me after that show, 'I've never seen you that quiet', and I replied, 'What did you want me to do?!' Scott was at his most bombastic, absolutely loving it, so instead of trying to compete with him, I thought it best that I be his foil and let him shine.

I like to perform, especially on a live show, but after appearing with Scott, I thought to myself, 'Well, I get a lot of opportunities to shout and joke and generally do what I want, so spending one night playing second fiddle isn't a problem.' And as time has gone on, I've become more comfortable reining things in in the studio as well. Sitting back and asking questions, trying to work people out, is as much part of my personality as the shouting and joking.

Having said that, I could never do what Payno does. There are nights when we do the live tour when he barely says anything beyond teeing the rest of us up, but he does it so well. That night in Cardiff, he had to sit there for about five minutes while Scott and I gave him shit, before making him neck a pint of lager. It's not easy to adopt that role and enjoy it, but Payno is such a pro that he plays it beautifully.

# 5

# LADS ON WORLD TOUR

**JH:** I was originally asked to DJ at the opening ceremony of the Hong Kong Sevens, right in the middle of all the fancy dress and heavy boozing in the South Stand. Then the organisers contacted *The Good, The Bad & The Rugby* to see if we'd be up for hosting the podcast and some promotional stuff out there.

I was there for five days in total, and even managed to fit in some corporate work with Wallabies legend David Campese. I get on very well with David and I really like him, despite him being one of the most negative people I've ever met. This might sound odd, but it's not bad negativity. I don't dislike him for it, we all have mates who are just a bit negative over certain things. His negativity is directed solely towards rugby. All the rest of the time he is great, but when he gets a question about rugby, then my god he is like a little cartoon thunder cloud with a frowny face, just bringing doom and gloom to everyone's door. While we were in Hong Kong he didn't once stop complaining that professionalism had ruined rugby and that everything in his day was better, and I ended up saying to him, 'Fucking hell, Dave, give it a rest. Can't we go back to taking the piss out of each other again please?'

There were all sorts of rugby characters doing the rounds, including Scottish duo John Barclay and Kelly Brown, neither of whom I knew that well but who I ended up having a whale of a time with. I ended up DJing in a couple of random bars for people and at one point with John Barclay and the Weasley twins (aka the Phelps twins) in my DJ booth. It's not every day you get on the piss with Harry Potter's mates. They awarded me 50 points to Gryffindor for good DJing. Kelly Brown and I ended up going from box to box at the stadium drinking and eating everyone's food while avoiding being asked any serious rugby questions. But mostly I was being sensible before my set because I take my DJing very seriously and didn't want to mess it up.

Rugby fans are not always the best crowd to play for, if I am honest. Generally they are great, but often they are very aggressive and entitled. I think it stems from the fact that many of them can't decide what they want players to be. Every fan has their own expectations and perceptions. They like players to be humble, but also want them to have a personality. But not too much personality, because that would mean the player is getting above himself. That being the case, many rugby fans have no idea what to make of me, while some actively want me to fail at anything I do (not so much the younger ones, I've noticed, they just want to have a good time, dance to my tunes and probably have no idea who I am anyway).

When I say to them that I'm a DJ and producer these days, some people seem to think I'm a like a wedding DJ and expect me to turn up with a set of traffic lights and a smoke machine. Now this is normally reserved for the uneducated among us, however it's not often that I turn up for a professional paid gig and they appear to have assumed that I was bringing my own gear. When I turned up for a soundcheck at the Hong Kong Stadium the day before the opening ceremony, they kept saying, 'Where's your equipment?', and I kept telling them that I only had a pair of headphones and a USB stick, and that everything else was meant to be supplied by them. I was getting the feeling that something had been lost in translation. Luckily someone appeared out the ether and said yes of course we have your equipment and then set about unboxing bits and plugging them in. Not ideal when you are supposed to be doing a soundcheck.

I was taken through what was meant to be my 'big entrance'. No one had mentioned anything about a big entrance to me before. Now, for someone who clearly likes the sound of his own voice and some serious self-promotion, I am not always comfortable putting myself out there for some mad hatter's scheme that has all the hallmarks of going down badly. I am especially reticent when it comes to grand entrances when I'm DJing.

The Hong Kong Sevens organisers had come up with this mad plan, which involved putting me in one of the entrance tunnels right in the middle of the South Stand, which, as anyone who knows the Hong Kong Sevens, is like a physical representation of Dante's Inferno. Every level takes you further into the depravity, sickness, die-hard drunken fans, all of whom are soaked in alcohol and piss (that's right, people piss in pint glasses and throw it). And they wanted me to walk right through this before my set. What could possibly go wrong? They were going to block off the tunnel and a 50-metre staircase through the hubbub to the pitch, with burly security guards. They were then going to fill the tunnel behind me with smoke, and on cue they would backlight me with a huge, burning bright light, like something out of a Michael Jackson performance. I was to walk through the smoke counting to 30 in my head, stand on the top of the stairs and give it the BIG I AM. Think of *Gladiator*, where Maximus screams, 'Are you not entertained?' as he surveys the ground, then replace

Maximus with Me, surrounded by pissed-up fuckheads blinded by smoke, and me in the middle of it all giving the big 'un. I would then descend the stairs and walk down through the crowd, everyone able to demand high fives and fist bumps while I made it onto the pitch.

For whatever reason, people aren't comfortable with me just turning up and playing music, they always feel the need to come up with some ludicrous theatre. For example, I was recently booked for a corporate event and asked to ride into the room on an electric scooter with flashing lights and fireworks attached to it. I told this very aggressive female organiser that I wasn't mad about the idea, and it all depended on the scooter and the access and everything else, because I really didn't want to make myself look like a dick. She said, 'No worries, we can get you down to check it out and it's just an idea at the moment, but we will come back to you asap.'

When I rocked up to the event three months later and they showed me the scooter, I immediately told them I wasn't going to do it. Instead of just the one central foot plate, this scooter had flaps on either side, so my massive feet didn't fit on it properly. And it was electric, but it also required you to manually push it to get it going before the motor kicked in, so I was worried about getting caught on the carpet and falling off, in front of a room full of people with iPhones. It turned out that the runway to the stage that they wanted me to 'ride' along on my battery-powered, firework-shooting, flashing-light-covered scooter was about 10 metres long from the door to the stage. Hardly even worth it, as by the time the motor kicked in, I would be at the stage. When I pointed that out, I was told maybe I could do a loop and go back around again. So now I am doing a display.

Imagine the scene: this big, burly meathead, trying to push a scooter along a carpet, wobbling from side to side because his foot wouldn't fit on the plate, so the thing is veering from side to side, firing fucking fireworks into people's faces, while neon lights flash, and dancing girls follow behind, like I'm some sort of unhinged Pied Piper. At the same time, I am wearing a huge helmet with some company's branding on it, looking like I have missed the sunshine bus and have somehow set my mind on getting back to my carer. No doubt about it, I would have been an internet meme for the rest of my days.

When I told this woman I wasn't doing it, she got very flustered and called in the big boss, who said to me, 'I gather you're not going to do the scooter thing. Can I ask why?' I replied, 'Because my foot doesn't fit on it, it's wobbly as fuck, the chances of me falling off are pretty high, I've got arthritis in my ankle, I'm a former rugby player who doesn't ride a scooter, and it looks really cheesy. No serious DJ would be seen riding something into their DJ sets, and what's it got to do with anything anyway? Tell you what, let's compromise: take the lights off and I'll walk with the promo girls holding the light sticks, hyping up the crowd and making a big fuss.' She replied, 'That sounds pony, and I think you are being stupid.' 'What?' I shot back. 'As pony as me riding a scooter lit up like a Christmas tree on fireworks night, with a helmet that makes me look like SpongeBob SquarePants, while I push and wobble all of the 10 metres to the stage?'

She crossed her arms, looking all arsey, and said something about me having a bad attitude and that I had messed them around, that I was unprofessional and a borderline moron. There was a prolonged silence between us, her eyes boring into mine as she channelled her best Cruella De Vil, while I stared back doing my very best silent Borat impression – you know, the one where he interviews those angry feminists and one of them tells him off and he says back in response, 'Why you not smile, pussy cat?' I obviously didn't actually say this out loud, as I would never be that rude nor would I be unprofessional, but by God, I thought it. I eventually explained to her as the stand-off continued that if my ex-wife couldn't get me to do what she wanted me to do, and I loved her, I certainly wouldn't be doing anything I didn't want to do for her. She left the room and my agent, who had been sat panicking in the corner with this shocked expression on his face, suddenly found his voice and was like, 'Wow, she was so rude to you, that is not on. I will go and speak to her and give her a piece of my mind.' I laughed and said, 'Calm down Rocky, where were you when I needed you? The words horse and bolted come to mind.' He shuffled off after the irate woman anyway to wreak horrible revenge to save my honour, or more likely mumble something incoherent to her, while the whole time not looking her in the eye.

Eventually, I did things my way and she ended up apologising. Needless to say, I had the last laugh à la Alan Partridge.

You might expect me to have a massive hard-on for grand entrances, but while it's true that I like being the centre of attention, I want to do things my way and not become a caricature.

Which brings me neatly back to Hong Kong. It turned out I was only booked to DJ for 15 minutes, which hardly seemed worth it. That's three songs, at most. But I still wanted to have another soundcheck on the morning of the opening ceremony, because the way things had been set up had made me jittery. However, second time around was even worse: one of the decks was randomly selecting stuff on its own accord like it was possessed by some Chinese demon and generally having a meltdown. When I told the supposed engineers about the problem, they suggested I turn it on and off again, which didn't go down well. And even when they went off and returned with a replacement deck, it was still a bit of an issue and I was concerned that things were just not being done properly. I actually ended up getting another deck from the stadium DJ who played the music between scores and breaks. I happened to mention to my fellow DJ the *Carry On* film that I appeared to be an unwitting star in, let's call it *Carry On DJ Disaster* or *Hong Kong Goes Wong*, and he said, 'Take the spare deck and God be with you.'

I now had three decks set up, which is what I was always supposed to have. I had faith in one and a half of them but thought, 'Never mind, I think I can style things out …'

When I turned up for my set, everyone was absolutely shit-faced as far as the eye could see, especially in the South Stand, which looked like the last days of Rome. My team of engineers, security and chaperones all looked tense. Just getting to the tunnel was a nightmare, I was accosted left, right and centre, and one very pissed bloke couldn't work out whether he wanted a photo or to fight me. He had his shirt off, his tattoos looked like they were bought at Asda and he had a proper mean expression. He kept trying to pull me towards him as he shook my hand, then he tried to fight security. Meanwhile others were asking for photos, high fives or shouting amusing things like 'Chris, Chris, Chris, it's Chris Robshaw!', turning to their mates, giving them a nod and a wink and pissing themselves laughing.

Getting out of the tunnel for my actual set was a nightmare; they had cleared everyone, the moment was upon us, the light rig was ready and the smoke was filling the tunnel. I had a bloke with a headset behind me and another one in front of me. One started telling me to 'go, go, go' while the other was saying 'stay, stay, stay'. I knew I only had limited time to play my set, so I decided to go. I started thinking of Bridget Jones when she goes down the fireman's pole only to be told, 'No, wait', and to much hilarity she tries to shimmy back up, only to crash-land on the reporter and camera below.

I was halfway to the pitch when the lights ignited, and the tunnel was lit. I got the photographs from the event, and you can see the brightly lit tunnel and me halfway down the stairs, fuck knows what went wrong, but judging by the fact I ended up DJing for less time than I should have done, the guy who was saying 'go' was right and the bloke behind me wrong. During my walk down, there was much cheering and a real positivity, which was great. It's at these moments that I realise how lucky I am to do the job I do. That being said, I was offered out once again to fight some bloke for no reason, or no reason I could see. There were also plastic cups flying all over the place, and I was thinking, 'If any of those cups have got piss in them, I'm going to fill someone in …' I don't mind a golden shower but it's usually on my terms and doesn't arrive in a plastic cup delivered by a cretinous, pissed rugby fan.

I finally made it to the decks, mixed the first song in and everyone went wild. But halfway through, the song skipped out of time. I thought maybe I'd nudged the decks – there were 20,000 people in the South Stand and I could see the whites of people's eyes, so I was a bit nervous – but having fixed things on the jog wheel and started waving my hands in the air, it suddenly sounded very briefly like someone was back-spinning the song, as if with some vinyl. (For the keenos out there, that's a vinyl break essentially.) The sound team and floor manager were flashing me quizzical looks, and I was looking back at them as if to say, 'I haven't touched anything, I've got my fucking hands in the air!' I was less than pleased as I had done three soundchecks and flagged issues, but when you are up there it's all on you, very much like when you are out on the field playing rugby. No one knows you have a slight injury, or your missus has done your head in, or you feel a bit sick. All they see is your shit performance. I was getting more and more livid, as it was nothing whatsoever to do with me.

That set was a struggle, to put it mildly. There must have been about 10 skips in 15 minutes – maybe it was water damage, because Hong Kong is notoriously humid, or maybe it was vibrations from the speakers going into the table that the decks were sitting on. My contract rider states the DJ desk has to be a certain height, but if they weren't going to provide the right DJ equipment, they were certainly not going to get the table height right. So, the desk had been put on wooden blocks to make sure I didn't suffer a spinal injury. Whatever was happening, the decks were malfunctioning and causing me all sorts of grief. I was dancing around and trying to force a smile, but inside I was furious and very embarrassed. I felt like a little kid and wanted the ground to swallow me up. I actually thought about lifting the decks in the air, smashing them on the floor and storming off, rock 'n' roll style. But then I remembered I wasn't Pete Townshend from The Who and me doing that would be much more of a story than me having a few sound issues.

Luckily, most people were pissed anyway and everyone seemed to have enjoyed the music. I got loads of amazing messages, but I knew it had been shit. I cut a very despondent figure back in the dressing room. I used all the tools my therapist had taught me over the years and I snapped out of it very quickly, but if it had happened a few years earlier, when my confidence wasn't as robust, it probably would have taken me weeks to get over. As it was, I still thought I'd blown what should have been a very big moment for me, but I said to myself, 'It's done now, I've no control over it, so move on.'

I have this dream of being a respected DJ and the more I shared that dream, the more people were desperate for it not to happen, or so it appeared, especially from those in the rugby crowd. I love my fans, most of them are great, and it's amazing how much positive love I get. I was recently at Glastonbury, and so many people asked me if I was DJing there. The tide is turning, but I do still get older men from the rugby fraternity saying, 'How's the DJing going?' before roaring with laughter and walking off in their brown shoes, bell bottom jeans and Superdry hoodies.

Social media can make you believe that everybody knows everything about you, but most people don't see the things I post. As a result, they don't know that I did MMA, or stand-up, or make music and DJ. As far as they're concerned, I was and always will be a rugby player, and if they find out that I'm doing something different, they'll openly mock me. I'll be behind the decks and someone will come up to me wearing his Fat Face fleece, cargo shorts and hiking boots, looking like he's about to walk up Scafell Pike, when he's actually 10 pints deep, standing in a nightclub at 2 a.m. He will then lean over and shout, 'Do you have any Eric Clapton?' and then say, 'I didn't know you're a DJ! Hahahahaha!' Then he'll try and tell me some story about his son playing for Saracens academy when I am mid-mix between two songs and unable to hear a word, and everything is going off around him, like flame cannons and confetti, yet he is still trying to tell me this inane rugby story. I am only saved when security lead him away.

So, I felt like the haters had a big win that day in Hong Kong. If it hadn't been a rugby crowd and there was no legacy, it would have been very different. There is a stark contrast between DJing for a rugby crowd and actual music heads. I try to only play in front of the latter now, as the difference between the two is like night and day.

A few weeks before the Hong Kong Sevens, a DJ called Grimes had experienced a load of technical issues at the Coachella festival and spent most of the second half of her set screaming in frustration, which was excruciating to watch. She then took to social media to explain what had gone wrong.

But most people aren't interested in why things go wrong, which is why I decided against doing a social media post of my own. Never complain and never explain. I decided to drop it and go out on the town with the lads. Win or lose, get on the booze.

We recorded the podcast from the stadium the following morning, although my voice had almost gone. I sounded like that guy with the electronic voice box from *Alan Partridge*, Dr No … Vocal Cords. Luckily, we had a good gang of guests, including DJ Forbes (the former New Zealand sevens captain, not actually a DJ), Rob Vickerman and David Campese. We let Campo rant about how rugby is shit nowadays, and how Fiji's Waisale Serevi, widely regarded as the greatest sevens player of all time, said that the reason he played rugby was because of Campo, and he put him down as his sole inspiration for taking up the sport. (We edited out the Serevi stuff because we didn't want to embarrass him, as that's a punchy thing to say. I'm sure it has merit as they are great mates, I just think it was worded a bit wrong. Luckily, we are not in the business of stitching people up.)

It was a fun last day in Hong Kong, but not without issues. I was a bit delicate after the night before, still a bit annoyed about my DJ set, and we had to record from the South Stand, which meant walking through a load of pissed lunatics again, while being filmed by a Chinese production crew. I had to keep saying to them, 'You're not putting that in!', including when some chopper full-on shoulder-barged me as we were walking along one of the concourses. I was so taken aback that I said, 'Oi fuckhead, say excuse me!' to which he replied, 'What?' in a vacant way and then 'Oi mate, don't you play for Exeter? I'm a big fan', and proceeded to try and talk to me. I kept walking and he kept following, but before he could ask for a photo and say how much he loved Sandy Lane, Payno had to step in and say, 'Come on mate, give it a rest.' Sadly, the bloke was not even being ironically funny, he thought I was someone but who I have no idea.

I'm sometimes asked, mainly by Payno, if I'm worried that I'll completely lose it one day and iron someone out, to which the answer is yes and no. I am actually very controlled and calm most of the time. I don't think I am some hard nut, nor do I think I can fight. I just don't really back down once things go turbo. But I normally try to avoid conflict. If people want to start a problem, more often than not I can equally get filled in. That being said, there is always some drama close at hand as some men seem to react in an odd way to me. It's like when you see dogs run up to each other and one always tries to alpha the other. I get alpha'd a lot, which is odd as I normally mind my own business.

In Monaco recently, someone I was walking past punched me on the arm while I was out with a mate. I said to him calmly and with a half-smile, 'Fucking hell, do I know you?' 'No,' he replied, 'we've never met.' To which I said, 'So why are you fucking punching me on the arm?' He was with a group of lads who all stopped and he looked a bit shocked at my response and mumbled something about the lads and rugby, and I ended up laughing it off. All his mates weren't sure where to look. I tried to keep it all tongue-in-cheek, but it would never cross my mind to punch someone when they walked past.

I have been working on not being reactive in lots of areas of my life, especially in situations like this, with my psychologist. He's trying to get me to go with the flow a bit more, instead of swimming against the tide. Acceptance is a massive part of life: if you accept your reality then you can move on much more easily. If someone is an idiot, don't rise to it. It's easier said than done, but my life would be better if I did that all the time. As it is, I spend a lot of time feeling like Larry David from *Curb Your Enthusiasm*.

Having finally taken our seats, a load of people started chanting 'Haskell, Haskell, give us a wave!' I was sat there thinking, 'By the power of Grayskull, get me out of here!' Meanwhile, Payno was reminding me, in his most soothing voice, to breathe and stay calm and to think of the money … just as someone puked up next to me.

**AP:** In Hong Kong, people were literally running after Hask and Tins, and it was very interesting to see how the two of them dealt with the attention. Hask spends most of his life in the public eye and is very active on social media, but while he's courteous towards anyone who wants a chat, an autograph or a selfie, he's also perfunctory. He'll chat, but usually while still walking, and probably for five seconds max. He'll give you a selfie, but that will be your lot. Lots of people leave comments under the podcast saying how much they dislike Hask, but whenever we're out and about, he's like the Pied Piper.

When we do big match days at Twickenham, we'll have lunch in the foyer, and people will be continuously banging on the windows, trying to get our attention. Tins and I will get up and have a chat with them, but Hask gets really pissed off about it and won't even turn around unless we tell him there's a little kid and then he always makes time. If they have a Barbour, walking boots and look rugby, he will just pretend they aren't there. Paradoxically, if nobody was trying to get Hask's attention, he'd start touting himself around – 'Would anyone like their picture taken with me? Anyone?!'

Tins is very different. He'll ask you where you're from, what rugby team you support, your views on the world in general. That's why we call him 'the reverse pothole', because while people go out of their way to avoid potholes, Tins is so keen to talk to people that they end up avoiding him.

# 6

# WORLD CUP 2019, JAPAN

**AP:** Japan was where our friendships really kicked on to another level. My wife might not be too pleased to hear this, but those three and a half weeks were among the best of my adult life. I don't think I've ever laughed so much, and as that old saying goes, people who drink together stay together.

If my memory serves me correctly, we didn't have anything to do but the podcast for the first two weeks. We were out 10 of those 14 nights, and the earliest we went to bed was 4 a.m. That might sound as if we were totally out of control, but you don't have to go chasing things in Japan, it will just pick you up and carry you, because the culture is just so different and invigorating.

Hask is always up for a night out and Tins needs no second invitation as he is either coming from a night out or going to a night out, so he just jumps on board, while I spent a lot of time feeling like I was in a sidecar – goggles and gloves on, scarf billowing in the wind, wondering where on earth we were heading.

It became a running joke that at eight o'clock every evening, someone would say, 'I think I'll just have a quick bowl of ramen for dinner and go straight to bed.' But we'd be sat in this little restaurant down a side street, they'd slide three little sakes in front of us, and we'd think, 'Well, I suppose one isn't going to hurt ...' Suddenly, it would be three in the morning and we'd all be belting out karaoke in a bar on the other side of Tokyo.

One Monday night, after we'd recorded the podcast in a pub, Tins, a mate and I ended up in a karaoke booth with a very nice Japanese lady we'd got talking to (remarkably, and to his eternal regret, Hask had gone home). Tins sang awfully, I sang slightly better, and then this lady sang absolutely beautifully. It transpired that she'd won the Japanese version of *Pop Idol* and had 80 million followers on social media. That was the podcast in a nutshell, in that it was constantly leading us into extraordinary situations, to the extent that those extraordinary situations soon became strangely normal.

Hask will tell you that I spent a lot of my time in Japan tipping and sipping drinks and hiding in the loo. Such talk is all white noise as far as I'm concerned, and no amount of brutish bullying from two alpha males will change me. I know what my game plan is and I stick to it, and I'm almost always there at the end of the night. If I didn't take that approach, I'm not sure the podcast would remain upright.

I did lash out at Hask one night. That was an unfortunate incident, but I'd like to think of it as a moment when respect was earned. We were in a taxi and I invited him to call my son, and somewhere along the way things got muddled up, I got very cross and threatened to rip his eyeballs out. If that sounds like an overreaction, you have to appreciate that there was a lot of muscle on the other side of the ring, and Hask has martial arts training, so if things did ever kick off between us, I wouldn't have a choice but to scratch and bite for as long as it lasted.

**JH:** The 2019 World Cup in Japan was an amazing experience. I'd lived in Japan, having played for Tokyo's Ricoh Black Rams in 2011–12, but the World Cup was a chance to travel the country and really get to know the place.

We were there for almost a month, attending games, recording the podcast, hosting events in bars and drinking far more than was healthy. There were times when I thought I might die, and Justin Marshall almost did – the tournament lasted for 43 days and he was on the piss for 40 of them (he only took those three days off because he went down with glandular fever, which only took him down for a day before he dosed himself up and was back out on the piss).

Tins and I did 22 days straight, including the time he went out for breakfast on a Tuesday and got back to the hotel on a Friday night. Very early on, we had what we thought was the brilliant idea of following every Asahi lager with a sake chaser, but that turned out to be a recipe for disaster (as anyone who has seen monumentally drunk Japanese men at post-work drinks would already have known). We nicknamed the drink combo a dragon ball. You would think after the first hangover from hell that we would abandon the combo, but we felt it had legs and with the right balance it could be a powerful combination. We are yet to find the balance.

One night, we all went to a restaurant that one of Payno's mates had recommended. We knew it would probably be expensive, because this guy owns something like 130 pubs in the UK, and most of Payno's mates have quadruple-barrelled names like Ambrose-Bertram-Waddle-Dudley. When you spend time with Payno, it's like an afternoon around Jacob Rees-Mogg's house. We were hugely underprepared for how weird this meal out was going to be. The first thing I saw when I walked in were two fat blokes dressed as Samurai warriors sitting on an island counter, surrounded by pots and stoves and a huge moat of water. The diners were arranged in a square around the island, and the two Samurai would cook whatever we ordered right in front of us before serving it up. However, they didn't just serve up the food and drinks, they had to deliver it on what looked like huge wooden pizza servers, with long handles to cross the moat of water. You see them being used in Italian restaurants to take pizza out of the oven, except these were bigger and longer. They would load them up and then hold them out, you would take off the proffered items and they would retract them until they needed to serve something else.

We decided among ourselves that it would be a good plan to start with some dragon balls. We let one of Payno's mates – Roderick or Rupert, I forget his name – make the order of sake. Let's go with Roderick: he was wearing head to foot tweed – and I mean head to foot, he had tweed shoes, socks, trousers, shirt, jacket and hat all made of tweed. It was an impressive sight. He put on his monocle, surveyed the sake list and made some incomprehensible posh noises, sounding like Brian Badonde from Facejacker, which I can only assume was from years of inbreeding. I bet his family tree resembled a wreath rather than a tree. We had to get Payno to translate the order as he speaks Etonian, which he duly did. I should have known that it was expensive when the maitre'd took in a sharp intake of breath and rushed off smiling and positively vibrating with happiness.

Five minutes later they dimmed the lights, a gong sounded, a puff of smoke erupted from a doorway and this bloke appeared like a genie from a lamp, in full ceremonial outfit, including a huge headdress adorned with gems and feathers. He carried a hand-carved wooden box which he set down and opened, revealing an ornate green bottle carved in the form of a geisha. He then opened the bottle with a massive Samurai sword, then just like that there was another puff of smoke, he disappeared and the lights went up. Everyone was watching us with a newfound respect. The sake was served and went down a storm with all the lads except Tins, who'd had enough by then.

The sake was so good and worked so well with the beer that about 10 minutes later, we had to go through the whole rigmarole again. Lights dimmed, smoke bellowing, swords flying and gongs sounding. Meanwhile, the fat lad on the island kept playing silly buggers – whenever I ordered a beer, he'd place it on the wooden spatula, hold it out for me to take and when I went to take it, he would move the board and I couldn't get it. That old trick. It was funny, I mean the other Japanese dinners thought it was fucking hilarious; honestly, for them it was like the greatest thing they had ever seen. I mean I laughed the first time, the second time he did it I smirked, but by the eighth time the joke had really worn thin; half the other diners were on the floor unable to move with laughter and some of them were pointing at me and mugging me off. Payno was saying, 'Breathe James, calm down', as I was about to dive into the moat, swim over and insert this sake bottle where it hurts into this Rik Waller look-a-like's anus, when the chef must have read the room – or Payno's imploring looks, which involved him mouthing, 'Please, please, stop' and giving the chop gesture over his own throat, the international signal to cut it out, as he offered up the beer for me to take on the ninth time of asking. The chef had no idea how close he came to getting a samurai sword through the Derby.

The food they served up was top drawer. However, in among the good gear there were some borderline criminal items that appeared to be used to pad the whole feed out, or so I thought. I had lived in Japan for eight months and never seen some of the rascal items being served up that night. The issue was that sashimi and yakitori skewers can only fill you up so far, and I was starving hungry, I couldn't stop myself from eating it. Gourmet restaurants are great, but they are not built for the professional grazer. The primary crime against food was something called abalone, which are basically giant sea slugs that taste like slivers of wetsuit. I'd need half a bottle of Asahi and a couple of sakes just to get one down me. But I hate wasting food, and there were bloody loads of them on the table, so once I scoffed all the good stuff like sashimi and yakitori and was looking at what else there was, I kept seeing this thing (abalone) and just kept eating it.

I have a habit of forgetting who's around me, especially after a few drinks, so I was doing my usual thing of being too noisy and swearing far too much. Payno thought that was funny, but not so much Tins, who was having as I have mentioned a rare night off. It's so rare it's the kind of night you would see in a *Marvel* movie when all the universes, planets, stars and fuck knows what else has to align, and Dr Strange is trying to stop the world ending. It's that kind of rare occurrence when the Lord is off the sauce and he was very quiet and wanted everyone else to be down on his morose self-loathing level. However, I had just downed four pints of lager, a litre of sake and half the contents of the ocean, including a fuck ton of sea slugs. I was shutting up for no man, especially one who kept threatening to make a call to you know who, who would then speak to MI5, who in turn would reach out to their Tokyo office, who would arrange for me to get a portion of tainted puffer fish or to have a Ninja knife me in my sleep.

There was an English couple next to me with two kids, so I felt the need to apologise for my language. 'We've heard worse,' they said, to which I replied (realising these people could take a joke, that even if they did learn some bad language off me, it was 10.30 and the kids should probably be in bed anyway),

'It's actually not my fault. I say blame the parents. It's past the watershed after all.'

To Tins' annoyance, I was soon rolling around on the floor pretending to die, one of the kids having picked up a sword off the wall and pretended to stab me. That's one way to get the parents onside and smudge over any potential complaints: show you are a man of the people and let their kids fake stab you. (I had to take the sword off him in the end, as my patience was beginning to go. At one point I was contemplating putting him to sleep while his parents weren't looking. He was also getting giddier with each run through, he was so excited he was going to burst, and I was worried he was going to actually chop one of my arms off.)

Between me forcing down slivers of wetsuit and mucking about with these two kids, Payno realised that he knew the dad from school. And like most of Payno's posh mates, this bloke called him 'Beetle' (I've no idea why, you'll have to ask Payno, but I'm assuming it's got something to do with a since defrocked school chaplain). I know what you're thinking – 'How can Haskell call Payno posh when he went to Wellington College, one of the most expensive schools in the country?' – but there's Wellington College posh and there's Eton posh. For example, when we started doing the podcast, we'd all meet up for the start of a new season and Payno would say, 'Did you summer well?' I'd have visions of Payno riding around his family estate on a Victorian velocipede.

It was a great evening until they handed us the bill, which was for the equivalent of $4,500. It turned out we'd had five bottles of the most expensive sake known to man, and the abalone, which we hadn't even ordered, were $500 each. It turns out that the two fat bastards serving the food had the last laugh on us. I should have just kept letting them take the beer away when I tried to grab it off the serving board. I should have bowed my head in deference at their superior humour, smiled and thanked them for being so, so funny. Instead of giving them evil looks and showing them my 10-metre swimming badge signalling their water moat was no match for me, and if they carried on I would dive in and go *Kill Bill 2* on them all. It had cost me dearly.

Look, $500 is an awful lot of money for a load of giant slugs, especially as they tasted like a combination of garden hose and wetsuit. As you can imagine, Tins was more crestfallen than the rest of us, because he'd hardly touched a thing. Then when I tried to pay the bill, my card was declined, which everyone thought was the funniest thing they'd ever seen. Even the kids were pointing and laughing, until I mouthed, 'I am going to fucking kill you' to one, and they ran off crying to their parents. At least I won a small victory that day. That will teach the 10-year-old not to mess with James Haskell. For those worrying about me and my financial prowess, I used another card, and my honour was restored. Payno tried to pay in gold doubloons, which upset the owner, but not as much as his other mate, the vision in tweed, who tried to pay in negotiable bearer bonds.

We had done a live show in a bar and were ready to get the train back to Tokyo, only to discover we'd missed the last one. However, it wasn't just us three, it was our crew as well. You can imagine that if someone had fucked the travel up they certainly weren't going to have come up with a contingency plan for where we would stay or have booked a hotel. Now there were a lot of sheep and not a lot of shepherds; the only bright idea someone came up with was to go and work things out in a McDonald's next to the station, with a plan being mooted that we could stay in there until the first train arrived and then jump on it at 7.30 a.m. We had finished the show and watched England play so it was 10.30 p.m. That is a fuck load of time to be spent in a McDonald's and I wasn't going to sleep in one in a million years. I didn't think there was any need and to be honest I haven't reached a stage in my life where that seems like a sensible and rational course of action. The day I wake up in a fast-food restaurant with a gherkin stuck to the side of my face is the day I kill myself. Being the shepherd I am, I said, 'Right, let's google a load of hotels and go door to door until we find a room. Then we can use the company card.' This is where the camp split. The crew led by Simon were saying no, they couldn't afford it, and all for one and one for all. Most of the support staff were what you would call liberal left leaning, practically communists. Ok, I'm joking, but not really. They were very much 'We are equal, what is mine comrade is yours' etc. With the group who shared that mindset, there was no convincing them. So, I led a team blue of Payno and Tins one way, while team red went the other way to a McDonald's to discuss how unfair the world is.

After traipsing the streets for hours, our team finally found a hotel with a room. We stayed in comms with the other group and when I told the crew they said they couldn't afford it. I did suggest using the company card but that was glossed over very quickly. The chap on reception, happy to have sold two rooms at that hour of the night, actually suddenly found a bigger room and upsold us to a suite. He kept banging on in broken English about 'Huge room, lots of space, big minibar, loads of drinks, amazing view'. It was 11.45 now and views were the least of our concerns. We had visited eight hotels and not found one room anywhere, and the thought of sleeping under the gaze of Ronald McDonald was making my skin crawl; I hate fucking clowns and especially ones that are situated in a place that smells of grease, ketchup and broken dreams. I suggested that with a bigger room the crew could all bunk in with us (like one big commune or gulag, depending on how they wanted to see it). I thought it would appeal to them. However, the proletariat were never destined to mix with the bourgeoisie, and they turned it down.

At least that's my version of events. The producer's version is that we abandoned them. That it was all for one and one for all until the heat came on and we dropped them like Jeffery Epstein's friends vapourised on him. They got a bit arsey and mutinous about it, there were some cross words, a lot of side-eyeing and talking in corners when we met at the station the next day. Not by us of course, we had slept if anything too well and were chipper as hell the next day. There was only talk of adventures for us, while the B team were nibbling a communal nugget and blaming the haves for not helping the have nots. The producer even collated my voice messages for a segment that he played out as a surprise on one of our live shows, in an attempt to prove that I never made the offer, and that we were all bastards. (I had made the offer! But he still goes on about it to this day.)

Now I said we slept well, but it wasn't as simple as that. Our 'suite', which if you had listened to the hotel receptionist would have rivalled that of the presidential suite at the Ritz or the Waldorf Astoria, allegedly came with so much extensive square-footage we would have our little English minds blown and would have very little time for sleep, considering all the incredible amenities at our disposal. I will be honest here, he had me hook, line and sinker. A great salesman, he was, as well as a proper bullshitter, as it turned out.

So to say it was underwhelming would be a grave understatement. The disappointment was palpable when we opened the door. The only thing I can liken it to would be being in hospital in the 1980s and hearing Jimmy Savile's visit had been cancelled only to hear the sound of a didgeridoo coming from down the corridor. I was fucking livid but too tired to do anything about it. It had one double bed, a camp bed and a sofa in one room, and a single bed in the other. As for the 'fully stocked mini-bar and facilities', that was a fucking joke. There was one can of Fanta and tube of Pringles. There was coffee and tea but no kettle, and the bathroom had a half-used bottle of body wash. You couldn't swing a cat in there, and it was 2,000 degrees, as all shit hotels appear to be.

Payno, who is used to Jeeves warming his bed with an old-fashioned bed warmer and taking his toilet in peace and calm while nanny tends to the children, was not happy to find out he had to share a room with me and was beginning to think he might as well have taken his chances in McDonald's. Sadly, he wasn't sure what a McDonald's actually was but assumed it must be part of a hotel group with a similar name or a gentlemen's club like White's. His aristocratic mind could not have comprehended the reality of it. No sooner was he tucked up in bed in his monogrammed pyjamas and little eye mask when, apparently, I started snoring like a grizzly bear in hibernation. He tried to shush me, but he wasn't sure how as he normally has someone on his estate to do that for him.

So, he did what he does best and panicked and sought refuge in the other room, only to find that Tins was snoring just as loudly, and also simultaneously whistling through his nose, which is no mean feat. When he really gets going, he sounds like an old-fashioned kettle about to boil. If you remember, Tins was the only rugby player who could smell around corners as his nose was at right angles. He got it fixed but we're not sure it was done properly, as his heavy breathing would give any nuisance caller a run for their money.

Payno again got all overcome like a Victorian woman and was about to get the vapours and collapse onto a chaise longue, only to realise there wasn't one, so he just folded himself up like a pretzel into the airing cupboard and slept like a big posh cat under the towels. For a normal man that would be awfully uncomfortable, but it helps when you have no discernible muscle on your body and you are just bones and sinew. The result is you have unreal flexibility, which made Payno a firm favourite with his choirmaster at school. I shall say no more, only that as it was an awfully long time ago and according to Payno all forgotten, water under the bridge etc. Payno's hotel stay was so awful that he's been trying to tell our producer that he had a lucky break ever since.

In Tokyo I went out with some old mates one night and didn't leave the bar until 5.30 a.m. It had started to piss down, I was in shorts and a T-shirt, and no taxi driver would stop for me. They'd pull up beside me before raising a gloved hand and waving me away. I wasn't really surprised – the driver who did finally let me into his taxi must have been pumping out water for days.

Chloe was flying in that day, and I'd planned to pick her up at the airport. But I spent most of the day dying in bed, nursing the worst hangover I'd ever experienced, and also had to appear at an official England travel club event. So in the end, I decided that it was best for Chloe to jump in a taxi and come to me. She actually told me not to come and pick her up as it was so far and I had work, it was all 'fine'. Which actually means I should have either been there to greet her as a surprise or after being told not to come, come anyway. If you want to take a lesson from this, fine does not mean fine. Fine means you have fucked up and you will pay for it later on. If you think your partner would expect you to do it, do it. Even if they say don't do it, do it. No means yes, yes means yes.

That being said, things may have worked out as I did have work, and putting the earth-shattering hangover to one side, I would never have actually made it back in time. So this might have been a non-issue, but Chloe's taxi got stuck in terrible traffic, a journey that should have taken an hour took four hours, and she had to get out on the motorway and have a piss on the hard shoulder in a massive queue of traffic. She eventually turned up with the raving hump, completely understandably, and her mood got worse when she saw what condition I was in. Nowhere on the internet has anyone said the cure for a hangover is to be brutally and repeatedly bollocked until your headache is now pulsing in time with your heartbeat. Once I had thrown up and mumbled the 85th sorry to Chloe, I then had to attend this England travel club event with Payno, the prospect of which made eating $500 slivers of wetsuit sound like an absolute fucking picnic.

I spent the first hour at the venue sitting at a table with my head in my hands, groaning. I kept saying to Payno, 'I won't be able speak to them. I won't even be able to look at them ...' The organisers kept asking Payno if I was alright, and Payno would say, 'Just leave him for now, he's not feeling very well, he'll switch on when he needs to ...' But when people started filing into the room, I didn't switch on, I panicked and hid in the toilet for 45 minutes. The toilet seat was heated to perfection – not too hot, just enough to warm some crumpets – but I spent the whole time muttering, 'Please, why won't they all just go away ...'

Payno came and found me, gave me a pep talk and I did my bit on stage. It went quite well, all things considered. But by the time I was finished with all those octogenarians and full-on rugby nauses – and told the tale of the time I ran into a post in Cardiff for the millionth time – I was in the foulest of moods. And when I got back to the hotel, I had the row to end all rows with Chloe.

# 7

# WORLD CUP 2023, FRANCE

**JH:** Since Payno has raised the subject of alpha males, if he is the alpha male in his group of friends, then imagine the fucking state of his mates: a group with indeterminate genders, some resembling a bunch of Georgian fops. I imagine they wear ruched cravats, have frilly cuffs on their big open shirts and attach nosegays of flowers to the lapels of their coats. I can also imagine them always challenging people to duels when they get upset, slapping each other with leather gloves and bringing out pairs of duelling pistols handed down the generations. I bet their idea of a good night out is either sitting around basket weaving, or talking about Jean-Paul Sartre's works. Failing that, they can be found in an opium den reading each other poetry.

Whenever Payno claims to be an alpha male, I tell him he's a zeta male on a good day. It then turns into a version of that famous sketch from *The Frost Report*, with Payno taking on the Ronnie Corbett role: 'I know my place …'

Payno, Tins and I haven't argued much, if at all, but we have butted heads over various things. If I have a falling out with someone, which admittedly happens every now and then (but if you believe Payno, Chloe or Tins it happens every second) Payno might say, 'Look, Hask, you don't have to be so scorched earth in your approach, you don't have to blow everything up, there are other options', and I'll tell him that I was just saying what I felt, but it won't go any further than that. However, I have had words with Tins, who can be quite blunt. Well, after he has consumed the next bottle of red wine, he might be Annoyingly Honest Mike, but most of the time to me he's just Blunt Northern Mike.

Tins can be like a big brother. He's adamant that I do too much and is always telling me that 'less is more'. At one point, I was doing three podcasts, writing a book, DJing, doing three or four talks a week and spending hardly any time at home, so I could see where he was coming from. But I'd usually reply, 'Tins, you might think that less is more, but I like doing more for more.' I told him I enjoyed doing all those things, and I enjoyed living in chaos as it's how I made money. He cares for me a lot and it always comes from a good place, but on one occasion I told him to wind his fucking neck in after he had misunderstood something around some podcast stuff I was doing. To be fair, he is always good at putting his hand up and saying he got it wrong, just as I hope I am.

When the three of us were at the 2023 World Cup in France, we watched Scotland's opening game against South Africa in a beach bar in Marseille. I'd had a bit of a mad one the day before, involving a very long and boozy lunch and almost drowning in the sea. I hired one of those electric scooters, the ones you stand on, to get me back to the boat we were staying on, but I had no idea where this boat was. And when I put an SOS out on all my WhatsApp groups – 'Where's this fucking boat?!!!' – I had Richard and Judy replying to me – 'What boat are you talking about?' I ended up going the wrong way down the road, fell off the scooter about eight times, went into the back of a car, had a row with the driver, forgot that cars in France drive on the other side of the road, and so pulled out of a junction looking the wrong way and was nearly toast. I made it back home, sweating, bleeding, in shock and still pissed, just in time for my two-hour DJ set, which I forgot I had until I went to see what was going on and they ushered me behind the decks and said, 'You are on in fifteen.' The set went very well, I thought.

As you can imagine, I was feeling quite precious the following day, but I was also looking forward to it because Payno, Tins and I rarely socialise as a threesome – it's usually me and Tins, or me and Payno, or very occasionally Tins and Payno. It's a running joke that the three of us can never be together for too long: the universe won't allow it. And when we do all get together for a drink, Payno and Tins bicker. They won't admit it, but I think they're quite competitive with each other. I'm competitive, obviously, but not in that way, so sitting back and watching them chipping away at each other makes me giggle. They both like to point fingers at me, and I take it because I have the self-awareness to see it and accept it. Payno is actually really fiery and is always having words, but he pretends he doesn't. Tins is never around but always says he is. If you told them any of this, they'd both just come back firing. So I am the team scapegoat, but those two fusspots are always a bit head on head with each other.

South Africa beat Scotland comfortably, but it was a pretty shit game. So to lift the spirits, and because I'd only nibbled away on a cheeseboard all afternoon, I suggested we all go out for a nice dinner on the boat. Of course, while we were eating, Tins suggested we had some rosé. When Tins says have some rosé what he means is he will get through a bottle, I will have a couple of glasses and Payno will pretend to drink but will in fact nurse the same glass until we leave and it will still be three-quarters full. He once nursed a pint for so long, it caught fire in his hand and set all the alarms off. When he isn't pretending to drink, he is tipping it in plant pots or over his shoulder. He is the original drink tipper.

Having found a decent steak restaurant tucked away on one of the decks, I put Tins in charge of the wine. He'd already drunk three bottles of rosé on his own (maybe it was one, but we'll not let the truth get in the way of a good story), so probably wouldn't have noticed if they'd served him Blue Nun, but he was always posting photos of him and his mates drinking Petrus and Margaux, so I assumed he knew what he was doing. Payno was very enthusiastic about having some red wine. 'Oh, I love red,' he said in his slightly camp public school accent. I rolled my eyes as we all knew it would end up on the carpet or still in its glass. I reckoned it would take him that long to drink it, it would probably turn back into grapes before he finished it or asked for a top-up. The same way Payno thinks he is an alpha male; he also thinks he is Oliver Reed on the piss when he is in fact much more like Rowan Atkinson's Blackadder in series 2 when he challenges Lord Melchett to a drinking competition and ends up throwing up in front of his puritanical fat aunt and singing about Merlin, the happy pig. Which is how Payno ends up in most of our sessions, that or offering to remove my eyes.

We all have that mate or partner who says, 'I am not having a big one, I will only stay for one drink and then be home.' Before you know it, it's 6 a.m. and they come swaying through the door off their head, as if this was always the plan, and get the arse when you point it out. I'm not sure why they say it, it's probably to justify it to themselves, but they always do the opposite. Well, Payno actually never has a big one and always just goes to bed. It's always quite surprising as you think he is just making himself feel better by saying he is not going to drink and needs to be home early, but no, he actually goes home, has a Horlicks, reads a sonnet and goes to bed in his huge four-poster with silk curtains around it.

Anyway, back to dinner on the boat. Tins ordered a lovely bottle of wine, the starters arrived and we had a very pleasant time chatting about all the characters on the boat. They seemed to have every rugby player who had ever lived on board, including former Scotland scrum-half Andy Nicol. My experience of cruises is that people just want to stuff their faces and get bang on it, booze-wise, but the organisers had gone turbo and were getting their pound of flesh out of the talent. There were activities with Andy about 10 times a day: 6.30 a.m. – sunrise yoga and engaging rugby chat with Andy Nicol and Mike Tindall; 7.30 a.m – breakfast with Andy Nicol; 10 a.m. – shuffleboard and croquet with Andy Nicol; 12 noon – lunch and rugby chats with Andy Nicol and Dwayne Peel; 2 p.m. – basket weaving with Andy Nicol and Noel Edmonds; 4 p.m. – high tea and scrum talk with Andy Nicol and Gethin Jenkins; 7 p.m. – haggis, neeps and tatties with Andy Nicol and Kenny Logan; 9 p.m. – how to smoke a cigar and clear a ruck with Andy Nicol. I imagined him announcing to a group of old people, 'I might as well say this now, Sue Cook has pulled out and I was made promises about storage, so the tie and blazer sets are slightly damaged,' and half of them getting up and leaving. I walked past the theatre on a couple of occasions, and it was just Andy sitting in half-darkness on stage, with no crowd in sight, silently sobbing, and every now and then begging his chaperone, who was standing ominously close by, to please let him leave or just put him out of his misery. The chaperone remained impassive and emotionless, watching the clock in case he tried to leave before the time was up. Rumour has it they never let him off the boat and he is currently doing five shows a day of *Peter Pan* for the kids' club, where he plays Nana the dog.

Anyway, Payno suddenly says, 'Oh, just to let you know, there's a real problem with this boat. I'm hearing a lot of people haven't been paid and they're going to go bust.' I was looking down at my steak at the time when I heard a big bang, I looked up and saw that Tins had stabbed his steak knife through the top of table. He turned to Payno frothing at the mouth, with his mortgage eyes on, one fixed and one variable. 'That's the problem with you, Payno,' he said, 'you're just so fucking negative. There's always a problem with everything. Why can't you just be positive for once?' He was pretty merry by now and to be honest, with his eyes rolling all over the place I couldn't work out initially whether he was talking to me or Payno. He looked like Mad-Eye Moody from *Harry Potter*, one eye revolving around the room. Even the waiter and a woman three tables away thought they might be in the firing line, only to breathe a sigh of relief as the eye tornadoed away to a new target.

Payno knew that Tins could get frank after a few drinks, but he hadn't expected knives to be involved. He tried to explain – about the boat being only half full, despite every hotel in every major city in France being booked up, which had left them deep in the shit – but Tins was having none of it. They paid us before we boarded – I demanded it, because I'd been burned far too many times – and as far as Tins was concerned, that's all that mattered. He kept saying, 'You're just so fucking negative', like a cyborg with a glitch, although he did occasionally throw in a 'You're such a fucking catastrophiser'.

Once Tins had stopped with his recriminations, there was an awkward pause. I pretended to have found something super-interesting on the carpet as I couldn't deal with the awkwardness, while Payno looked on the verge of tears. Tins was putting food into his mouth and sipping wine at the same time, which was a new tactic I hadn't seen before, but I didn't dare to say anything in case the steak knife found its way into my neck. Alex looked like a fish out of water with just his mouth opening and closing and no sound coming out, looking at me for help.

He was like Joe Pesci's character in *Lethal Weapon*, just floundering around and not sure what to say or do. He finally piped up and said, 'Okay, okay, move on, move on', as he always did in those situations, and I started talking about the curtains. 'Wow, have you guys noticed them? I wonder where they got them from. How much do you reckon they spent on curtains for the entire boat?' That's how bad the shit got; I started talking about the fucking curtains, anything to detract from this awkward hell I was trapped in. With that, the Eye of Sauron fell on to me, as Tins said, 'As for you, you fucking dickhead, you're still doing far too fucking much. When are you going to learn that less is more?' I thought, bloody hell the waiter is only doing his job, then my blood ran cold, as the now revolving eye of the Dark Lord was fixed squarely on me. The tiny black pupil in its bloodshot alcohol bath was piercing through my soul. Not sure what to do, I said, 'Oh look, a dolphin', which distracted Tins for just enough time for me to get up and go to the bathroom. The fact it was 10.30 at night, pitch black outside the windows and we were 60 feet in the air didn't stop Tins looking around for a dolphin for a good five minutes

We carried on with the meal, although the atmosphere had dipped somewhat. Tins kept saying, 'I'm just being honest, I'm just telling it like it is', while Payno wasn't saying a word. And once we'd polished off our main courses, Payno walked out of the restaurant ahead of us, like a flustered bird.

Tins had now finished his wine and was all hunched over, like Frankenstein's lab assistant Igor. I said, 'Tins, it's time for us to leave,' and he said, 'Coming, Master.' His ability to walk was slightly impaired, so I was half holding him up as he waddled out from the restaurant. Then he said to me, 'I know what I'm gonna do', before breaking into a sprint, spear-tackling Payno ahead of us and very nearly putting him through a shop window. Understandably, Payno was somewhat perplexed. As was I. And after Tins had crawled off to bed, I had to talk Payno down from the roof. Not literally, but he was quite put out, acting like Lynn, when Alan Partridge crashes into that bollard, and she jars her neck. 'Calm down! Air! Air! Air! Calm down Lynn, you're suffering from minor women's whiplash.' Just replace Lynn with Payno and suffering from whiplash with suffering from an Annoyingly Honest Mike attack. Payno was near to tears and hyperventilating. I soothed him by singing an old choir song he likes and rubbing his palm like the black widow does to the Hulk in the *Marvel* movie. After a bit of time, he was back to his posh old self, reciting sonnets and getting ready for a big day of flower pressing.

Zara came out a few days later and when we mentioned this to her, she confirmed that this had happened before. It turns out this was one of Tins' trademark moves: to become bluntly honest, whether anyone wanted it or not.

**MT:** Payno overthinks things – he's got one of those creative brains that never switches off – and he can either be very positive or a negative Nelly, there doesn't seem to be an in between. And when he starts catastrophising and I've had a few drinks, Annoyingly Honest Mike appears. And he comes on strong.

There was a lot of stuff going on with the boat company, which everyone was calling the 'sinking ship'. People hadn't been paid, and Payno started panicking about us not getting paid in the middle of what had been a good, long, boozy lunch. I'm the ultimate optimist who always sees the good in people. Until someone has burnt me, I trust them. And if someone starts being negative about something that hasn't happened yet, I can get quite irritated.

So when Payno started going on about us being in trouble, I grabbed my knife, drove it into the table and said, 'All you do is moan, Payno. Why can't anything be easy with you?'

'Well,' he replied, 'what do you expect when I'm dealing with you two? I've always got to plan for doom.'

'You're a catastrophiser!' I said. 'That's all you fucking do! Everything is either rosy or shit, never in between.'

I don't think I'd ever seen Hask looking so awkward, and after we'd paid the bill in silence, I started to feel a bit bad. I thought, 'You know what, a hug will make up for it.' But it wasn't really a hug, it was actually a rugby tackle that nearly broke Payno's spine. It wasn't my finest moment. When I woke up the following morning, I was a bit worried that Payno would hate me. Then I remembered him stopping me drinking an ill-advised shot – I think his exact line was, 'Maybe you don't want to do that.' But when we met up, he was good as gold, as if nothing had happened. We're very good at getting past our occasional disagreements, and we often save each other from making mistakes. That's how good friends work.

I don't worry about any of our shenanigans getting into the papers because we tell most of the stories on the podcast anyway. I am what I am, which is a typical rugby lad, even though the media has tried to portray me as some kind of heathen monster in the past. My stag do in Florida proved to be quite controversial, but all we did was drink a lot, which is just what rugby lads do. One of the points of going on tour with the podcast is getting into interesting situations every now and again, because that makes for some good stories. Like when Hask almost drowned during a heavy liquid lunch – he has to swim upright, like a seahorse, because his feet are so heavy and sink to the bottom. Or the next day, when he forgot he was meant to be DJing and almost killed himself making his way back to the boat on an electric scooter. It's not the most grown-up behaviour, admittedly, but rugby lads never really do grow up.

**AP:** We'd seen glimpses of Annoyingly Honest Mike before the 2023 World Cup. You know how you have certain friends you seek advice and feedback from? Well, I find that before you ask for advice or feedback, you build up to it, there's a bit of dancing to be done. And usually when it's given, it's given gently. That's how most normal friendships work.

But Annoyingly Honest Mike works radically differently. It might be a lovely sunny day and you'll be talking about something totally incidental, and suddenly Annoyingly Honest Mike will appear in the middle of one of your sentences and give you a complete breakdown of your failings. Because you're completely unprepared for it, and didn't ask for it in the first place, it's really quite shocking.

Before that infamous dinner on the cruise ship, which we'd been on for what felt like an eternity, Tins had already had three bottles of rosé. Meanwhile, I'd been sipping and tipping, because it was a baking hot day and I wanted to pace myself. Having gone for such a deep reach on the wine, ordering a bottle that cost as much as a car, you would have thought that Tins would nurse it through the meal. Alas, he got stuck into it as if it was mere Ribena.

I didn't invite Tins to offer a comment. In fact, I was in the middle of explaining that the cruise company was very close to going bust, which I thought was quite an important detail to share with the group, when he suddenly transformed into Annoyingly Honest Mike and slammed his steak knife into the table.

It ended up being a horribly awkward supper, with Tins and me not talking to each other and Hask attempting to play peacemaker, which is extraordinary in itself. Then Tins tried to make up for the fact he'd rather spoilt dinner by almost tackling me into a shop window. Imagine the headlines if that had gone wrong.

It's also worth mentioning that the cruise company did go into administration a couple of months after the Rugby World Cup, and we were one of the few people who ended up getting paid in full. Needless to say, after the tears, I had the last laugh.

# 8

# MORE PARIS MAYHEM

**JH:** On the night of the semi-final between England and South Africa at the Stade de France, Payno and I went out for dinner. We drank lots of wine, spent a couple of hours laughing our heads off, watched brave and brilliant England agonisingly lose, before queuing outside a bar for 45 minutes. The people on the door kept pretending they were going to let us in, but they never intended to. You know, the sort who would not have looked out of place in a *Zoolander* movie: headsets, outlandish outfits all in black and faces like smacked arses. They all had single names like Seal or Avicii, and one of the door women was so cool she just had a sound for a name. I think it was blarhsssh. I kept nodding and winking so it looked like I had Tourettes. I think it was Payno's outfit that put them off. He was in his best cagoule and cravat combination with red trousers and Gucci loafers. But because we didn't have Tins with us, they wouldn't let us in. None of them would have pissed on us if we were on fire (Tins, of course, would have been waved to the front of the queue at Studio 54), so we ended up paying 50 euros each to get into a shitty nightclub near the Eiffel Tower where everyone was way younger than us and we couldn't hear each other over the Euro-gash music. Think of the works of scooter and Mr Worldwide, combined together with a French twist. Basically, the music ear-fucked you into submission, until the only choice was to buy more drinks to make it tolerable. We had a couple of drinks and a deep and meaningful conversation before leaving at around 3.30 a.m.

When Payno turned up to record the podcast the following morning, he was all wrapped up in a big coat, looking very pale and feeling very sorry for himself. Meanwhile, Tins was nowhere to be seen, so the two of us recorded it without him. Tins does have a habit of disappearing every now and then. He always has a multitude of excuses, from the King needing his back scratching, or a Corgi had shit on his laptop so he couldn't access his emails, or the moat cleaner hadn't arrived on time and Zara was going mad. Sometimes he would eventually turn up, but it would always be a couple of weeks too late.

That was our last day in France, and I wasn't bowing out without one final swing of the bat. A lawyer friend of mine had invited me for lunch, but Payno really didn't fancy it. 'No, no, no,' he said, 'I feel a bit sick and I need to go for a poo. You go on without me …' It was pathetic. 'Payno,' I said to him, 'don't be such a pussy. Like every other establishment in France, this place has toilets. Just one beer, hair of the dog. I promise you'll be back home in time for *Antiques Roadshow* and I'll even give you a cuddle before you go to bed.'

'Are you sure?' he replied weedily.

'Listen, Payno, you're a 45-year-old man. Grow the fuck up and come for a bit of lunch …'

He muttered something in a tearful voice about ruddy well needing a poo and that it just wasn't cricket to drag a fellow out who needed to make toilet. I didn't understand most of what was said, but reminded him that if he didn't come, I would cause some sort of ungodly drama and bring the business down just to spite him. That got him up and out, albeit slowly and gingerly.

We turned up at this bar, met my mate Will and a couple of his mates, and got stuck into the Bloody Marys. And once Payno had had his poo, he was a man reborn. He had a spring in his step and like a good pedigree dog his nose was wet and his eyes were shining once the first drop of alcohol touched his lips. I texted a few of the England lads and soon they started filing into the bar: Danny Care, Jamie George, a few others. Then Tins turns up, closely followed by former All Blacks scrum-half Justin Marshall, whose autobiography should be called *My Life Between Drinks*. Springbok legends Schalk Burger and Bryan Habana were next to show, and we immediately got stuck into Bryan for ordering a Malibu and pineapple. He was told to fuck off and sit at another table if he wanted to have that sort of drink. A few lads started asking what his pronouns were. True, the rest of us were drinking rosé, which on home soil is not really play on, but it's acceptable on the continent, but there is a time and place for Malibu and pineapple on a boys all-dayer and that's never and in the bin.

It was one of those wonderful impromptu drinking sessions that sprang from seemingly nowhere, with cigar smoking, daft cocktails and shots, storytelling, much laughter and industrial levels of piss-taking. We must have been 30 bottles of rosé deep by the time Owen and Andy Farrell rocked up, and Big Faz immediately started having banter with Justin Marshall, after Justin decided to pick a battle over who had played the most games. Justin did actually play quite a lot of games, including 81 internationals, but Big Faz put him back in his box with, 'Mate, I fucking played 700 games pal, union and league.' I had sidled over to see what the bigger boys were doing and chatting about. I heard the convo so decided to throw some petrol on the fire by pointing out that Big Faz had also been rugby league's Man of Steel. Big Faz shot back with, 'Twice, Hask! Man of Steel fucking twice!' That pretty much finished Justin off for the night. You can't even on your best day argue against 700 games, dual code international player and two Man of Steel awards.

Colleen Farrell (Big Faz's wife) was also there and she thanked me for all the support I'd given her boy on the podcast and in the media, which was really nice of her. A lot of shit had been written about Owen in the media, which his mum thought was out of order, as did I. I mean at times it was borderline criminal the amount of heat he got and what people were saying about him. Owen's a great bloke and an amazing family man, and all that flak had really worn him and his family down. Big Faz also said thanks, and I felt the need to tell him and his wife that I had stood up for Owen not just because he was a mate, but also because he was a good man, a leader and a brilliant rugby player.

By the time I got back to the big table, Tins was shirtless and straight-arm pouring a bottle of rosé into his mouth, well near his mouth, eyes and nose. It was like he wanted the rosé in his body all at once and just putting it in his mouth was not enough. I think he was trying to drink it through his eyes, nose, ears and pores in his skin. Which I have to say was a novel approach, but you could see the drunken science behind it. So, when he could see and breathe again and the bottle lay empty, he said to me, 'Oh, there's Owen, I'm gonna go over and have a chat.' I was stricken with panic, because when Tins is replaced by Annoyingly Honest Mike, anything can happen. I wanted to say to him, 'Tins, nobody wants to hear your honesty now', but you've got a better chance of stopping the Incredible Hulk than Annoyingly Honest Mike.

Rugby-wise, Owen only cared about playing well and winning. He didn't want to be a media personality or play any games. But I knew Owen to be a fun, light character, and Tins and I thought there was mileage in him giving the media at least a glimpse of his personality. Because if a sportsman doesn't reveal anything of himself, people will fill the void of silence with a load of negativity. However, for some people all they want to do is win, work hard and be a leader, a great team man and a dad. I had always respected Owen for being the polar opposite of me. That's perhaps why he is one of England's greatest ever players and I am in the *Daily Mail* for groping Payno at the World Cup or upsetting yet another section of society by making a mistimed joke.

Anyway, Tins staggered over to Owen, and what he meant to say was, 'I think you could do a bit more of the media stuff, let them see who you really are as we all love you, but don't let the bastards grind you down, you're doing an amazing job.' But instead it took him about 10 seconds to say, 'You could do more', while prodding a finger into Owen's chest and coming across as a very dour northern man with an axe to grind, and by the time he'd said it, Owen's mum had flown across the table like a spider monkey and screamed, 'What do you mean, he could do more?!'

Mrs Farrell chewed Tins out for about half an hour, melting one side of his face. He kept apologising for the misunderstanding and tried to explain what he'd actually meant, and every now and again he'd look over at Big Faz as if to say, 'Are you gonna help me with this or what?' Big Faz would smile wryly and shake his head and reply, 'No, been there, it will end when it ends'. Meanwhile, I was thinking, 'I can't save him either, I'm not sure anyone can, I think it's time to shuffle off home …' So, I did what any good mate would do, I just left him to it and hoped he would be ok. I knew what Northern birds could be like and it was touch and go if I am honest.

**MT:** I'm in a WhatsApp group of former World Cup winners from all over the globe, which Hask and Payno obviously aren't a part of (not that I remind them very often). And whenever it gets to the knockout stages of a World Cup, they see very little of me, as the group gets very active with meet-ups.

The day after England's semi-final loss to South Africa, I met up with a few South Africans and Justin Marshall (who, I should make clear, never actually won a World Cup but was out there doing media work). I went to meet Hask and Payno where they were and suddenly it was like someone had blown one of those big Viking war horns. Former and current players, plus wives and girlfriends, started filling this bar up, and about six hours in, Faz Sr, Faz Jr and his mum Colleen turned up.

I love Faz Jr, he's such a good person, but I can understand why people aren't sure about him because he doesn't seem to have much craic and often looks like an angry northerner. He had the most horrendous treatment from the media and fans before and during that tournament. He was vilified for the high tackle in the warm-up match against Wales, which meant he was banned for England's first two pool games, and when he did start playing again, he was criticised by journalists and abused on social media. He couldn't win.

On the podcast, we'd discussed what Owen could do to make people like him, including smiling every now and again and being more amenable and open with the media, maybe even showing them what a good husband and dad he was. And now he was there in person, I decided to tell him to his face, except it came out all wrong. After a bit of small talk, I said to him, 'I think you can do more', and his face changed completely. 'What do you mean, you think I can do more?' he said. Then his mum appeared from nowhere and screamed in my face, 'He's given fucking everything to the game!' I turned to Faz Sr, who I played with for England and is a good mate, and said,

'Are you going to help me out here?' He replied, 'No, I'm not.' And when I asked him why, he said, with a wry smile, 'Because I've been there myself ...'

So for the next half an hour, I had to stand there and take it, like a schoolboy being upbraided by a headmistress. I simply couldn't get out of it, there was no way of trying to explain myself, and in the end I said, 'I'm sorry that didn't come out as intended, I'm going to leave!' I think Faz Sr saw the funny side, and I don't think Owen holds it against me, and I learned a valuable lesson: it's good to be passionate about rugby and people, but when you've had a few drinks, and your timing is a bit off, that passion can get you into trouble.

**AP:** When we were at the Hong Kong Sevens, Mike's alter ego was at it again when he took on Scotland legend John Jeffrey, who will probably be the next chairman of World Rugby. After 15 minutes of Mike decrying the state of world rugby – and, for that matter, World Rugby – poor John looked traumatised, like a man just returned from war having seen far too much.

To Tins' credit, he acknowledges that this demonic alter ego exists within him, although he's yet to learn how to handle him, let alone anyone else. Hask is probably least fazed by Mike, presumably because he could deal with him physically, should he ever get completely out of control. As for me, Annoyingly Honest Mike sometimes crops up in my night-mares, usually with a steak knife in one hand and a bottle of Petrus in the other.

Am I catastrophiser? No, I'm a realist. I have peripheral vision and like to make everyone aware of potential pitfalls, whereas Tins and Hask are like a couple of wild beasts with tunnel vision, rarely thinking about what they're charging into. To be fair to Tins, he has a more nuanced outlook than Hask, but he's so busy and disorganised – with a very, very laissez-faire attitude – that I need to be much more into the weeds of our business than either of the other two. But when I give them bad news, or simply tell them something they haven't got time to deal with, they accuse me of being 'a negative Nelly'.

# 9

# THE LIONS LEGACY TOUR

**JH:** A couple of years back, Payno, Tins and I went on a Lions Legacy Tour, taking in Aberdare, Dungannon, Westbury and Bannockburn rugby clubs. It was sponsored by Vodafone, and the idea was that we'd do various events during the day and a live show and auction in the clubhouse in the evening.

The evening before the Bannockburn gig, we fitted in a live show at Payno's old club, the Edinburgh Accies, in their clubhouse. It was a great event, and we were well looked after. Post-show I don't normally like to hang around as I hate being naused up, but I had met a group of lads and we were chatting away and smashing down some free Blackeye and tonics. Payno, bless him, kept coming over to try and rescue me, as I do get naused into oblivion at times or forced into some long-winded character assassination of myself by a fan who wants me to know that he used to think I was a dick but now doesn't, and would then ask if I wouldn't mind doing a video for their partner who would be well jealous that they were speaking to me. But this time I'd have to keep telling Payno to leave me alone because I was having such a good time.

One of the lads worked for the drinks company Diageo, and he invited us back to his offices to sample some fine wines and spirits. They had some serious gear down in the basement

– Napoleon brandy, a bottle of Churchill's favourite Johnnie Walker whisky from the 1940s – so we ordered in some pizzas and got stuck into it. Well, I did – Payno was long gone and Tins spent most of the night asleep with his head on the table.

I didn't leave until 4.30 a.m., when I proceeded to drunkenly walk back to my hotel through Edinburgh, but ended up going down alleyways, through fences, into the back of buildings and out the front of others. I am not sure how I did it but Google Maps appears to work very strangely in Scotland. What made matters worse was, I had to be up at 7. The taxi journey from Edinburgh to Bannockburn was absolute hell, at least for me. Tins was fine, while Payno was fresher than the freshest daisy, as you will have read, he avoids drinks like Jimmy Carr avoids taxes. Tins calls him 'The Squirrel', because he hides drinks like squirrels hide nuts. And whenever we do shots, Payno's go straight over his shoulder. He actually blinded an elderly couple by throwing a flaming sambuca over his shoulder, it set fire to the wife's blue rinse and the flaming hot liquid scolded both their eyes. Luckily, Payno has powerful lawyers that quashed it all and the couple were paid off, given a small holding on one of Payno's many estates and each given seeing-eye dogs. (I'm joking of course, all that never happened, my legal representatives have told me to say, as did the extremely posh man who is holding my daughter hostage at point-blank range with an antique musket.) But when Payno does get on it, his favourite tipple is gin and Dubonnet, with a slice of lemon under the ice, like the Queen Mother.

We turned up at Bannockburn and I headed straight for the green room, such as it was. A young kid from the production team called Tommy presented me with a list of stuff to do and I had to say to him, 'Listen, Tommy, when it's time to do what I have to do, I'll be on it, I will deliver 100 per cent but will give no more or no less. I'm not hanging around and meeting people in the meantime.' I eventually emerged to referee an under-5s game, which was fun – I yellow-carded three of them for backchat, which I think was a first for an under 5's, and I think through all their crying, they probably knew it was the right decision. I think lessons were learned, and I don't want to give myself too much credit, but I think those children will in future put their successes down to me teaching them a valuable lesson at an early age, i.e. 'Don't be a gobby little shit.' Sure, some of the parents were angry, and may have sworn at me, but those are the blows you have to take to be a pioneer – then I had another lie-down in the green room, exhausted from my good works.

Then the Army turned up with some tanks and guns (I was going to post a photo of myself brandishing a big machine gun but was told that might be a bit insensitive, what with Russia having just invaded Ukraine the day before), but when I got back to the green room, a soldier was in there. At first that was fine, because he seemed like the silent type, but then he started gypping. I had to say to him, 'Mate, you can't be in here, I'm horribly hungover, I can't have you being sick in the corner.' But I couldn't get rid of him. He was like some malingering relative who comes to stay and just won't stop moaning about life and their ailments.

This bloke stayed for two hours, turning greener and greener and retching every few minutes, so I barely got any kip and my hangover, instead of abating, went turbo. This soldier may have at some point defended the country I love and our freedom on some foreign battlefield, but on this day, he was being a fucking nuisance and really nearly pushing me over the edge.

I then watched Tins play in an actual game and chop one of the local heroes in half. I thought he might have killed him. And once that was done and dusted, they dressed me up as a

Scottish piper, with a kilt, long socks and one of those furry hats. I looked like Fat Bastard from *Austin Powers*.

It was all fun and games until the bloke who was looking after me handed me his bagpipes. The end of the blowpipe was crusted with white mouth scum, and I could smell it from three feet away. I had to ask one of the crew to get me a wet wipe, using Covid as a convenient excuse, but no antibacterial product known to man would have eradicated this monstrous odour. I could almost see it. When I eventually put the blowpipe to my lips, I could taste this man's mouth in my mouth, which is a sentence I never wanted to write, especially given that this man's mouth smelled of Satan's bottom. He had what could only be described as some deep-seated halitosis. Which is perhaps why he professionally wore a dress and played the bagpipes, I don't imagine there was much shagging in his life with breath that could set the fire alarms off.

I didn't want to upset this young lad who had lent me his pipes for the day, and probably had no idea that he had dog breath, I suspect the fact that flora and fauna desiccated in front of him every time he breathed out may have given him a clue, but his glasses were awfully thick so again perhaps he just didn't know. So I gamely blew away while people snickered, because they knew exactly what was going on. I was worried what might happen if I vomited down the blowpipe – maybe it would have filled the bag up, so that the next time this young lad squeezed it, the crowd would get splattered, like in *Bugsy Malone* – but I managed to get through it without any terrible incidents. I then returned to the green room and scrubbed my tongue with Dettol. Mercifully, the gypping soldier had gone.

# 10

# LEADING LIGHTS

**JH:** People say there are no characters in modern sport, but that's simply not true. There are plenty of characters in rugby, it's just that the sport has no clue how to promote them.

Rugby clubs and the RFU are so paranoid about getting bad press that they think it's best for players not to talk to the media at all. And when they are allowed to talk to the media, it's under strictly controlled conditions.

When I was playing for England, we'd have media days, and there would always be four or five random people wearing fleeces, telling us what we could and couldn't say. They'd pop up from nowhere, we wouldn't even know their names, but they'd hand out fact sheets with a list of topics to steer clear of. If we were coming off a bad defeat, we might be told to ignore it completely. I'd think, 'This is bullshit. Why can't we talk about it? Are we meant to pretend we played well?' It was all manufactured, there was no realism. Plus, journalists will write whatever they want anyway, so why would it matter if somebody said the 'wrong' thing?

The people in charge of the game wonder why big companies don't want to get involved with the sport, but why would you give millions of pounds to a sport that actively prevents its participants from showing their true selves? And why would you give millions of pounds to a sport that says no to everything? At the last World Cup, World Rugby kept reporting people to Twitter for posting clips of the action. It made no sense – why wouldn't you want people to share clips of the action? That summed rugby authorities up: they attach stupid, arbitrary rules to everything, which they can't afford to do.

Don't get me started on the fact that you can't actually use the words 'World Cup' to promote the tournament unless you have paid world rugby or are an official sponsor. Which makes life very difficult for, say, a rugby podcast to hype up the tournament and let people know what to look out for with the rugby players when we can't refer to it by name. Really? And I am the mad one apparently. I just told everyone to fuck off and just use it. That's half the reason the boat wasn't full, as they couldn't promote the fact they were selling rooms or stays for the World Cup. How can you promote a World Cup party boat without saying 'World Cup'? The answer is, you can't.

Of course, as a business (basically everyone else but me) we didn't want to upset the applecart. So, we had to re-film stuff and find creative ways of promoting and executing. I have to say I find World Rugby are about as scary as a dial-a-ride bus full of elderly people who have been told that Radio 4 will no longer be played in the nursing home. Yeah, sure, they will make a lot of noise, wave their arms, offer a few pointed words, but I'm pretty sure judging by the fact they can't do anything else effectively, they would just either give up, fall asleep or forget why they were there in the first place. If you dragged it out long enough most seniors on the board would pass away due to old age. So if you do use the words 'World Cup' you will get fined and your content taken down. How can you promote something you can't talk about? I still haven't worked it out, perhaps you need to ask the brains trust who work at World Rugby.

By contrast American sports champion their characters. When you watch interviews with NFL or NBA stars, they're open and honest. They are, to use a slightly naff buzzword, authentic. Look at that famous Chicago Bulls team led by Michael Jordan: they had Dennis Rodman, who was a complete lunatic; Scottie Pippen, who was a bit of a weirdo; and Jordan himself, who was the most competitive bloke who ever lived but who nobody seemed to like. But their head coach Phil Jackson knew how to manage them and never even dreamt of telling them what to say and how to be.

Meanwhile, British rugby players often look terrified when microphones are shoved under their noses. It's true that they don't have the same life experiences as lads from the amateur era, because they've only ever been professional rugby players, but they still have personalities and outside interests, whether it's music, cars or cooking. Unfortunately, they're trained to be defensive – 'Remember, you can't say this, and whatever you do, don't mention that' – rather than open their shoulders and play a few strokes.

England isn't as bad as New Zealand, which is the spiritual home of tall poppy syndrome and whose rugby media and fans hate players with even a hint of individuality. But I know from experience that if an English player has outside interests, people will tell them to stop fucking about and concentrate on rugby. That breeds players who either don't want to have outside interests or, if they do have outside interests, are reluctant to talk about them.

Because journalism has become so lazy, with lots of articles being just repetition of opinions off social media, and publications love clickbait headlines, you're liable to be stitched up whatever you say, which makes players think, 'Maybe these random people in England fleeces who keep prompting me on what to say are right when they tell us not to say what we're really thinking.' I did more interviews than most, and sometimes met up with journalists for off-the-record chats, but I grew more and more wary, because I kept getting turned over. Then again, I do have some sympathy with rugby journalists. Since the advent of social media and comments underneath articles, they get hounded by readers whatever they write. If they criticise a player, people will slag them off for being horrible. If they don't criticise a player, people will slag them off for being soft. And the sport gives them less and less access, which breeds a 'them and us' mentality.

The more access you give journalists, the less likely they are to be sensationalist, but media officers think it's part of their job to panic. In fact, everyone seems to be a catastrophiser in the workplace nowadays. People are always saying to me in meetings, 'But what if such and such happens?' To which I'll reply, 'But what if such and such doesn't happen? What if everyone loves it? And even if such and such does happen, we'll just move on in the knowledge that nobody actually cares, they're just desperate for attention.'

All in all, it makes for a boring environment, but I like to think that our podcast has made things slightly more interesting, for our guests and for fans. By creating a comfortable environment for players and coaches, we've revealed depths that were previously hidden. The long-form format enables them to speak from their hearts, to get emotional, to tell stories they'd never tell some strange journalist on a media day. And if they say something that upsets some of our fans, we don't start panicking, we stick by them. And we tell our fans that if they don't like it, they should watch/listen to something else instead.

Before Jonny May started appearing on the podcast, very few people outside the hardcore rugby community had any idea he was one of the game's biggest characters. Actually, most people had never heard Jonny speak, which is a great example of how poorly the sport is promoted by those in charge.

Jonny is very different to me. People always assume I was a prankster, but I didn't have time for that nonsense. However, because I was always so wrapped up in other things, I was very easy to prank. If you jumped out on me, I'd get scared. If you said something to wind me up, I'd always react. But I'd rarely get involved in a prank war. In contrast, Jonny was constantly being pranked by teammates (usually by Joe Marler) and couldn't resist pranking them back, often with disastrous consequences, at least for him.

Jonny was and is a perfectionist, which means he overthinks everything to the nth degree and becomes fixated with routine. In England camp, he'd be in a perpetual loop of training, stretching, icing, massaging, eating, and he'd wander around with a stopwatch in his hand, so that he would have everything managed to the second: the perfect amount of stretching time, followed by the optimum amount of time in an ice bath. He even timed how long he ate and how long he allowed himself idle chit chat. He still is incredibly professional. So Jonny was a prankster's perfect victim. As it would not have taken much to upset his equilibrium.

Jonny had orthotic insoles in his shoes, which Joe Marler would steal from time to time and on one occasion never gave back. As a result, Jonny developed plantar fasciitis, which is a terrible pain in the arch of your foot. In other words, Joe Marler disabled Jonny May, although Jonny had probably done something to deserve it.

Other times, Joe and a few others would break into Jonny's room and tip everything upside down. Jonny would play some weak practical joke on Joe in response, only for Joe's revenge to be doubly painful. I'd walk past Jonny's room while he was getting filled in, strung up and cocooned in medical tape, and he'd look at me pleadingly for help, his little upside-down head going redder and redder as the blood drained into it. One time, I just shrugged and said to him, 'Jonny, you know I don't get involved in that nonsense.' After that, Jonny would constantly say to me, 'Nonsense is it, Hask? I know, I know, Hask doesn't do nonsense …'

When Joe wasn't filling Jonny in, they'd be naked wrestling. It wasn't some homoerotic sex thing, like Oliver Reed and Alan Bates grappling in front of a roaring fire in *Women in Love*, they just had too much time on their hands (meanwhile, I'd be working in my room – doing what the lads liked to call my shpizness, as in 'shit business'). The closest I got to that kind of behaviour was at the 2011 World Cup in New Zealand, when we got a big delivery of chocolate and Chris Ashton would bring a bar of Dairy Milk to my room every day in exchange for a wrestle. I'd fight him, one of us would win, he would hand over the chocolate say, 'See ya, pal' and walk off sweating and panting. I never asked him why he did it, but he suddenly stopped when the chocolate ran out.

Now Joe Marler liked a prank, Jonny liked a prank, but no one did a prank like my old mate, Joe Simpson. Taking him on was like Accrington Stanley taking on Manchester City: you would always lose and sometimes by a huge margin. I've never met anyone as committed to pranking as Joe, he'd go to incredible lengths. He once joined a housing community group on Facebook and caused absolute havoc, just to get back at two teammates who lived there. He pretended to be an elderly gay gentleman and would constantly complain that these two lads were having noisy parties, fly-tipping and upsetting his cats and dogs, or that he'd seen ladies of the night leaving their flat at all hours. He would pit people against each other, it was amazing to watch. He once took me through all his posts, and

I was crying with laughter while making a mental note to never mess with him. He made the housing forum so toxic that the whole thing had to be disbanded pending an internal investigation by the housing authority. They of course realised at some point that there was no 'Mr Simpkins' and threw him out of the forum and blocked him, by which time Joe was on to his next prank. He'd also send envelopes of glitter to people, which would explode upon opening and end up all over people's clothes and hair and lead to their partners accusing them of being in a strip club. And when they tried to explain that it was probably just Joe Simpson playing a prank, their partners simply wouldn't believe that anyone would go to all that trouble.

One time on a Gloucester night out, Jonny lost badly on the wheel of misfortune and had to clean one of the lad's cars. I said Jonny was professional, I never said he was smart. He is shrewd in some areas, a clever one with money, but has very little common sense. He used steel wool and a Brillo pad and completely wrecked the car. Then there was the time that Jonny came home to find that someone had parked a van in front of his drive. After a day or so, Jonny hammered nails into this van's tyres, before discovering that it was his brother-in-law's and his wife had given him permission to park there. What makes it worse is I think Jonny had OK'd it but then forgotten.

Jonny for some reason decided to bring a chicken into the club. My recollections of why he did it are hazy, but he did. He also used his car as a home for his feathered friend during training, which obviously resulted in the car getting covered in shit, feathers and the odd egg produced under duress. Again, I am not sure why this happened but Jonny thought he was possessed by the chicken, whether through some sort of transference or maybe the chicken died, and his soul went into

Jonny. Make sure you ask him when you see him. Whatever the reasons, Jonny for a long time thought he was possessed by a chicken. The lads had a field day with all this. When a few of them locked him in a cage with some chickens, he screamed the place down, and from then on he would do that horrible scream when you least expected it. We'd be on a plane, he'd scream and everyone would shit themselves. Well, I'd just roll my eyes, because as Jonny used to say, 'Hask doesn't do nonsense.'

One pre-season, Gloucester went to an Army training camp, the go-to place for most of Premiership rugby, which involved sleeping in tents. Each player was told to bring training clothes, a toothbrush and their own sleeping bags, the Army would provide the rest. When one of the lads unfurled his sleeping bag with unbridled confidence, a big black dildo flew out the end. What made matters worse was he'd borrowed the sleeping bag off his missus. This dildo was not your run of the mill fanny tickler it was about 15 inches long, like the one Hatchet Harry used to beat someone to death in *Lock, Stock and Two Smoking Barrels*. Strictly for professional pleasure seekers only. As you can imagine, this bloke got terrible abuse for the fact that his wife, when he was away or out training, was sitting on the equivalent of Nelson's Column. When they weren't abusing this bloke, which was only for meals and toilet breaks, the lads were running around hitting each other with it, or laughing at the camp dog running around with it in his mouth (just to be clear, the dog wasn't camp as in Liberace, he just lived at the Army camp).

Jonny was still hitting people with this dildo when everyone else had had their fun and was trying to get some sleep. And in the end Ben Morgan, a man not to be trifled with, grabbed Jonny, dragged him out of the tent, tied him to a tree and gaffer taped the dildo to his mouth. He either had to gnaw through the tape and the big black dildo or freeze to death, as Ben never came back to untie him; he just left him there to die, or get very cold – you, dear reader, can decide the nature of his intention.

The other day, Jonny was late for an appearance on the podcast because he'd been doing work experience as a fireman. He got a bit defensive when I started taking the piss out of him. 'Why are you laughing at me?' he said. 'You should support players who try to forge new careers after rugby.' But I wasn't laughing at the fact he was looking at other careers, I was laughing specifically at the idea of him being a fireman. And not just any fireman, a fireman at RAF Brize Norton.

'Jonny,' I said to him, 'you've never wanted to be a fireman. And you're the last person I'd want in charge if an airport full of planes went up in flames.' I imagined him running around like Corporal Jones in *Dad's Army*, shouting 'don't panic!' and trying to put the flames out by wafting a towel. Knowing Jonny, he probably woke up the day before, thought 'I want to be a fireman' and using the Rugby Players' Association he quickly got an appointment to go and see how being a fireman works. I'm not really sure how or why it had to be a fireman at an RAF base, that's a pretty niche thing to want to do. God knows what he will dream up next, but rest assured the idea will burn as bright as phosphorus then die just as quickly, to be replaced with him wanting to clean the outsides of submarines or be a surgeon.

Having said all that, Jonny's much more astute than people give him credit for. He's fully aware of what he's saying most of the time, it's just that the more you laugh at him, the giddier he gets and the more nonsense he speaks, much of which our poor editor has to cut out. Much like me, to be fair.

**MT:** When Jonny May came on the podcast the first time, I thought, 'Oh my God, has no one seen this side of him before?' I played with Jonny at Gloucester for four or five seasons, so knew what a character he was. But Jonny would say that he wanted people to be talking about his rugby rather than anything else, especially not the fact that he once got invited to North Korea.

Jonny gets obsessed with stuff, including North Korea for some reason. He was fascinated by the fact that people in North Korea are only allowed to have one hairstyle and that laughing and celebrating birthdays was banned for 11 days to commemorate the 10-year anniversary of the death of Kim Jong Il. A rugby journalist found out about Jonny's North Korea obsession, asked him about it during a Six Nations, and when he returned to Gloucester, he had a letter from the embassy in his pigeonhole, sealed with wax, like something from *Harry Potter*. They loved the fact that he was so taken by North Korean culture and wanted him to visit their embassy in London, meet some dignitaries, chat about the country's history, and maybe even visit North Korea itself.

Jonny's quite neurodiverse, so if his normal routine gets interrupted, his head blows up. As Jonny put it on the podcast, 'What does a 27-year-old with autism, ADHD, anxiety and post-traumatic stress disorder do in a moment like that?' Jonny being Jonny, he phoned his mum, who told him to tell the RFU.

Jonny phoned England head coach Eddie Jones about it, asked what he should do, and Eddie replied, 'Tell them to fuck off, mate.' Jonny phoned his mum back, told her that Eddie reckoned he should tell the North Korean embassy to fuck off, and his mum couldn't get her head around it. She thought his life might be in danger if he didn't respond, and maybe she saw her son as rugby's answer to Dennis Rodman, hanging out with Kim Jong Un and chatting about the time he played a round of golf in 18 shots. As it was, Jonny didn't tell them to fuck off, he decided to just ignore the invitation instead.

**AP:** What can I say about Jonny May? Well, a lot of things actually. Jonny is a strange one, in that he's a supremely talented athlete and England's second-highest try-scorer, yet not many people, outside of hardcore rugby fans, knew much about him until he appeared on our podcast for the first time. Suddenly, everything came pouring out, and the rest of us were sitting there thinking, 'What the hell is going on? Where did all this come from?'

He needed a pee after about 10 minutes, started having a meltdown after about 20 minutes, and lost his voice after about half an hour. He gave everything of himself, in a hugely chaotic fashion, including much that was unusable. If the full recording of that episode ever leaked into the public domain, we'd go up in flames and none of us would ever work again.

People describe listening to our podcast as like earwigging a table full of blokes in a pub. I like that analogy because it means we must sound natural. But while we do have to push the boundaries to get the content we want, plenty ends up on the cutting room floor, and you can probably guess who has the biggest dossier of inflammatory outtakes (clue: it's not me or Tins).

The podcast was originally designed to be an hour long, but it started to stretch to an hour and a half, sometimes longer, when alcohol was introduced. We could get away with that back then, because the podcast market was a lot less congested. But now, we'll normally record for about an hour and a half and edit it down to 55 minutes. And most of what gets chopped isn't actually inflammatory, it's just pauses, repetition and Hask saying, 'I don't really give a shit about this'. Or in the case of Jonny May, wild detours that lead nowhere.

What was lovely about Jonny's appearance was the adulation he got from our audience. We had so many messages saying, 'Where has this man been? Why haven't we seen him before?' They couldn't understand how a man who had flown under the radar for most of his playing career could be so unique. Here was someone who was unable to suppress his inner monologue, but the stuff that came pouring out of his head was completely relatable.

Jonny has been on loads of times now, and we'd love him to do lots more episodes. We might have to do without him for most of next season because he's just signed for French second division side Soyaux Angoulême, but he'll be brilliant for us in the future, because he still knows most of the players in the England team and is able to take us into the changing room.

Failing to market its players properly, if at all, is one of rugby's biggest problems, and the reason why it produces so few household names. We did a show after the 2023 World Cup, based on the top 10 superstars in rugby, and it wasn't an easy list to compile. The rugby establishment doesn't seem to want tall poppies, it prefers to promote itself as the ultimate team game, in which everyone has a role to play and no single player can earn success on his own (unlike football, which has always celebrated outrageous individual talent).

Similarly, rugby likes to celebrate modesty, the idea that however talented a player might be, they should still be 'nice' self-effacing girls and boys off the pitch. That's why Danny Cipriani got so much flak from the media simply for dating celebrities, and why Hask got so much flak for having lots of interests outside the game. It's also one of the key reasons for *The Good, The Bad & The Rugby*'s success. We give players space to tell their stories, instead of them writing 140-character tweets, which tells the public nothing, or their thoughts being written up by a journalist, accompanied by a clickbait headline.

Sonny Bill Williams came on the podcast primarily to promote his book, but we chatted for an hour and a half, really drilling down into the details of his life. And at the end of it, he said something along the lines of, 'That is the most fun I've ever had in an interview.' That's one of the ironies of the podcast: on the face of it, it's a few lads chatting. But because it's so relaxed, our guests give more than they would in any other media environment. At the same time, we've had some robust discussions with rugby administrators, talent agents and the like. I like to think we sit outside the city walls, 'holding the powerful to account' and providing a safe space for those who want it.

**JH:** Another regular guest is former France international Ben Kayser, who I played with at Stade Français and is one of the best rugby pundits out there (on a par with Dylan Hartley, Sam Warburton and John Barclay, in my humble opinion).

Ben's a great guy and we get on like a house on fire. He can actually get quite loose after a few beers. (Unlike Owen Farrell, who you will see suddenly catch himself having too much fun, calm right down and go into professional mode. I've watched it many times.) But Ben's far more intelligent than me (he recently completed an MBA at Oxford University and works for an investment firm back in France) and can be quite serious. If I go off on one of my tangents, he'll look at me as if to say, 'Why can't you just shut the fuck up so we can get back to the point?' And because he's a very proud Frenchman, despite being married to an Englishwoman and speaking better English than me, he gets arsey if I say anything negative about my time playing in Paris or take the piss too heavily.

I'd get Ben to translate for me at Stade Français, including the time the head coach was screaming in my face while waving my contract at me. I kept saying to Ben, 'What's he saying?', and Ben kept replying, 'I'm not translating! I don't want to be involved with this!' In the end, I said to him, 'Well, you better translate, because I'm gonna knock him out if he keeps screaming at me', and Ben reluctantly responded, 'He says you're shit, Martin Johnson thinks you're shit as well, and he's going to tear your contract up if he's still in charge next year.' Luckily, the coach himself was shit and never lasted the pace. So needless to say, I had the last laugh and bounced back.

Another story Ben likes to bring up is the time I hosted an auction at the Dubai Sevens and, in his words, ended up offending half of Dubai.

I'd done it the previous year with no hitches, while raising a ton of money, but after the tournament boss Tom Burwell rebooked me, he was replaced by my old England teammate Mat Tait, who was a lot less experienced and slightly more sensitive.

It was a big room full of very loud, aggressive, entitled expats, mostly from South Africa and New Zealand, and they annoyed me from the outset by talking all through the keynote speech. They were meant to be there for charity and they couldn't even shut up and listen for five minutes, so I thought I had to take control of the room, by hook or by crook. It didn't help that the prizes weren't much cop – football and rugby shirts with a handful of signatures on, that kind of thing – but I still managed to get something like 200 grand out of them. Unfortunately, I managed to upset one or two people along the way.

I honestly didn't think I was that bad. I even kicked off by saying, 'Listen, Ladies and Gentlemen, I'm going to become the worst version of myself for the next hour, but I don't really believe what I'm saying, it's just a bit of fun.' I'd dig out a table of lads for having no women on their table, then joke that they'd probably be paying for them later. Or I'd address a table of women and joke that it was good to see them dominating proceedings, instead of trailing 10 feet behind the blokes, as is sometimes the case in Dubai. But it was mainly the usual bidding schtick: one bloke would bid and I'd say, 'Sir, you are Billy Big Bollocks in the room. Your wife hasn't looked at you like that in 10 years'; or I'd say to a lady who'd put a chunky bid in, 'Very good, madam, I'm right behind you. It's about time you women put men back in their proper place.' People were laughing, everyone seemed to be enjoying it, but unbeknown to me, I was everything some of the women there hated in a man. Honestly, I had everyone's attention, nothing I said wasn't true and it was all tongue-in-cheek. I pushed up the bids, created battles between tables, kept the people in the cheap seats entertained. I was happy with what I had done.

But I should have known I'd overstepped the mark when I saw Ben looking at me open-mouthed, and later when I was accosted by two women in the bar, who were fuelled up on lady petrol and forgot they weren't behind their keyboards. I'm not sure what they thought I was going to do, but I didn't give them the reaction they wanted. They proceeded to call me everything under the sun, and that I had misjudged the room. I pointed out it was entertainment, a joke, and I had raised more money than anyone. They weren't having any of it and proceeded to tell me to go fuck myself and said I wouldn't be hearing the end of this.

Clearly, they weren't the only ones who felt upset as some high-ranking women who worked for partner companies complained to Mat Tait. Now Mat is a good man, but it was also his first week on the job and he did what anyone would do under pressure, he crumbled like a soggy rich tea biscuit.

He messaged me when I got back to the UK and said I was being stood down as an ambassador but was still able to DJ. Which, if I'm honest, suited me fine. I would DJ all day every day rather than do corporate work.

I hate this new corporate world. I speak all the time in it, and you can't please anyone. Everyone has a voice, and they think by complaining they are fixing the world and making a difference. For them it feels like profound action, but it's actually a distraction from them doing anything themselves. If they wanted to make a difference, they would worry about themselves, work hard, take responsibility for their own actions and be better humans. There is nothing that is more deplorable than getting offended on another's behalf. Just fuck off, and get on with your own lives, because if you took five minutes to actually see how much you had to work on, whether that's body, mind, self-development or mental health, you would realise your side of the street is a mess. Did complaining that I made jokes about prostitutes or that women have to walk 10 feet behind men, change any of that? No, it just changed me ever working again in Dubai. So, the problem remains, but the person pointing out something off-key and making light of an issue gets stopped from working or earning a living. Their actions made no impact, but they feel like they have done a great service to the world.

I must run everything by everyone before I do anything in the corporate world, with endless conference calls, checking and re-checking. There is always some busybody who comes up to you at the end to share their views. I will never forget the woman who wanted to feed back to me that my story about my father and son trip was non-relatable and needed to be changed because she took her son on a 'mother/father trip', and I should have used this more inclusive language. I pointed out there were no women on my trip, and the fact it was my story not hers, I couldn't add this stuff in as it didn't happen. I explained how a story works: I tell it in such a way that I create pictures in her mind through my use of language and she then relates to them and makes them her own. When I speak at a rugby dinner it's amazing to see women's rugby growing and I am super-happy it's going great guns. I just don't have any relatable stories, as from the age of 5 to 35 I never once played at a club with a women's team, or had anything to do with women's rugby, or any stories that might cross over. I was invited to a dinner recently to speak and there was a chairwoman, which was great to see, and I was sat with the women players. It was a really fun lunch, but you could see them looking at me and listening to my stories, and it was plain to see there was a huge gulf between my world and theirs. It's no one's fault, but don't blame me if you don't like what I have to say. You know who you booked.

Getting stood down by your old mate was interesting because I'd raised a shitload of money, which was my primary job. It got even more interesting when Mat effectively fired me (not face to face, obviously) and I had to write an apology letter.

I'll let you into a secret – I didn't really mean everything I said in the letter. However, it was the right thing to do, and everyone loves an alpha male showing the error of his ways. Being honest, I did steer close to the line, and I could have played it safer, but I was making people laugh and that's what gets me going. But if I had my time again, I wouldn't make any jokes about women. In fact, having spoken to quite a few people in the corporate world, I will never even mention any banter relating to women in a corporate environment again. You only have to piss one woman off and you're cancelled, while you can carry on taking the piss out of men, within reason, until the cows come home. Apparently, that's progress.

However, there's no point thinking you are right while sitting at home poor and out of work. I clearly needed to change what I was doing, learn and adapt. It's always been one of my strengths. Self-analysis is the key.

# 11

# ALWAYS MEET YOUR HEROES

**AP:** I covered Ben Kayser a lot while working for Sky and I could see that he had the makings of a brilliant pundit. He speaks better English than Hask and Tins, which is lovely for those of us who like our pundits to be articulate, he's extremely bright, and he's a very hard worker. Plus, he played with Hask at Stade Français, and against both Hask and Tins for France.

Ben didn't want to commit to a weekly podcast, but he did agree to do between five and ten shows a year, which was perfect for us. He's done a couple of live shows and usually joins for the big events, like the Six Nations, World Cups and European finals. I sometimes see him frowning, sighing and rolling his eyes when Hask is speaking, but that's all part of the pantomime.

I worked with former Ireland winger Shane Horgan for years at Sky and he's one of the best pundits in the business. Like Ben, he's smart and lucid, but he's also got a broad range of interests. His sister, as many readers will know, is the hugely successful comedy writer and actress Sharon Horgan (*Pulling*, *Catastrophe*, *Motherland*) and his brother Mark is a very talented radio and podcast producer, so it's hardly surprising that Shane takes us to some interesting places whenever he appears on the podcast. He's also very honest and forthright and will happily disagree with other people on the show, which adds a bit of spice. On top of all that, he's got a great sense of humour and Ireland fans love him, so he brings a whole new audience with him.

Another guy I have a real soft spot for is Joe Marler, partly because he's one of rugby's biggest characters, but mainly because he's a really good guy.

I had a godson who died of brain cancer a few years ago, and while he was going through his treatment, his father, who is one of my oldest friends, put on a fundraising event in London on the South Bank. He asked if I'd do a Q&A with someone, but Hask and Tins, the obvious choices, were otherwise engaged. So I asked Joe if he'd be up for it, and he said yes immediately.

Joe drove up from Brighton, wouldn't accept any money and stayed well beyond his allocated time, chatting with everybody and doing selfies. You might think, 'Well, players should do things like that, they have enough time on their hands', but they're professional athletes, always knackered, and are constantly being told to rest properly. So I was very grateful for Joe doing that.

Another cherished memory I have of Joe is when he was playing for the Barbarians and he came into the pitch-side studio after the game. He brought along his kids, and they were running all over the set, doing roly-polies, pinching the make-up kit, making funny faces into the cameras. Joe kept saying, 'Sorry, I can't control them', but he was very comfortable all the same.

Joe is a very unique person, not afraid of the microphone, not afraid of giving a strong opinion or of what people might say about him. For all those reasons, he's one of the biggest characters in the game, a genuine non-conformist in a game that seems to prefer its participants to conform. It obviously helps his cause that he's incredibly good at rugby – if he was a rubbish prop, none of that other stuff would matter – but the sport could learn a lot from how Joe has flourished by being allowed to be who he really is. And his club Harlequins have to take some credit for that. They realised very early on, when Joe was turning up to games with adverts for sausages shaved into the side of his head, that by letting him be himself off the field – the person he, his wife and his kids needed him to be – they got the best out of him on it.

Joe has also been very open about the challenges he's faced, including a very good documentary he did for Sky, *Big Boys Don't Cry*, in which he talked about his battles with depression. We live in a time when people want public figures and especially their heroes to be real, and Joe is that. By articulating his challenges in such a down-to-earth manner, and by showing that even a tough rugby player can have vulnerabilities, he's helped a lot of people.

He has also demonstrated that rugby isn't just for middle-class public schoolboys. There are plenty of players from working-class backgrounds, and always have been, but the stereotype persists. However, there is no mistaking Joe for anything other than what he is, which is a state school boy from Sussex. My 11-year-old lad loves Joe Marler, proof that he's done his bit moving rugby forwards and connecting the game to a new generation of fans.

**JH:** We've had Joe Marler on the podcast a few times, and he's undoubtedly been the biggest character in English rugby for the last few years. He's a brilliant player, has been on one hell of a journey, and I love how he talks so openly about his mental health and love for his family. Having said all that, it took me quite a long time to get to grips with him. I'm not sure I ever have.

Joe first came to my notice when he had a fight with my best mate Paul Doran-Jones, when Harlequins played Northampton. Not long after that, Joe turned up to England training with a red mohawk and the words 'jolly hog' and 'sausage' written on either side of his head (he was advertising his Quins team-mate Olly Kohn's Jolly Hog meat business). He was only 21 and I was already a bit of a veteran, and I remember saying to Dozzer, 'Who the fuck is this guy?'

I found it difficult to work out if Joe was being serious or not. He'd start a conversation, suddenly stop, say something weird, then walk off. I'd be standing there thinking, 'I don't really get what this bloke's all about.'

People assume that Joe and I are similar personalities, but we're not really. We're both non-conformists, no doubt about that, but in very different ways. He's quirky, can seem off the wall at times, which I think might be a defence mechanism. However, he is hugely loved and always goes above and beyond for the fans. In contrast, when people meet me, they're often surprised by how different I am to the perception they have. I am fairly boring and quiet most of the time. I mean, don't get me wrong, I'm far from normal, it's just that they are surprised that I am quieter than you would think, and I don't say 'lads, lads, lads' and 'banter' on repeat. I am more serious than you would expect.

Joe and I became closer over time, especially after Eddie Jones took over as England head coach. It helped that both of us were good pals with his fellow prop Dan Cole, and the fact that he had such a great attitude on the field. He was obviously a very good scrummager, but he was also a destructive, under-rated tackler. But we didn't always click, including the time he squirted water at me during a Wasps–Harlequins game and I put him in a Vulcan death grip. Hardly a day goes by without some joker either asking me about Joe or saying, 'Be careful no one squirts you with water', before proceeding to snigger or cackle as if they have said the funniest thing known to humanity. I give them the tightest smile possible; you couldn't even fit a Rizla between my lips, they are so tight.

While we're both performers (Joe's got his own podcast and has done stuff on TV), we're not the same kind of performer. And if you're into Joe Marler, you're into him 100 per cent. There's no halfway house, as there is with me. The queue of people who hate me is as long as the queue of people who enjoy what I do, and there's a third queue of people who can't make their minds up.

As well as Joe's appearances on *The Good, The Bad & The Rugby*, I interviewed him for my *What a Flanker* podcast. I wanted to speak to him about his mental health, partly because I wanted to understand how he could have been a teammate for so long and I didn't know he was struggling.

I was a bit worried that we'd just end up talking shit and be quite destructive for an hour and it would turn into a cock-off, so I said to him before we started recording, 'Look, this isn't *The Good, The Bad & the Rugby*, I need you to be serious today.' He was serious, he was so amazing and it was one of my favourite conversations with a rugby player I have ever done. I felt like we really bonded that day, and I'll always have a lot of respect for him. When Joe and I are clicking, I can't stop laughing.

**AP:** Jason Leonard is nicknamed Fun Bus for very good reason. He's lived a very rich and varied life, has a million and one stories, and is just a lovely man. Every time I meet Jason, he gives me a big smile and a firm handshake and asks how me, Tins and Hask are getting on, and how the podcast is doing.

When the Lions toured South Africa in 1997, Jason was expected to start the Tests, especially given that he could pack down on both sides of the scrum. But when Ireland's Paul Wallace and Scotland's Tom Smith were picked ahead of him, Jason didn't sulk, he did everything he could to help Paul and Tom prepare. That's why head coach Ian McGeechan called him the 'ultimate Lion'. He was the heartbeat of any squad he was in, and he's still the heartbeat of any room he's in.

I'd describe Jason as Hask without the edge, which is meant as a compliment to both of them. When Jason came on the show, it was tale after tale, including the time Canada's Norman Hadley sorted out a couple of young yobbos on a Tube train and his first England tour to Argentina, just eight years after the Falklands War. That involved the locals burning Union Jacks and pelting England players with oranges, whisky bottles and bathroom taps, and England enforcer Wade Dooley punching almost everything that moved.

Jason was very much a mentor of Tins when he first came into the England set-up, while Tins has mentored a lot of England players since, and that unbroken bloodline, if you like, is one of the special things about rugby.

JH: I always look forward to seeing Fun Bus because he's one of the warmest guys in rugby. When I was introduced to Jason as a young fan at Twickenham, I was struck by how down-to-earth he was, being a proper geezer (born and raised in Barking, East London, which is not your normal rugby pedigree) and a carpenter. I remember I was a young player at Wasps, and I would always bump into Jason at internationals, and he would always give me the time of the day, with a big smile and a hug. That was the time when Twickenham used to be like the wild west. The international lads would be going all over the stadium pre and post-match doing appearances, speeches and photo ops. I remember one year Simon Shaw had a Vespa, so he could get in as many jobs as possible. He would be whizzing around the stadium and the surrounding area, going to people's private houses and doing bits. It was insane, it was back when cash was still king. I would always ask Jason how he was getting on, how the work gigs were, and he would smile and wink, opening his blazer to reveal several hidden pockets in the lining bulging with envelopes. On most normal people, that size of jacket with that amount of cash stuffed into it would have made them look like the Michelin Man, but Jason obviously had a great tailor and enough mass to hide all the reddies.

Jason is one of England's greatest players (114 England caps, World Cup winner, World Cup runner-up, four Grand Slams, three Lions tours), one of rugby's finest drinkers (he once put away 20 pints to recover from a hangover) and a magnificent storyteller, which I'm sure is partly down to the fact that he had a career before rugby. He's been part of the blazer brigade for a while now (former RFU president, former chairman of the British & Irish Lions) but has never lost his authenticity. He's about as old-school as you can get, but he gets on just as well with people from the new school, which is a rare gift.

One of my favourite Fun Bus stories concerns the time he got lost in Rotorua in 1993, while touring with the Lions, and accidentally threw a goat into a ravine (which reminds me of the story Michael tells Alan Partridge, about throwing a monkey into the sea because it ate all his fags). And Jason's got hundreds more where that came from.

I never played with Jason, but I did have a chance meeting with him after my England debut against Wales in Cardiff. I'd just had a tactical chunder in the toilet, which must have sounded like a rhinoceros being gang-banged, and had left the toilet looking like a combination of Chernobyl and Middlesbrough town centre. I walked out in a daze, thinking how I can possibly have 25 more drinks with the rest the squad? (That was the England initiation: you had to have a drink with each member of the squad if they asked you to. The only catch was they had to drink what you drank.) Jason was the first person I saw when I stumbled back into the conference room. He grabbed my arm, very hard, and growled, 'Congrats on playing for England, now get a pint of Guinness down you', at which point Wales prop Gethin Jenkins appeared over my shoulder. Soon, I was pinned between the twin stomachs of Jason and Gethin, and all I could think was, 'Jesus, this is how I'm going to die, crushed by the Fun Bus and a minibus with a face.' Either that or I'd have to hack myself free with a butter knife, a bit like that American climber who cut his own arm off after getting stuck between two boulders. Mercifully, I was saved by a passing waitress carrying a tray of canapés – while Jason and Gethin were steaming into them, I managed to escape, no butter knife required. The fatties can't resist free food.

MT: Fun Bus encompasses everything that's great about the game of rugby. He started out as a carpenter playing for his hometown club Barking. He has hollow legs that enable him to drink for days and a ridiculously good memory that enables him to remember pretty everyone he's ever met and every place he's ever been to (I usually remember faces, but I struggle to remember their names or where we met). Everyone in rugby knows and loves Fun Bus because he's such a likeable human being and just loves to chat and tell stories.

Jason and Lawrence Dallaglio took me under their wing when I toured Australia with England in 1999, which was a nice place to be. After the game against Queensland, which Jason also played in, he gave me his shirt so that I didn't have to swap mine. I thought, 'What a nice touch, I love this guy already.' Some veteran probably did the same for Jason when he first played for England in Argentina in 1990, and a couple of years later, I did the same for another new player.

**JH:** Journalists sometimes say to me, 'I've interviewed that person a hundred times and he's never opened up like that', and the reason we're able to do that is because our guests don't see us as journalists, and we don't put any spin on our chats.

Journalism is too often someone's interpretation of what a person said or who a person is, and that interpretation is often a result of a journalist's life experiences and prejudices, even if those prejudices are unconscious. I've been on the end of those prejudices myself, with people seemingly more interested in how much my house cost or what car I drive than in what I have to say; the subtext being: if he lives in a £1 million house and drives a Range Rover, he must be a wanker. In contrast, we record a podcast and then it just exists, it's not possible for it to be our interpretation of what our guest said. Of course, you could try to be clever and edit stuff, but to be honest the record of the show will always stand. It gives listeners the ability to see the context of what was being said, as there's no clickbait.

That's why we were able to get Exeter's finest Jack Nowell on a live show dressed in a floral onesie (that made him look a bit like Roy Chubby Brown) and talk about his stag do, hiding from his family in the gym, surfing and diving for scallops; or get Ireland great Seán O'Brien to talk about his childhood catching sheep and crashing tractors (when he should have been at school) and that he thought I was a wanker before we roomed together on the Lions tour (he stole all my sweets, had a shit with the door open and taught me Irish farmer songs, which was definitely different from my usual room-mates) – the fact that he vocalised that shows you how comfortable people are. If you know you're not going to be stitched up, you're more inclined to tell daft stories, without fear of being judged.

Returning to Nowellsy, he and I spent most of the disastrous 2015 World Cup hanging out together, learning to play football and doing extra weights. He was of those guys who plays the game with a smile on his face, even though he openly admits that he'd often rather be doing something else.

Exeter players can get a bit indoctrinated if they spend a long time at the club, because it's quite isolated down there and head coach Rob Baxter likes to do things his own way, and that way has been very successful. I think Jack going was a great decision, the right decision, and while I think that moving to La Rochelle was a bit of an eye-opener for him, and would have been very, very different to Cornwall and Exeter, he's carved it up since joining them in 2023.

I'll never forget our drinking exploits, if you can call them that, at the end of the 2017 Lions tour, with me, Jack Nowell, Rory Best, Dan Cole and Joe Marler playing various drinking games. All the fun was dictated by Rory. He came up with a couple of games: the first one wasn't sophisticated or clever, when he said 'drink' we had to finish our drinks. That was it. That was the entire game right there.

Then he came up with another one. He would say 'One, two, three' and then stick a toothpick in his head. And we had to do the same. That was it. Three-dimensional chess it wasn't. By the end of it, we all looked like characters from the film *Hellraiser*.

I am sure you are sensing a theme here. Anyway, as the hours ticked on, we got more and more pissed. We were so drunk that Paul Gascoigne would have said we were overdoing it. We were more shitfaced than the stars of *2 Girls 1 Cup*.

So Rory, who had not been to bed, was looking a bit worse for wear. On one occasion when he shouted 'Drink!', he finished his beer, but the froth was a little too much and he did a little foamy sick on the carpet, which I found hilarious and gave me a chance to finally take him down a peg or two. I was like, 'Aargh, the legendary Rory Best has done a sick on the floor. You did a little cat sick Rory. Blurrgh.'

I said I would start calling him Felix (as in Felix the Cat from those old adverts), to which he was not best pleased. By this stage Rory was absolutely steaming. The last world-class athlete to be this legless was Oscar Pistorius. Nothing has been this wasted since someone bought Gemma Collins a salad.

After a while, sensing him fading further, I got the lads to wheel in Jack Nowell's hospital bed from the team room. Why did he have a hospital bed you might ask? Well, Jack had come home so steaming the night before he was unable to walk, so the hotel had got a special bed on wheels for him and put him in the team room to sleep it off. So weirdly, he spent the entire night literally off his trolley. And ON his trolley.

When Jack eventually woke up and found himself on a hospital trolley in a hotel meeting room, he took a long hard look at himself. He apologised to the hotel staff for all the inconvenience he'd caused, cleaned up the mess he'd made, and vowed never to drink again ... Did he fuck! He slid off the trolley, stumbled into the breakfast room and continued on the lash with the rest of us.

So, by now we had the hospital bed in the breakfast room and empty beer boxes on our heads with faces cut into them. If you have read my book *What A Flanker*, you will know what happened next, but it's too good a story not to tell again.

I said to Felix (Rory), 'Listen, I think you need a little lie-down. 'No I feckin' don't, feck off Hask and stop calling me Felix!' But after chipping away at him for an hour or so, I managed to get him to just have a little lie-down on the trolley bed next to the table, so he still felt part of it. We tucked him in, so just his little bald head was sticking out the top. We kept on drinking and telling stories and eventually his eyelids got heavier and heavier until he nodded off. He was like a bald, drunk Sleeping Beauty.

We waited a little bit to make sure he was fully asleep, then I pointed to the French windows that opened out to the road. We were on the ground floor of the hotel that opened out onto a road at the top of a hill in Auckland. Picture the scene: seven drunk men, giants, with cardboard boxes on their heads trying to quietly push a sleepy Irish rugby hero towards some French windows, the steepest hill in Auckland, and to certain death.

It was hilarious.

Everyone was giddy with excitement, which meant we were being really loud. I kept saying 'Shh' but then we were shushing each other louder and louder and making more noise trying to be quiet than if we had been just talking.

Rory was so deeply asleep that we could have got someone to tattoo a cock and balls on his face and he wouldn't have woken up. Which in retrospect, seems like a missed opportunity.

We got the doors open and pushed Rory out into the street. We were laughing so much than none of us could speak. His little bald head was the only thing on show. As everyone else wondered what to do next, I went, 'Fuck off' and gave the bed a friendly kick. The bed started to move. Slowly at first. But then it started picking up pace.

We were inconsolable with laughter, some of the lads couldn't stand up. As I watched Rory on his little bed disappearing down the hill towards a busy road, with tears running down my face, suddenly the enormity of what I had done started to kick in.

He was heading down a main road to a junction and then to God knows what. He was going so fast that we now couldn't catch him. What would happen if a car came? Or a lorry? Or a car AND a lorry? I was like, 'Fuck, fuck, I've killed Rory Best.'

Then reality kicked in. Suddenly I was sober and realising the enormity of the situation.

So I started running after him. I say 'running'. I had been drinking cider since 8.30 a.m. so now I pretty much had all the sprinting ability of a lazy Stephen Hawking. The rest of the lads pulled themselves together and started trying to catch him too. Rory was getting faster and faster, all the while sound asleep.

The harder we ran, the harder it got. It was like a *Carry On* film – they would have called it *Carry On Manslaughter*. We kept running. Ever more desperate. Ever faster. The trolley was always just out of reach. But on we ran. Until finally, unbelievably … We gave up.

We were never going to catch him. All we could do now was stand back and watch the slaughter. I would have to go on the run. I would have to change my name. I could never visit Ireland again.

I had destroyed the Lion's legacy for everyone. All I had wanted to do was let my hair down. But in the end, I had let myself down. My team down. And my country down. I fell to my knees.

Then something miraculous happened. Almost imperceptibly the camber of the road started to take over and little by little, the bed started to edge to the side of the road towards the curb. He was still flying along, but it became clear he was going to veer off the road into a curb and fly at speed into a bus stop full of pensioners. Thank God. They would cushion the impact. Like a row of wrinkled human airbags. It looked like Rory Best was about to take out more old people than Covid. The bed flew straight into the bus shelter, catapulting one of Ireland's greatest hookers up and into the shocked and screaming Kiwis. Old men and women were running around screaming and shouting, 'It's a dead body, it's a dead body!'

They had mistaken Rory for a runaway corpse from a hospital. But not only were all these nannas running around in a state of frenzy, Rory himself got the shock of his life when he suddenly woke up to find himself at the centre of an OAP Armageddon.

Rory was saved. I was flooded with a sense of relief and knew I would live to fight another day. Looking back now, the whole incident represented one of the biggest regrets of my life. No, not pushing a comatose Rory Best into traffic. Admittedly, that would have been hilarious. No, what I really regret is not taking that opportunity to tattoo a cock and balls on his face. It was a once in a lifetime chance. And I'll never ever have that opportunity again.

So, the moral of this story is 'Carpe Diem'. Seize the day. And draw a cock on your mate's face.

On a sidenote to this event, while he was back on the piss, Jack Nowell did prevent the hotel from burning down when we played the classic family game 'fire pussy', displaying surprisingly smart footwork, given his alcohol intake, to stamp out a bonfire built of cardboard and Johnny Sexton's shirt sleeves. Again, see *What A Flanker* for more detail.

Former South African star Bob Skinstad was another interesting guest, and not just because I grew up idolising him. Bob was one of the original playboys of South Africa's professional era, a good-looking, barnstorming loose forward with all the skills, but there is a lot more to his story than that.

Bob's family fled Zimbabwe when he was a child, he spoke English as a first language when most of his teammates conversed in Afrikaans (he tells a great story about misunderstanding the Afrikaans for 'let us pray' during a team talk and going around slapping his teammates around the face), he suffered a bad car accident in 1999, walked away from the pro game for a couple of years (he even played part-time for Richmond in London South-East Division 1), before returning to the Springboks fold and winning a World Cup in 2007. Bob is such a warm, funny, engaging character, nothing like the stereotype of a South African player, and I loved having him on the show.

**AP:** We're getting more and more past legends on the show and even have a new series called *Rugby's Greatest Unions*, which reunites famous partnerships. One of my favourites was with Scottish half-back pairing Gary Armstrong and Craig Chalmers, who had plenty of stories about the violent nature of rugby in the amateur era and, of course, that momentous day at Murrayfield in 1990 when Scotland upset England in the Grand Slam decider.

On the morning of the game, Craig's room-mate John Jeffrey, a farmer who was used to rising ridiculously early, woke him up at 6 a.m. by throwing a shoe at him. And the morning after the post-match celebrations, which went deep into the night, Craig's sleep was rudely interrupted by Jeffrey again, this time because he'd agreed to play in a charity football match in Melrose. A few hours later, he was running around a pitch dressed as a nurse.

There was also the story of the Romanian rugby player Cristian Raducanu, who, in a story worthy of a John le Carré novel, defected after a Test against Scotland at Murrayfield in 1989. After the post-match dinner, the Scotland and Romania players moved to the nearby Tron Tavern, which was run by former Scotland international Norrie Rowan and connected to the recently rediscovered Edinburgh Vaults. The Romanian secret police were guarding the Tron Tavern's exits, so Rowan led Raducanu down into the Vaults and Raducanu resurfaced a few hundred yards away, flagged down a policeman and asked for political asylum. Some of Raducanu's teammates died during the Romanian revolution, which started a few months later, while Raducanu spent the next decade playing rugby in the UK, while carving out a very successful furniture business, with links to his homeland.

Craig also told an amusing story about rooming with England back-row Mike Teague on the 1989 Lions tour: Teague had a few mates over from Gloucester, and instead of staying in their own hotel, they slept on his and Craig's floor. And on the eve of Craig's Lions debut, the first Test in Sydney, Teague and his mates came crashing through the door at 3 a.m. Teague, I should point out, wasn't playing in that game because of an injury.

We also did a show with that classic England centre partnership of Will Carling and Jeremy Guscott, who weren't the greatest of friends while they were playing together but time has shown them what they had. It was fascinating hearing about the evolution of their relationship, which started with Guscott strolling up to captain Carling on the first day of his first England camp, patting him on the arm and saying, 'Thanks for keeping my shirt warm …'

They didn't get much closer before Carling resigned as England captain in 1995 (although Guscott and the rest of the England lads very much enjoyed their skipper being on the receiving end of a Noel Edmonds 'gotcha', which involved him trying to teach Mr Blobby how to play rugby for a fabricated children's TV programme). But nowadays they can share a bottle of wine and look back at what they achieved together with great pride and joy.

I found their story reassuring and heartwarming. I'd like to do more of those shows, because too often these legends are taken for granted. For example, how I would have loved to have done a show with the likes of Barry John, JPR Williams and Phil Bennett, all of whom have passed away in recent years.

MT: Will Carling never had a nice word to say about me in the early part of my England career, which was ironic given that he wasn't dissimilar to me as a player. The first time I met Will, I made the mistake of mentioning that I was only 10 when he was made England captain in 1988, to which he replied, 'Just fuck off' (to be fair, my Bath side had just hammered Will's Harlequins at the Stoop). He wrote quite a few very unhelpful columns about me back in the day, but I speak to Will quite a bit nowadays and have grown to really like him.

Jerry Guscott was my mentor at Bath, if you can call it that. The first thing he said to me was, 'You're slow, you can't catch, you can't pass, you can't kick. I can't see much of a future for you, what's the point of you doing it?'

We used to play 1st XV v 2nd XV on the Thursday evening before Saturday's game. That was complete madness because if you were in the 2nd XV, you'd obviously try to injure your opposite number. I was part of that first generation of big, physical centres and in one of those games, I ran straight over the top of Jerry, looked down at him and said, 'That's how I'm going to play rugby.' (I think it was actually Mike Catt I ran over, because I remember people shouting, 'Ooh, Jonah's back!', a reference to Lomu stamping all over Catty at the 1995 World Cup. However, it's my story, I'll do whatever I want with it, and Jerry works much better for me.)

That's what rugby was like back then, older players constantly putting younger players down, which was essentially a test. If you sat back and took it without firing back, the abuse would get worse and you'd be labelled as weak. But if you did fire back, they'd think, 'Right, this lad's got something.' Some people would consider that bullying nowadays, but it was actually a test of a young player's resilience. If you weren't able to cope with robust banter on the training ground, chances are you'd give up too easily on game day.

**JH:** Eddie Jones did us a big favour when he agreed to help us launch *The Good, The Bad & The Rugby*, and he'll always be one of my top guests.

Eddie's legacy was tarnished by what happened towards the end of his time in charge of England, not least when he was asked to leave before his contract was up. But the fact is he took the job after 12 years of mediocrity from the England team, during which the coaching and mindset had been pretty awful, and created an environment that produced excellence.

Eddie's certainly not perfect, but he was very good at getting the best out of players. His England team equalled the most consecutive wins by a tier 1 international team (18, shared with New Zealand), he had the best winning percentage of an England head coach (73 per cent, which is better than Clive Woodward, the man in charge when England won the 2003 World Cup), he created one of the best captains England have ever had in Dylan Hartley, he led England to three Six Nations titles in seven years, their first Grand Slam since 2003 and a World Cup final in 2019. That's an amazing legacy.

Unfortunately, his methods are frowned upon nowadays. People want to be told they're amazing and that they'll succeed if they work hard enough, but that's just a lie, not everyone can. So instead of taking the 'kind' approach that the media seems to like, Eddie would just tell players and coaches that they weren't good enough. He was demanding, ruthless, and that wasn't for everyone. It rubbed people up the wrong way, created a lot of disgruntled individuals who thought they would have made it had Eddie not been in charge. But that's exactly why he used those methods, to weed out people who lacked the necessary steel and would rather blame other people than themselves.

The media are constantly banging on about the need to be kind nowadays, but I never wanted my coaches to be kind. I wanted them to be honest, give me the tools to get better, and then help me do that. That's all you want, no nonsense or mind games, and if they preferred other players for no other reason than they did, then say that, don't give me a list of work-ons and then say keep going, when you are always going to go with other players. Professional sportspeople are meant to be comfortable being uncomfortable; they're meant to go to dark places and hate what they're doing; they need to be told that they're shit from time to time; they need to understand that professional sport isn't about being friends with everyone, it's about respect. And I always thought that Eddie got the balance between bloody hard work and fun just right, while conceding that I wasn't around for the last few years of his reign.

Dylan Hartley tells a story about his first meeting with Eddie. Eddie said, 'Mate, I like your attitude, I like your determination. But you're a shit player, which means you'll have to work doubly hard.' Dylan did work doubly hard, and became a better player and an amazing captain, but he almost burnt out. If I'd had to do what Dylan did, I wouldn't have lasted a year under Eddie. In fact, quite a few players briefly burned bright during Eddie's regime before being discarded. Not Jonny May, however. One time, Jonny wrote that he was tired and injured on a form that specifically asked if he was tired and injured. Eddie called him in and said, 'Tired are you, mate?

Injured are you, mate? There's no fucking room here for tired, injured players, mate. Do you fucking want it or not? Because if you don't, you can fuck off. I'll call you a taxi now.' Jonny thought about it for a millisecond and said, 'Actually, I think I'm fine.' Lo and behold, Jonny stopped feeling tired and injured and went back to work. Now don't get me wrong, Eddie would pick and choose who he did this to. He would never have done this to an older player or someone that had a lot of miles on the clock. This was about setting a precedent and testing out to see if Jonny was tired and unable to train or if it was just a mindset thing. You don't always get it right doing things this way, but if you give players an out then they will take it. In sports teams a coach can say, 'No, fuck off, I'm not interested that your cat has died, either you want to play, or you don't; if you don't then no hard feelings but don't come back.' Sport has no place for passengers and energy sappers.

For every player who hated Eddie there was another player who liked him, and Eddie's methods weren't a problem when he had strong people around him, like John Mitchell, Paul Gustard and Steve Borthwick. They only became a problem when his support staff became weaker and Eddie stopped being checked and balanced. He was also dealing with a younger generation of players towards the end, people who just weren't used to his directness.

I think the main reason things went downhill was weak support staff. From the outside, it often looked like Eddie spent three years after losing the 2019 World Cup final to South Africa trying to avenge that defeat. That meant changing the way England played, which just didn't work out for him. I have no real idea what was going on in camp and everyone I spoke to was always very positive about it, but whatever happened it didn't end how anyone wanted. I will always love Eddie, and he was by far and away the best coach I ever worked with. That period of time with England with that group of coaches and players was the best I have ever experienced.

The less said about his time in charge of Australia the better. I could see that by attacking the press, he was trying to distract from and motivate his team. And when his team didn't back his words up, he ended up looking a bit foolish and out on a limb. But that short stint with the Wallabies was an anomaly. Over time, people will reassess Eddie's time in charge of England and realise that we were very lucky to have him for as long as we did. I know things with Japan have not gone well. I can only comment on the man and person I know, and I will be honest and open, but whatever anyone says, he is a good and caring man and the best coach I ever worked with.

**MT:** There are few more enigmatic and polarising people in rugby than Eddie Jones, which is why he's always good value when we have him on the podcast.

Eddie's reign as England head coach was as mysterious as the man himself. He had great success with England overall, including leading them to a World Cup final in 2019. Their semi-final win over New Zealand was probably England's greatest performance in a World Cup. But he got a lot wrong in his last few years in charge, and the opinions of those who worked with and played under him are very mixed.

Hask is a big fan of Eddie because their personalities fitted. Hask wasn't intimidated by Eddie and Eddie loved that Hask was the ultimate team man, which is why he kept picking him. But plenty of other players found Eddie too abrasive and the environment he created too fearful. He burned through coaches and backroom staff at an alarming rate, and the fact that Eddie's captain Dylan Hartley seems to both love and hate him is telling. Eddie pushed Dylan to the absolute limit, physically and mentally, but he probably wouldn't have won 97 England caps had Eddie not been in charge.

I suspect Eddie's old-school approach with England was influenced by what happened at the 2015 World Cup. I reckon he looked at that group of players and thought, 'How have they gone out in the pool stage at their own World Cup? There must be something up with them mentally, they need toughening up.' I think he genuinely cares about his players but also believes in taking them right to the edge, to see what kind of minerals they've got. I guess it's his way of filtering out the weak from the strong. If, like Hask, you pass through the filter, he'll do everything he can to support you. If you don't, Eddie will discard you, and it's those players who dislike Eddie most.

I've always thought that England losing the 2019 World Cup final in the manner they did – they didn't really turn up against a very powerful South African side – left permanent scars on Eddie. Every game after that, until Eddie got sacked, it looked like we'd prepared for the Springboks, which is probably why we almost beat them in the semi-finals of the 2023 World Cup.

Spend time with Eddie in an informal environment and I guarantee you'll like him – take rugby out of the equation and he's just an affable Aussie bloke – which makes his relationship with the media in recent years baffling.

When Eddie's England were doing well, which was most of the time between 2016 and 2019, journalists could have a bit of banter with him. Eddie always had an edge, but he could also be fun. I even enjoyed some of the stuff he said about Wales head coach Warren Gatland, and vice versa. I know some people think that kind of stuff demeans the game, but it also sells tickets and gets the game onto the back pages. But when England started losing, and journalists wanted proper answers to serious questions, quips suddenly weren't enough.

Eddie seemed to go down the José Mourinho 'everyone is against us' route. He no longer had a twinkle in his eye, and his press conferences were no longer much fun for anyone. And if you don't answer journalists' questions and try to embarrass them, they will turn against you.

His time as head coach of Australia was a bit of a disaster, and I think it tarnished his legacy a bit. He handled his exit particularly badly – during the Wallabies' disastrous World Cup in 2023, he flatly denied he'd already interviewed for the Japan head coach job, only to resign the day after the World Cup final and re-join Japan a couple of months later. It's a shame, because he's still so knowledgeable about the game and can't have become a shit coach overnight.

I really don't know where I stand on Eddie. I've heard so many negative stories about him and I disagree with so many things he does. But when I ask Eddie about this stuff, he's very good at explaining his reasoning. And I'll find myself thinking, 'Yeah, now I think about it, that actually makes sense …'

**AP:** Two great examples of guests who revealed themselves to be completely different people than their on-field personas were Ireland and Wales fly-halves Johnny Sexton and Dan Biggar.

Johnny had a reputation as someone whose competitor levels were often in the red zone on the pitch, and by his own admission he crossed the line on occasion. But those kinds of disciplinary lapses are perhaps to be expected from a man who has had to battle back from more injuries than most. Johnny is unbelievably driven and obsessed with winning, and when you play as close to the edge as he does, occasionally you'll overstep the mark. But when we had him on the show, he was hilarious. He told us about a game he played for the Lions against Queensland in 2013. Just as he was about to go on as a replacement, a fan shouted, 'Sexton, you've got shoulders like a snake!' As Johnny tells it, his teammates found it funnier than his abuser's mates in the stand.

Hask will tell you that there were few chippier, gobbier players than Dan Biggar, and he was convinced he wouldn't get on with him on the 2019 Lions tour. I'd occasionally worked with Dan during my Sky days and always found him not only a fantastic analyst of the game but also a gent with it. And that's exactly how he was when he came on the podcast. I actually think that part of the reason Johnny and Dan come on the show is because they recognise a kindred spirit in Hask, another bloke people assume is a dickhead.

People tend to form opinions about sportspeople, often very aggressive ones, based on snapshots, but they fail to understand that they're essentially warriors without the guns and the armour, and they have to put on a mask every time they cross the whitewash. On top of that, the sporting world needs those characters with rough edges and spikes on, because it would be pretty bad for business if everyone was whiter than white like Roger Federer.

**JH:** The first time I played against Johnny Sexton, he got right into my face after I gave a penalty away playing for Wasps against Leinster. You know how he loves some afters – he really tried to mug me off. I was not feeling well during that game, and we were under the pump, so I reacted aggressively as I always do and said, 'Fuck off you shit cunt and mind your own business.' Nigel Owens was the referee and he called me over and said to me, 'James, we can't have that, I've never heard language like it. There's mothers and children watching.' I replied, 'I learned it from my mother', and Nigel looked shocked and said, 'I don't believe that James …'

But when I went on the 2017 Lions tour, I got on really well with both Johnny and Dan Biggar. They were just ultimate competitors who demanded the highest standards, much like Owen Farrell, who is a nightmare to play against as well.

I got to know Dan well when we played together at Northampton, and he's a lovely guy. I'm interested to see what he does next because while Johnny was born for coaching, I never got the same impression about Dan. I'm not sure he had much of a fun ride playing for Wales, and I think he breathed a sigh of relief when he signed for Northampton and escaped that fishbowl. The Welsh are so passionate about their rugby, but that passion can turn quite toxic. Life was more enjoyable and less stressful away from it all, and maybe Dan will decide to leave rugby behind altogether. I wouldn't blame him. That being said, I think towards the end of his time with Wales things did start to swing back for him and he got the appreciation he deserved.

I was going through my phone the other day and came across the 2017 Lions tour photos and there are some real gems in there. I've got a picture of Johnny on a night out drunk wearing a beanie, and he looks absolutely awful. No one would know it was him, he looks like a teenager serving an ASBO. He could be a down-and-out, a scaghead, or someone with a terminal disease. Actually, he could be all three. Had I posted that picture on social media, someone would have started a Just Giving page for him. I also found a video of the fire pussy game, and Rory Best asleep on that bed. All of which will never see the light of day but remind me of one of my best times as a rugby player.

During the tour Johnny shared a room with Owen Farrell, and one night Ben Te'o turned up shitfaced and kicked the door in as both the lads had dodged another night on the piss and were being consummate professionals in their room. Ben came into the room and jumped on their beds and started fucking them up. He was getting into them for being boring: 'You two are a couple of pussies.' Both lads have been very serious operators for a long time and found love early, which as you can imagine in a group of meathead alphas makes for boring reading. Ben went on to say, 'You've done no shagging, you've had one bird between you, fucking pathetic.'

Once he had knackered himself punching them through their duvets he left. What he didn't know is the lads had recorded what he was saying in his pissed state and it made for hilarious listening in the WhatsApp group the next day. It was made even better in his Aussie accent: 'You fucking morons, don't even drink, you don't have sex, what's the fucking point of you?' He isn't wrong. On the last day of the tour Ben, as our WhatsApp administrator, which everyone else had forgotten, without a word just emptied the group and deleted it, leaving no evidence of anything, especially no record of the night of the long nauses, but also binning all the lovely photos and other bits from the tour. In hindsight, probably for the best though.

**AP:** I'm not sure you're ever going to get All Black legends like Richie McCaw and Dan Carter to open up completely, partly because New Zealand rugby is all about humility and the importance of the team over the individual, but also because Kiwis just tend to be quite reserved. But by doing a bit of poking and prodding, we did manage to get McCaw and Carter, as well as Sonny Bill Williams, to reveal more of themselves than they usually do. Including Richie maintaining he was never, ever offside.

**MT:** Sometimes a guest will come on and really not want to talk. You'll get five minutes in and realise they're treating it as a media interview, instead of an informal chat. That was certainly the case with Ma'a Nonu, who was very wary. It took a lot of coaxing to get some giggles and stories out of him.

It took me ages to persuade Dan Carter to come on the podcast, even though we're ambassadors for the same company and good friends. He'd say to me, 'You guys are going to make it so relaxed that I'll probably say something I'll regret.' We got Dan to loosen up a bit towards the end, but some people are just never going to open up completely.

**JH:** I'm of the opinion that there's a bit of gold in everyone. That said, there are the guests who have lots of great stories but aren't able to tell them well, which can be tricky, especially for the editor.

There are also guests who don't get what the show is supposed to be, while others do know what it's supposed to be but simply refuse to buy into it. We're not asking people to admit to shitting in their coach's bed or sniffing cocaine off a stripper's breasts, but we do want them to be open and have a bit of a laugh.

We really wanted to get Steve Borthwick on the show when he got the England head coach job, and as you can imagine he was a bit hesitant in saying yes, but we did eventually get him on and he was great.

I played with Borthers, and while we were very different personalities (opposites, in fact), I always got on well with him and respected him. And when he was Eddie's forwards coach, I played some of my best rugby. I credit him with one of the reasons I played so well during that period. It was to do with the help and guidance he gave me and how impactful he was working with Eddie during that time. It wasn't just Eddie, it was the perfect coaching team around him. So I knew there was more to Borthers than met the eye, but when we finally got him on and I said we wanted to talk to him about what kind of person he was, and not just his role with England, he replied, 'I'm not sure anybody's interested.' I said to him, 'Borthers, when you don't say anything, other people fill the void by saying things that might not be true about you. Of course rugby fans want to know what you're really like.' He was eventually persuaded and opened up as much as he ever will, which was insightful and interesting. I think he showed his passion for the game and England. And we were the only podcast he did.

We recorded two hours with him and while it was tough going at times, some of his chat was great. Interestingly, Borthers was a real trash-talker on the pitch, which doesn't fit with his image. I remember giving a penalty away and him saying to me, 'Unlucky, Hask, you're fucking shit', before grinding my face into the turf (I felt like saying to him, 'Fuck off, Borthers, you've had 10 carries for minus one metre', but that wasn't really my style). He didn't seem overly happy when I brought that up, but he did have a wry smile on his face; he also didn't deny it either, which was telling in itself. It does sound like something I would make up, just to stir the pot as it's so out of character for him, but it's true. He was hugely competitive on the field. It actually ended up being a jumping-off point to explore where that competitive streak came from.

Borthers also opened up about previous England environments he'd been in as a player and coach, and not in a complimentary way. He wasn't treated particularly well by Martin Johnson's coaching staff; after they told Steve to get the knee surgery that he needed at the end of the season, they said they would have him back when he was fit, but they didn't and they never picked him again. Basically, they didn't want to have to drop him so just waited for the right time and binned him. He had a miserable time at the hands of the media and spent most of his international career looking over his shoulder, as did a lot of his teammates. But he wasn't telling us all this for the sake of it, he just wanted us to know how those experiences had shaped him and how his England environment was different. He wanted his players to feel at home, he wanted them to enjoy themselves. He also showed he liked a bit of romance when he selected Danny Care for his 100th cap. Borthers came across as humble, supportive and quietly inspirational, a man who cared hugely about England and its rugby team, which is why the comments under the podcast were overwhelmingly positive.

Sonny Bill Williams got a bit arsey about a couple of things I said to him, but I think that was down to a misunderstanding. I was interested in the fact that Sonny Bill obviously liked to entertain as a player and how that fitted in, or didn't, with Pacific Island culture, which tends to prize humility. There was a real dichotomy going on between someone who was a superstar, had a massive character, had done so much in the limelight but was also from a humble background, and culturally expected to be humble. I think he thought I was accusing him of trying to be something he wasn't, or being false, as opposed to what I was trying to get at: how do you manage the internal struggle to perform and then not, it must be tough. I am a performer, and I don't ever worry about anything other than that. Things got a bit strained for a couple of minutes and I think post-show there was some back and forth with his agent, but it was all cleared up when the context was explained. But I prefer that to guests who come on and give us almost nothing beyond bland statements about their team trying to do their best and not worrying about what anyone else thinks etc.

Then there are the players we regularly try to get on the podcast but who don't believe they need to do it. I find that frustrating because they're not doing themselves any favours long term. I know that's the case because I've spoken to players who spent their careers saying nothing before suddenly realising they'd made a terrible mistake after hanging up their boots. They're lost, don't know what to do with their lives, partly because they didn't want to have any dealings with the media. Fundamentally, no one gives a shit about them now that they're not playing, because they don't have any public profile.

Even players who were outrageous talents struggle in retirement. I met one such player at an airport recently and he just seemed a bit lost. He'd written a book (that at the time he didn't want to promote) and was involved in various business ventures, but he seemed to have lost his identity, probably because his identity had been so wrapped up in rugby. Now the horse had bolted it was very hard to suddenly get back in the mix and build a profile. I know first-hand how hard retirement is and it's tricky when you are no longer pursuing your passion, which had been rugby for as long as he could remember, but now he was meandering through life. Being humble is great, but it doesn't pay the bills.

The flipside of that is someone like Dylan Hartley, who wasn't really interested in anything outside of rugby until I would say the last half of his career, until he realised that he was actually a great networker. Dylan's now got his fingers in so many pies and makes me look like an absolute amateur. He has forged a great career for himself and is brilliant at it. Whereas I have gone the other way and don't really focus on networking, which I need to readdress as it's really about who you know, not what you know.

Then there's Richie McCaw, who was pursuing outside interests long before he retired in 2015, despite being one of the greatest players who ever lived. When we had Richie on the podcast, he talked to us about flying gliders and helicopters (he's even been involved in rescue and reconnaissance missions) and adventure racing, which involves trekking, mountain biking, kayaking and whatever else the organisers fancy throwing at teams.

I know people think I'm media hungry, but I take the view that if you're going to do something, you need to throw yourself into it 100 per cent. Otherwise, what's the point? When some people write a book, they can't be bothered to publicise it. But I'm all in, otherwise hardly anybody is going to know about it and hardly anybody is going to buy it. I'm not saying I don't have moments where I'm a bit all over the place and don't really know where I'm heading, but by fully committing to whatever I do, I'm in a better position than lots of others.

My life is chaotic, but it needs to be. If it wasn't, I'd quickly lose my mind. I recently had a week at home on my own, while Chloe was away with Bodhi, but I didn't put my feet up, like a lot of dads would have done. Instead, I spent most of that time doing things – writing a speech for a dinner, booking interviews, spending time in the studio making music, DJing. I always relax by reading, or watching a TV series while I eat, but to be honest, I always ask myself whether I could be using my time better, and if the answer is yes, I will do work. I find peace in chaos. Some people think that being busy all the time means you have no freedom, but freedom is being able to do the things you love doing – even if it's lots and lots of things.

On the podcast, we try to champion the benefits of having interests outside of rugby, as well as revealing your personality and having an opinion, because we know just how tough life can be once you're done with rugby and rugby's done with you. Promoting yourself through the media is like dancing with the devil, but it's a necessary risk. You have to play the game to a certain extent, even if it feels like the last thing in the world you want to be doing.

Of course, putting yourself about in the media doesn't just allow you to portray your real self, it also means you can make yourself look a better person than you are. I recently had a call from a supposedly squeaky-clean rugby great who was getting up to all sorts of mischief in a notoriously hedonistic European capital. But I wasn't at all surprised, because the same guy had propositioned Chloe a few years earlier while I was DJing a few feet away, and his teammate, another supposedly squeaky-clean rugby great, was groping her arse. Nobody's perfect, but if you're clever, you can make it seem that way. My personal choice is to be upfront and honest, warts and all. That way, if you get caught out it's not a surprise. I try to always be the same with everyone. I'm sure I don't get as much work as I could by being like that, but I would rather not be everyone's cup of tea than pretend my shit doesn't stink when it very clearly does.

# 12

# THE SUPPORTING CAST

**JH:** We used to have a feature in live shows which involved the three of us, plus guests, calling famous people in our phone books, with whoever got through to the most famous person being the winner. We'd text them beforehand, to make sure they were available when the show was on, and make it a video call, so that the person would be beamed onto a big screen.

Before a show in Cardiff, someone put me in touch with Tom Holland via his brother. Tom is a big rugby fan, and we exchanged a few private messages on social media. I was thinking, 'Oh my God, I'm fanboying over Spider-Man and Spider-Man is fanboying over me, how surreal is this?' He gave me his number and said he'd like to meet up, and I thought this was finally my chance to trump Tins. (I was on to a winner with Caitlyn Jenner, but she didn't answer and Tins pulled Rebel Wilson out of his hat. Caitlyn did call me back but while I was on the way home, so no good for anyone really, but it was nice that she responded.) Most of the time, though, I was left with no one responding and looking like Billy No Mates.

The day before the show, I dropped Tom a text asking if he'd mind helping me out with this feature, and he texted back saying he was up for it. But when I called him, he didn't pick up. That was an excruciating 30 seconds or so. The phone rang and rang, and a thousand Welsh people laughed harder and harder. I can't remember who Tins called that night, but he won again. And after the show, I discovered that Tom had unfollowed me on social media. Turns out he thought I was a wanker, and you won't be surprised to learn that we haven't spoken since. He is clearly a good judge of character, as having me as a mate could really damage your reputation.

**AP:** My favourite celebrity guest was probably Jamie Dornan, the ludicrously talented Northern Irish model, musician and actor.

Bizarrely, Jamie used to live next door to my parents-in-law in Gloucestershire. When he first moved in, my wife's mum, who had no idea who he was, popped a note through his letter-box inviting him round for a Christmas drink. The following evening, there was a knock at the door, and when my wife answered it, there was Jamie Dornan, wet through from the rain, holding a bottle of champagne. She immediately recognised who he was and wondered for a second whether he'd lie her down in the hallway and make love to her, à la Christian Grey from *Fifty Shades*, or batter her to death, more in keeping with his character from *The Fall*, who was a Belfast serial killer.

Jamie turned out to be lovely, as did his wife, the musician Amelia Warner. It was all very surreal, with Amelia wanting to talk to my wife about the best schools in the area, my wife wanting to talk to Jamie simply because he was Jamie, Jamie wanting to talk to me about rugby, and me wanting to talk to Amelia simply because she was Amelia. Jamie has been on the podcast a few times since, but that's probably because he already knew Tins, who also lives in Gloucestershire and is friends with every famous person in existence.

**JH:** Jamie Dornan was great, although I was slightly perturbed to learn that he cries when Ireland lose. I fancied him a bit before that, but it's definitely turned me off him. Jamie cares more about Ireland than I appear to care about anything else in the world, apart from my daughter.

How is that possible? I couldn't get my head around it. He's an amazing actor, one of the world's biggest heart-throbs, the sweetest, kindest guy, but also a massive nerd who lives and breathes Irish rugby. He must have been almost suicidal when New Zealand knocked them out of the last World Cup. It's good to know that even being the sexiest man on the planet can have its downsides. It made me feel better about my solid 5/10 set-up – there is hope for us average guys after all.

**AP:** Probably my favourite celeb show was during Covid, when lots of people were locked down at Christmas. Tins and Hask got very busy with texting and we had 15 to 20 people on a Zoom call, including the Reverend Richard Coles (formerly of The Communards), golfer Lee Westwood, TV presenter Vernon Kay, Ian Wright and Jonathan Davies. It was just about the strangest gathering you could ever imagine, but also a huge amount of fun.

**JH:** That Covid Christmas was proof that Payno is sometimes given free rein to cause chaos behind the scenes, not always with good results.

He still thinks that show was brilliant, but I just thought it was weird. It was such an odd mix of people, including a vicar (I thought it was the Archbishop of Canterbury until someone told me it was actually the guy who used to be in The Communards). Ireland prop Tadhg Furlong popped up in the group zoom, he looked like someone had set a firework off under his arse when he logged in. For those few minutes, he had the look of fear in his eyes and was like, 'What the fuck am I doing on here?', before pulling the rip cord and logging off. Since that call, he has never responded or come back onto the show.

**AP:** It's because of Tins and Hask's pulling power that we don't have a booker. And while it might be fun to employ one, I think we'd open ourselves up to a lot of criticism if we moved too far from rugby and started becoming just another place for celebrities to plug their latest wares. I'd love to have Daniel Craig or Chris Hemsworth on the show – both of whom are big rugby fans and friends of Tins – but it would lead to lots of grumbling about Tins and Hask getting above their station and flaunting their celebrity contacts.

**MT:** I'm always being told by the other two to get my contacts book out, it's one of my main roles in the unit. That time I phoned Rebel Wilson in Cardiff, not one of Hask's so-called celeb friends answered (which was funny, because he's always dropping names), but Rebel answered while she was visiting Disney World on her birthday.

I first encountered Rebel through the thoroughbred race-horse auction house Magic Millions. I met her at a New Year's Eve party in Sydney, before meeting her again at the races on the Gold Coast, and she also had a strange link to the Australian rugby team.

Rebel is a bit of a genius, and one of her talents is the ability to speak Afrikaans. She spent a year in South Africa as an ambassador for the service organisation Rotary International and while there had a malaria-induced dream in which she was an actress, which she then went on to be, rather than a lawyer. It sounds like an urban myth that the Wallabies asked her to translate line-out calls when they played South Africa, but it's true.

I like having other people, such as Rebel and Jamie Dornan, involved in the podcast because I'm fascinated to know why they're interested in rugby. Jamie loves Manchester United and golf as well as the Ireland rugby team, and he told us he cried three times during Ireland's win over South Africa at the 2023 World Cup – during the anthem, when the final whistle went and watching the team celebrating. We asked him what he'd prefer to do out of hitting the first tee shot for Europe at a Ryder Cup, scoring in a cup final for Manchester United or leading Ireland out for a Six Nations decider against England, and he chose the latter.

I'd love to have The Rock on, because I know he's a big rugby fan (his mum is Samoan and he played a bit as a kid in New Zealand), or fellow Hollywood star Jason Momoa, who is a huge fan of the All Blacks. South African UFC champion Dricus du Plessis was at the 2023 World Cup final, while Russell Crowe is interested in union, despite being a league man first and foremost. When it comes to all of the above, they're attracted to rugby because of its warrior spirit, and it's our job on the podcast to tell you more about the warriors who play it. Of course people want us to talk about the rugby itself, and we do that to a certain degree, but more people want us to dig deeper and reveal juicy personal nuggets that they're not normally privy to.

JH: Some of my favourite guests have been non-rugby players, including former soldier Jason Fox, from Channel 4's *SAS: Who Dares Wins*.

Foxy told some amazing stories, as you would expect from a former special forces soldier, including one about a certain unnamed television personality fucking about with a helicopter, with disastrous consequences. It's one of the best stories I have ever heard.

According to Foxy, him and a bunch of his Special Boat Service mates were flown to an old fort in Afghanistan, which doubled as a UK Army base, in a Chinook helicopter to prepare for a mission. Whenever they fly, they are always supported by two Apache gunships. This job was no different. While they were waiting to start their mission, chucking a rugby ball about or sleeping in the shade of the choppers, they spotted two jeeps coming along the road past them as they were outside the walls of the fort. They noticed that there was a well-known TV personality at the front of one of the jeeps, looking and point-ing at them. It's not a sight the SBS see every day while waiting for the green light and mission intel in the baking sun, before taking to the skies to bring death to their enemies.

This bloke emerged from the fort, wandered over and said, 'Hi guys, such and such celebrity is visiting, and he'd love to come and meet you.' The SBS lads replied, 'Fuck off, we're not meeting that bellend.' The solider marched back off and went into the fort. Ten minutes later the same solider reappeared and marched over to the two parked Apaches that were on a little rise some way from the Chinook carrying the troops. Foxy saw the army solider chat with the pilots and then go back into the fort. Five minutes later a jeep drove out the fort past the SBS lads and headed over to one of the Apaches. Once parked, the celeb got out looking red-faced and flustered.

As the jeep had driven past, half the SBS lads really got stuck into him, calling him all sorts of names; one of the lads remem-bered this celeb's character name from a TV series where he had played an SAS soldier (have you guessed who we are talk-ing about yet?). So they all shouted that at him among other things. The celeb pretended he couldn't hear them. He 100 per cent could. The SBS lads went back to killing time, chatting shit and generally just being lads. Foxy saw out the corner of his eye that the celeb was given a tour of one of the Apaches. The SBS lads could see him seated behind the controls, acting like a kid – yanking the stick, pressing buttons and probably making flying noises, machine gun sounds and pretending to blow up invisible enemies. After his playtime was over, the SBS lads took the piss out of him a bit more as he drove back past them before he re-entered the fort, perhaps for jelly and ice cream.

The SBS lads finally got the go-ahead just before dusk, at which point they got into the Chinook. The normal procedure is they load up, and within a minute they are up in the air and ready to roll. Obviously when a huge helicopter starts up there is a lot of noise and dust, you are aware of nothing else and can't see out the windows. Foxy was sitting in the back, he heard the engines start to rev and that it was ready to lift off, then two minutes went by and they had gone nowhere. Then the engines started to wind down.

Across the radio came the abort call, the ramp of the Chinook came down and the lads re-emerged to find chaos. One of the Apaches was upside down on the sand fucked, with the pilot and co-pilot of said aircraft kicking the fuck out of each other.

Foxy ran over and separated them, not before hearing the co-pilot shouting at the pilot while he punched him repeatedly, 'I fucking told you not to let him anywhere near it, you said he would be fine, that bald prick has fucked us.'

Apparently, as the call came in to go quicky, the Apaches needed to be in the air pronto to give cover while the Chinook took off. As they had prepared to take off, one of the Apaches had gone haywire and just flipped itself onto the sand knackering its tail and rotors. There were only minor injuries, mostly from the post-crash fight, but each of one those Apaches cost

£45 million. As for the SBS mission, it was scrapped, which Foxy wasn't very happy about at the time. Obviously, there was a huge enquiry as to why a mission was aborted and a helicopter gunship ended up arse over tit. If you google this story, you will find out more of the detail but essentially the reasons cited were that the unnamed celeb had got into the Apache and touched a load of switches and buttons which were not reset before take-off. In the haste to get the mission going as time was of the essence, the celeb's tampering went unnoticed. A huge portion of the blame was put upon this celeb's shoulders when the ruling came to pass.

While I'm on the subject of soldiering, I might as well tell you about the time I sat next to this same unnamed television personality at a dinner. I had heard stories that he was a bit intense, but I thought it was all for show and he was really going to be normal or even better it was going to turn out he was funny as fuck and had just been trolling everyone. How wrong I was.

I don't think we'd even finished our starters when he said to me, 'James, have you ever killed a man?'

'No,' I replied. 'Have you ever killed a man?'

The television personality scoffed, then said, 'Yes, of course. A few.'

Me and one of my best mates Jamie, who's a former world champion kickboxer turned jeweller, were kicking each other under the table, doing everything in our powers not to laugh.

'We were in Iraq,' the television personality continued, 'it was at night and I was next to one of the Special Forces guys who was manning the 50cal, and through the night vision we could see the locals were crop-planting ...'

'What does that mean?' I said. 'Actually planting crops at night? Because it's so hot in the day I suppose.'

'No! Putting in IEDs.' He said it in such a way to imply that I was a complete fucking idiot for not knowing this.

'Oh.'

'When we saw them planting, we'd radio to a fire team who would put mortar rounds into or near them, that would then make them run right into where we were sitting with the 50 cal. At first, I was just loading. But then they let me have a go on the 50 cal.'

He then mimed firing three round bursts from an imaginary gun in front of the other diners. He even made the noises. It was like he was transported back there; he had that ominous thousand-yard stare and a wry smile on his face.

He snapped out of it and turned to me. 'And like I said, I didn't just kill one of them, I killed a few. Don't ask me if I enjoyed it.'

'Did you enjoy it?'

'I fucking loved it, mate …'

'Oh.'

He looked over his shoulder, before adding, 'But don't tell my wife, she doesn't know …'

Me and Jamie had to take ourselves off to the toilets, to confirm it was actually happening and he was really saying all this. We had to hide in a cubicle and laugh or we would have exploded. I started taking notes on my phone as this was going to give me the best stories ever. I could not believe it was real. When we got back to the table, we were relieved to discover that the television personality wasn't quite finished.

First, he told me about the time he was in Ukraine before the war and that Vladimir Putin saw him as a person of interest and had hacked his phone, and when on the Ukraine visit he had put drones into the air to follow him. Then he told me about his jiu-jitsu, saying that while I was bigger than him, he would use my weight against me and that I would never see it

153

coming. He informed me that he had been told by a grandmaster that he could have got a 10th Dan black belt now but it wouldn't have been fair after such a short time doing it. Then he grabbed me and tried to move me, I didn't move and he was like, you see I knew you were going to do that, but actually I was going to do this! And again he tried something on me like an arm drag and I just moved my arm and he fell back into his chair. He shot up, 'Drink anyone?', and just marched off to the bar. Jamie was in tears in his napkin, I was like 'What the actual fuck is going on here?'

He returned as if nothing had happened and then he started asking me, 'Do the England team ever do hot debriefs?'

'What do you mean, do we have meetings in the sun or the sauna? No, not really, why?

He went 'No, once you have gone into battle or a game, do you just have a quick meeting and share everything before moving on?'

'Well', I said, 'sort of, but not like you are saying.'

He was blown away. 'What, you don't do that? Bloody hell, that's so backward, me and the SAS guys are always doing them. I can't believe the England team don't do them, God that's awful. Me and the boys sit around, have a pint and get things off our chests. We talk about all the mad things we've done and all the people we've killed.'

All the time he was saying this, he was aggressively nodding and nudging Jamie as if to say, 'God, what a bunch of fucking amateurs the England team are.'

'That's maybe why they aren't playing well, me and the SAS are always saying how important the meetings are to get stuff off your chest.' He was poking and backslapping Jamie so much, Jamie had to pretend to take a call to get away from the mad bastard. I thought Jamie was going to roundhouse kick this pillock into next week. It was like having dinner with Jay from *The Inbetweeners*, or what I imagine he'd be like in 30 years' time.

The more the red wine flowed the more absurd the shit got. Honestly, the celeb was madder than a box of frogs. Having watched him polish off a bottle and half of red, he now made the Mad Hatter look normal.

He had a lull for 10 minutes and then he tried to pitch me an idea for a new TV series. His rationale was he liked me and Jamie so much he wanted to do something with us. We were now the best of friends.

'James, I wanna make you famous,' he said. 'Tell you what, why don't we climb Everest and swim the Channel together?'

'That's quite a lot to take on, isn't it?'

'Are you not prepared to die?'

'What do you mean?'

'I only work with people who are prepared to die.'

'Oh, I see.'

'I like your mate Jamie, he seems like a tough man, we'll get him on the TV show as well. Tell you what, the only thing we're missing is a black lad. Who can we get?'

'Mo Farah?'

'What's he gonna fucking do?'

'We could try to make him eat chicken?'

'Why would we do that?'

'Because he's a vegetarian and it would be a challenge.' I was clearly taking the piss, but it went over his head.

'Nah, he's not funny. We need funny. Do you reckon he'd be prepared to die?'

'For God's sake, why does everybody have to die?!'

The more he spoke, the more intently I stared at him, trying to decipher a flicker of humour. Surely this had to be a wind-up? Surely he'd give himself away eventually? But no – on and on he ploughed, his face getting stonier.

'Thinking about it,' he said, 'we probably need a bird and a black bloke. Know any birds who'd be up for climbing Everest and swimming the Channel?'

'Mate,' I said, 'what makes you think I can climb Everest and swim the Channel? I haven't even got my 25-metre badge!'

'Look,' he said, 'unless you risk it all, we can't get this going. Are you in?'

There was spittle on his mouth and his eyes were glazed as he said this. He stood up and came around to Jamie and me and said, 'Are you fucking in?'

'Of course,' we said.

He hugged us both, kissing both of us on each cheek like a mafia boss.

'Excellent! I own a production company, and I'll be in touch in the morning.'

We swapped numbers and guess what? I never heard from him again. I even messaged him to say it was nice to meet you; he read it but never replied. So it looks like I won't be swimming the Channel after all.

# 13

# BUT SERIOUSLY

**AP:** Behind the scenes, we talk about *The Good, The Bad & The Rugby* being a place where you can tackle life head-on, which is a slightly cheesy way of saying it's not just about analysing the game. We've never been about deep dives into the weekend's action, we're about rugby and everything that happens to come into its orbit.

We've done things with the LGBTQ+ community and Fathers 4 Justice, spoken to people about suicide attempts, terrible injuries, depression, drink problems and death threats. It can be hard-hitting at times, but we don't set out to be agenda-setting or anything like that, it just sort of happens organically.

On a personal note, Tins has spoken about his kids and the death of the Queen and Hask has touched on his family situation, which isn't easy, and his retirement. That show when he announced he was hanging up his boots was raw. I could tell he was very emotional and the journalist in me wanted to squeeze a few tears out of him, but he held firm. And about six months later, he spoke about having lost his identity. He'd gone from being 'James Haskell the rugby player – Premiership and European champion, 77 caps for England, Lions tourist', to 'James Haskell – just trying to make his way in life, like everyone else.' To paraphrase Ray Liotta in the final scene of *Goodfellas*: 'Today everything is different. There's no action. I'm an average nobody.'

I was able to empathise with Hask because of my own loss of identity after leaving Sky. And I tried to impress on Hask that while I was roaming in the wilderness for a while, starting again and building something new was so rewarding. I was no longer a puppet on a string, I was my own man. I even had a boxing match in 2022 – it was all for charity, so give me a break – and if you'd told me that was going to happen 10 years ago, I'd have thought you were out of your mind.

**JH:** Things would often get serious on the podcast by accident. And one of the first episodes of the podcast to turn a bit dark was with Billy Vunipola.

The first time we had Billy on, he spoke about his issues with alcohol, which took me by surprise (that's why we can't just rely on notes, we have to be nimble and be prepared to go wherever the guest takes us); and the second time, he spoke about his sometimes tricky relationship with his brother Mako, his Tongan roots, his Christian faith, his guilt, and his support for Australia's Israel Folau, who had recently stated that 'drunks, homosexuals, adulterers, liars, fornicators, thieves, atheists [and] idolators' were destined for Hell.

That was one of the only times I fell out with our producer, because people were having a go at me for letting Billy, my old England teammate, off the hook. But despite our friendship, I did ask Billy some robust questions, it's just that they were edited out. I thought our producer had made me look dishonest, while he probably thought there was a bit too much darkness.

But those Billy episodes were great examples of what made the podcast so popular: yes, we went to some dark places, but there were also funny stories, including one about Billy eating a curry pizza sandwich (a chicken korma inside a folded-over 13.5 inch Mighty Meaty) washed down with a large bottle of Coke.

**AP:** I knew a lot had gone on in Billy's life that the public weren't aware of, but I wasn't expecting us to go to that place. Then again, Billy is another great example of a player who has lots of different dimensions, rather than being the cardboard cut-out the media sometimes portrays him as.

Billy did so much for Saracens in the decade or so he was there – he won five Premiership and three European titles – and the tributes that poured in after he announced his move to Montpellier were effusive. Sarries' director of rugby Mark McCall called him a 'thoughtful, supportive teammate and a fantastic mentor to many young players', yet there will be people who mainly remember him for being tasered in a bar in Mallorca (I have it on good authority that the first taser didn't floor him because it hit him in the wallet).

By his own admission, Billy can be a bit of a handful when he's drunk, but so can lots of people (Tins is an absolute nightmare after a couple of bottles of red), and there's so much more to him than that. He's a good family man who hadn't touched a drop for years before that Mallorca incident, and whenever he's been on the podcast, he's been fantastic value – open, honest and entertaining. That's what the podcast is all about, uncovering the real people behind the headlines.

We had former Scotland and Lions full-back Stuart Hogg on and afterwards we got a message from a Scottish journalist saying, 'This is the best interview with Stuart I've ever seen.' Stuart explained that his signature 'W' try celebration was a tribute to his best friend, Richard Wilkinson, who died in a car crash in 2009, and how it quite easily could have been him who died instead. Stuart, Richard and two others did rock, paper, scissors to decide who sat in the front, Richard 'won', and was killed when the car failed to take a bend and crashed through a fence.

I'm very proud that we've created an environment in which people feel comfortable enough to tell intimate and emotional stories like that, and not too surprised that Stuart hadn't opened up to any journalists before then, for fear of his words being bent out of shape.

**MT:** There are still one or two players in and around the England team that I played with and against, while Hask has played with quite a few of them. So we have a connection, we're mates, and that immediately puts people at ease.

I always say to guests, 'We're not the *Daily Mail*, we're not here to piss anyone off, so give it everything you've got and if you're worried about anything you've said, we'll just take it out.' That's why the podcast usually sounds like some blokes chatting shit in a bar, and the audience are essentially eavesdroppers.

We champion men talking about stuff they might normally keep a lid on, and it can be quite powerful getting deep with a guest on the podcast. And when we get it right, I feel good that we might have helped some people.

We're planning something around the 2003 World Cup winners, because as I mentioned earlier, quite a few of those guys are struggling. People make assumptions about sportspeople, especially those who have been successful. They think their lives must be rosy just because they won something 20-odd years ago. But look at my old England teammate Phil Vickery, who declared himself bankrupt and is not in a good place. Then there's Steve Thompson, who has early-onset dementia. Even Jonny Wilkinson, the most famous of all of us, has struggled with his mental health.

Even footballers struggle with life after hanging up their boots. They've spent however many years playing in front of tens of thousands of cheering fans every week, and suddenly that's gone. Yes, they've got lots of money in the bank, but they've got no real purpose or sense of self-worth. They're just sleepwalking through life, defined by what they used to be and can never be again.

**AP:** When we had Jason Fox on, he started talking about attempting to take his own life within 10 minutes, which none of us was expecting, maybe not even Jason. That episode highlighted that the podcast is essentially a chat rather than a prescribed interview. We always have a script, and my role is to craft the conversation, so that a show has a beginning, middle and end. But the best shows are often those where the script gets thrown out of the window after five minutes and we start freestyling.

Often the guests have no idea which of their stories are most interesting but if things take a sudden twist, I try to grab hold of the topic and peel back the layers, as was the case when Hask's best friend and former England teammate Paul Doran-Jones appeared on the show. The first half an hour was Hask and Paul just mucking about and desperately trying to top each other with more and more outrageous stories, which was quite exhausting, despite the fact I barely got a word in. But when James mentioned that Paul was a single father who had had a horrific time with custody battles, effectively ending his playing career over all of it, he spoke about how it tested his mental health and fortitude to the limit. When he talked about how the organisation Fathers 4 Justice had made contact with him, and how unfair the current system was – you can see why dads are scaling cranes dressed as Spider-Man to shed some light on how imbalanced the court system is – the chat went from being an almighty cock-off to a fascinating, emotional, deep dive into his sometimes painful journey as a single dad.

**JH:** Another guest who spun off in an unexpected direction was Ellis Genge, who admitted that he hadn't been as professional as he should have been because he was taking sleeping pills, playing computer games late into the night, not eating the right foods and therefore not training properly. He was not being a consummate professional and I thought it was quite brave of him to say that he wasn't where he wanted to be and hadn't been doing what he needed to do to fulfil his talent. He talked about how he completely changed what he was doing and how he built a routine and a plan to succeed. After a very short period the results spoke for themselves. He is now more dedicated than ever. It's refreshing for people to admit that they didn't always get things right at first, but then found a way to achieve their goals.

**AP:** Kevin Sinfield was incredibly inspiring, not least because he sat in a yoga position for the entire interview, which lasted 90 minutes. Only when we finished did he unclip his legs, and he didn't show a flicker of pain.

We spoke to Kev at the height of his fundraising efforts for his old pal Rob Burrow, who was battling motor neurone disease, and he was a great example of the incredible camaraderie that runs through both codes of rugby.

When I started at Sky, someone said to me, 'You are media, they are sport, and the two shouldn't connect. Don't try to have friendships with the people you talk about on a Saturday, because your job is to tell the story, and sometimes you'll have to tell the story in a way that people aren't happy with.' But since I started doing the podcast, I've really enjoyed the connections I've made with a lot of our guests, including with Kev. When I spoke to him afterwards, he was so grateful that we'd put a nice show together for him and Rob.

**JH:** A particularly emotional episode was with Welsh referee Nigel Owens, who spoke about his struggles coming to terms with his sexuality and wanting to take his own life. I had known Nigel for years but never knew of his story and just how close he came to not being around anymore. Then there was English referee Wayne Barnes, who spoke about the threats of death and sexual violence his wife and children had recently been subjected to, all over a decision he made in a game of rugby.

There was also the episode with former England prop Alex Corbisiero, who spoke about being diagnosed with and twice recovering from testicular cancer. I had always found Corbs a bit socially awkward, which is not me talking out of turn, yet he was also a bit of a dichotomy. He would be shy and nerdy one moment, but then would stand up at the front of the bus and rap freestyle with this insane riff that would destroy whoever his sights were set on. It was remarkable to watch and as you can imagine I was on the end of it a number of times. Corbs is also one of those people who when they walk and talk with you, they cut across you or meander into your path, it's so funny. I almost fell off a cliff in South Africa having a chat with him. I have seen him walk along next to lads, and they have ended up in a bush or have had to say, 'Corbs, fucking walk straight', and push him into line.

Corbs ended up working as a rugby pundit in America (where he was born). When you watch him, he's everything you'd expect an American sports pundit to be – very verbose, very loud, very upbeat. He is brilliant at it, and he has grown into a fantastic operator of his craft. I love having him on the podcast and listening to him – it's wonderful considering how low he must have been when he was going through chemo, his cancer having spread to his lymph nodes, wondering if he'd even be around for much longer.

**AP:** We had Matt Hampson on during Covid, and he provided some much-needed perspective at a difficult time for a lot of people all over the world.

Hask and I were there when Hambo suffered his life-changing injury at an England Under-21 training session in Northampton in 2005 – Hask was a teammate, I was a junior reporter – and I remember it so clearly. It was a scrummaging session and I'd just nipped off to get my cameraman and set up for the interviews. I was in the car park, helping the guy get his equipment out of the back of his car, when team manager Pete Drewett sprinted past. I said to him, 'You're in a hurry!', and he replied, 'Yep, we've had an accident …' A scrum had collapsed, severing Hambo's spinal cord. Two days later, I had to report from Stoke Mandeville, home to the National Spinal Injuries Centre, before covering the game on the Friday, which was against Scotland at Franklin's Gardens.

I find listening to Hambo's story more inspiring than tear-jerking. Despite that terrible accident leaving him paralysed from the neck down, he's gone on to do amazing things with his life, including founding the Matt Hampson Foundation, which provides advice, support and relief for anyone who has suffered a serious injury or disability. His Get Busy Living Centre, a rehab centre for sufferers of serious injuries through sports accidents, opened in 2018; he gives motivational speeches, has written columns for rugby publications, as well as an award-winning book. More than most people, I'm sure you'd agree.

Hambo was out at the World Cup in France, accompanied by a great gang of people and just getting on with life, which is typical of the man. He wasn't quite doing donuts in his wheelchair, but he was pretty bloody pissed.

**JH:** Another of my favourite guests was James Waterhouse, the BBC's Ukraine correspondent. James came through Wasps academy, like me, and played for Rotherham in the Championship, so was obviously a decent operator. He also played for Esher, and after a chance conversation with John Inverdale, the Esher chairman and former BBC rugby presenter, he did a journalism degree. Having kicked off his journalism career with BBC Essex, James ended up being posted all over the world, eventually pitching up in Kyiv. And when the Russians invaded in 2022, suddenly he was reporting from a war zone.

James didn't just talk to us about Ukraine, he also described what it was like to play in the lower leagues. He earned just 12 grand a year playing for Esher, while also selling sports kit to schools out of a portacabin, and at Plymouth Albion he played under former Bath and England hooker Graham Dawe, one of the hardest men in rugby who was still playing in his fifties. And all the while, he was thinking, 'There must be something else out there …' The funny thing was, we recorded a podcast with the great Australian scrum-half George Gregan directly beforehand, and while he was good, James' rugby story was just as interesting in its own way. That's why I love *GBR* so much, you never know what you are going to get until you press record. I always go into every interview excited to pull back some layers and see what's underneath.

James flew into Kyiv in January 2022, his bosses having told him a Russian invasion was unlikely (to be fair to them, hardly anyone predicted it was going to happen, including most of the Ukrainian people James spoke to). Then, six weeks later, it all kicked off: soldiers on the streets, jets screaming overhead, people trying to flee. As James said, 'You could still see Kyiv, but you couldn't feel it anymore.' And he thought to himself, 'What are the Russians going to do when they get here? Are we still going to be able to broadcast? Is there a way out? Oh my God, I haven't texted home …' A few people moaned that there wasn't enough rugby on that episode, but they always fucking moan about something, which is good. You want people to comment. Audiences don't know what they want; if you try to give it to them you will fail. There is a great quote from Henry Ford that goes: 'If I'd asked my customers what they wanted [before he made the Model T], they'd have said a faster horse.' I want to do more shows that leave rugby at the door and focus on the people we are interested in. I thought the James Waterhouse interview was brilliant.

**AP:** That episode with James was pretty hard-hitting (although Hask did still manage to shoehorn a few knob gags in) and a bit of a jaw-dropper. He'd gone from being a lower division rugby player whose dad kept telling him to get a 'proper' job to reporting from a war zone in PRESS body armour, seeing things that most people wouldn't want to be anywhere near. It was an amazing story which made Hask's career zig-zagging seem quite humdrum by comparison.

We also did a show with some Ukrainian rugby players who had lost teammates in the conflict, which was quite emotional. Apart from their descriptions of war, what really hit home was their complete and utter hatred for the enemy, which was almost impossible for someone like me, who has never experienced war, to comprehend. They were also very grateful to be invited on the show, which enabled them to spread awareness of the situation.

It's important to do those kinds of shows every now and again, even if they don't break the bank in terms of numbers. At the same time, we have to be careful not to lose sight of what we are. Our audience doesn't come to *The Good, The Bad & The Rugby* for war reporting – they get enough doom and gloom from the news – they come to us for a bit of light-hearted escapism.

**JH:** There are times when I want to dig deeper and push harder, but I have to remember that I'm not Jeremy Paxman (you'll never see me asking Eddie Jones 'Did you threaten to overrule him?' 12 times) and we're not in the business of throwing anyone under a bus or creating any tension. There are times when I interview people and they say stuff about themselves and others, and you know it's bullshit and you could push them on it. I often try to do it in a way that's non-aggressive, which is not easy.

Some people are ready to share and hear certain things, in which case I'll delve deeper. But some people don't take kindly to too much prying and I don't want to be starting any rows. Nevertheless, people have said to me that our podcast has ended up doing more proper journalism than a lot of the main-stream media, and I can see where they're coming from.

We do give opinions on the latest goings-on in the world of rugby, but we're not in the business of making grandiose, hyperbolic statements without any substance behind them, like some pundits I could mention. All three of us are steeped in the sport, have a pretty good idea of what we're talking about, and try to make sure our discussions are grounded in the truth. I'd rather be positive than negative, but in the UK it seems like unless you are being negative you aren't really doing your job. We often get hammered in the comments section under the pod apparently – I wouldn't know as I never look at them, but

Payno does – about not being direct enough or letting people off the hook. Payno gets all flustered about this, but I just say, 'Fuck them, it's not who we are, it's not what we are about, they can find a podcast that does that very easily.' Payno will say, 'Yes, but we should take the feedback on board', and I just go, 'Sure, sure, will do', and walk off. It's not who I am and not what I do.

The reason our guests feel able to open up is because they're comfortable in our company and know we aren't going to stitch them up. If a guest asks us to edit something out, we do it, no questions asked. Payno is right, we do provide a safe space, although that phrase makes me shudder, along with people who ask what my pronouns are. My response is normally fuck and off. I read a quote recently, something along the lines of, 'While Russia and China are expanding their armies and nuclear arsenals, in the West we're building safe spaces for men who are scared by words.' Even so, I don't want to be hurting any of our guests with words, so maybe I am a bit of a hypocrite.

**AP:** Back in the day, we had a Thursday highlights show on Sky called *The Rugby Club*, with 30 people working on it, but it eventually got binned because highlights started appearing online within a couple of minutes of a try being scored. So waiting five days for match clips was immediately obsolete. Sky no longer produces any such programmes, they just skip from live event to live event, but it turned out that not everyone's attention span had decreased, and podcasts like ours filled the void. People still want to hear stories being told well, and guests on *The Good, The Bad & The Rugby* tell better stories than most.

Funnily enough (or not, depending on how you see it), a lot of newspaper rugby coverage now consists of reporting what was said on podcasts. Only recently, the *Telegraph* did a whole article on our LIV rugby episode. Also, the written media has a limited ability to protect interviewees. Horse trading goes on, but newspaper journalists are ultimately in it for the scoop and the online clicks. It's funny where storytelling has gone since the dawn of social media in the mid-2000s. For a while, everything got shorter and more immediate, because the feeling was that audience attention spans were decreasing, but now tens of millions of people are listening to these long, sprawling podcasts.

**JH:** We do make the odd mistake, such as when we had Matt Dawson on and a stand-in editor cut up some clips to make it sound like he was slamming Ellis Genge and posted them on social media. It caused a big stir in the rugby world. Matt put out a social media post saying his words were taken out of context, which they were, and I recorded a video apologising. I also said to the social media team, 'Listen, we're not clickbait people, that's not what we do.' I was livid though, as I've been misquoted a lot in my career and fucked over by different parties, so for us to do it to someone else did not sit well with me at all.

Because it feels just like I'm talking to two mates down the pub, I sometimes forget how many people are listening in. I'll get texts from old teammates pretending to be furious that I put them in a bin juice XV or that I told a certain story. Because I never listen to a recording of the show, sometimes I won't know what they're talking about. (I should make it clear that I do ask the producer and Payno to give me feedback. I really care about everything that I do and getting better at it, but on social media it's always unqualified people offering advice and it's usually bullshit.) I chuck it all out there and forget about it, but it's not verbal diarrhoea, and I never say anything about anyone I wouldn't say to their face. If it seems like I have said something controversial or pointed, I meant to do it. I'm not some clumsy oaf who says whatever comes into his head, even if it seems like that sometimes. I have no problem crossing lines if I think more people will laugh than not.

The only person who got really upset about me telling stories about them was Will Greenwood. Several people had told me about the time Eddie Jones invited Will to work with England's backs. Apparently, Will kept going on about this wicked move that could unlock any defence, but the first time they tried it, a defender read it easily and smoked the guy with the ball. After I relayed this story, Will messaged me and asked why I was talking shit about him. Which is not what you want; Will is a really nice guy, and I have a lot of respect for him. I am never just throwing people under the bus for fun. I tell stories and people tell stories about me. I don't think I have ever told a really bad story about anyone, and this wasn't bad either. I think the fact the podcast has such a big reach means that people get rattled when mates start messing with them and it's like, 'Fucking hell, I didn't know this or that happened.'

I messaged Will back straightaway and said, 'Will, I really respect you and you are a mate, but I've been told that story by four different people on four separate occasions, they're not going to be making it up, and it's just a bit of fun. If it is made up, then you need to speak to the England backs as they are the ones telling everyone.'

Having said that, the podcast has a depth and honesty that others lack, and everything on it is presented through the prism of our own experiences. It's never simply a case of, 'Danny Care has been selected for England again, here's some tactical analysis'; it's more, 'Danny Care has been selected for England again, here are some personal stories about Danny Care from me and Tins, plus maybe a bit of tactical analysis.' So we don't put anything out there that hasn't been cast through the lens of our show; in other words, nothing is presented that we haven't put our mark or interpretation on.

Over the years, we've talked about relationships, fatherhood, family problems, mental health, physical health, all that stuff our own dads and granddads kept quiet about. Our ability to change emotional gears and get people to speak about themselves, not just their rugby, set us apart from other rugby podcasts. I sometimes get the tone wrong and come across as crass, but I think I mainly come across as sympathetic and empathetic.

On a personal level Payno, Tins and I have discussed injury, separation, parenthood, death and lots, lots more besides. Perhaps my most emotional episode was when I announced my retirement from rugby. I hadn't told anyone, not even my Northampton teammates, and it all came flooding out. The highs, the lows, the wonderful memories, the many regrets, my hopes and fears for the future (I was scared shitless, to be honest). Payno did his best to make me cry, and while he didn't succeed, he got close a few times.

I think we have a duty to be honest and respectful about those kinds of subjects, especially given that some of our audience will assume we've got it made. And through speaking about such subjects, Payno, Tins and I have become close friends almost by accident, in the way I imagine people in various support groups become close friends too. (It could be a case of Stockholm syndrome, but I am pretty sure we are mates now!)

Listeners were surprised that I wasn't some neanderthal who just wanted to bash people over the head with rugby tales and was able to ask insightful and challenging questions. I was at an event the other day and a guy came up to me and said, 'I just wanted to say I love your podcast. I love your honesty and hearing about the journey you guys have been on and it got me through a really tough time.' We get messages like that all the time, especially from men who I think look to guys like us to validate how they felt at times and take comfort in the knowledge that everyone goes through shit periods in life.

Human psychology dictates that you always remember the negative feedback more than the positive feedback, but the positive actually outweighs the negative a hundred times over. And it's particularly nice to hear those personal testimonies and imagine people putting the podcast on, listening to three men sharing their vulnerabilities, agreeing and disagreeing, laughing and crying, and forgetting their troubles for an hour.

We also get a large number of female listeners who love the show. You would think that the last thing they would want to listen to is someone like me, who on the surface is the dictionary definition of toxic masculinity. We met loads of female fans on our recent tour and one quote sticks with me. 'I started listening to your show in lockdown. I knew nothing about rugby and wanted a laugh. I listened to every episode, and I have still not learned anything about rugby, but you made me smile.' Mission accomplished.

# 14

# ROYALTY

**JH:** I was never worried that Tins might be a bit guarded because of his royal connections. I knew what he was like and had seen him speak at events, so I knew he pushed the envelope a little bit. He even got into a bit of trouble when he appeared on a live version of *A Question of Sport*: he told a story about him and Iain Balshaw pretending to punch Prince Harry at a post-World Cup final party in 2003 and joked that the royal family wanted to fill him in for real. I say trouble but it was a bit of a minor kerfuffle, nothing to write home about. It did come back into public consciousness when that very odd bloke Omid Scobie started sticking up for Harry and Meghan, and loads of trolls went in on Tins, especially about him wanting to fill in a young, defenceless Harry. All context, sarcasm and humour lost, when things are taken out of the zone they were meant to be in. To be fair to Tins he gives zero fucks about stuff like that, but it's very annoying for him. Royal fans can be mental. I think we all know that American royal fans are fucking nuts, especially Scobieites.

Rugby is Tins' bread and butter on the podcast, and even if I take the conversation to slightly uncomfortable places for our resident royal, he just sits there and smiles through gritted teeth, usually with his cap pulled over his face. However, he can't hide when he finds it funny, which is the best bit for me. Getting people to laugh who don't want to but can't help it.

I've even sat next to Tins on stage and made jokes about Prince Andrew. I tell a joke about being at Tins' wedding: the Queen and the rest of the royals have gone to bed, leaving just Prince Andrew on the dancefloor, sweating up a storm. After an hour or so, he looks around, realises that everyone else on the dancefloor is over 18, and fucks off to bed himself. This is not a true story, I made it up, but it's funny because it ticks a few boxes.

After Tins did *I'm A Celebrity* (and very well I might add, certainly better than me) I told this made-up joke when I ask Tins, 'What was your biggest fear going away into the jungle?', and I feign surprise when he says, 'Prince Andrew babysitting my kids.' Now of course he never said that, nor would he ever dream of saying that. Only a shitbag like me would say that, However, I made it up one night and took it for a couple of spins on the live shows and it went down a storm. People may say you can't joke about stuff like that. Well you can, it's quite easy actually.

I also talk about Tins going to the World Cup in Australia in 2003 and coming home with a winner's medal and a princess. Fuck me, if Carlsberg did holidays …

I love fleshing out the narrative that Tins' is a modern-day *Prince and the Pauper* story. From Wakefield to Windsor … if that isn't a Netflix doc I don't know what is. I did this whole made-up skit on tour and it always brought the house down. I ask the audience how the hell this working-class bloke from Wakefield ended up waving on the balcony at Buckingham Palace. It's a truly modern-day fairytale.

I paint a grim picture of Tins' childhood: his tiny, crooked house on a steep street, exactly like the Hovis advert; a small boy, no more than four years old, pushing a cart; an emaciated horse nibbling on grass between the cobbles. Then I cut to the sad scene in Tins' living room (the only room) – a single piece of coal on the hearth; one tiny turnip for breakfast, lunch and dinner; Tindall Senior staring blankly at the wall, just waiting to perish, like most people from up north (that's what I imagine it to be like even now); young Tindall Junior playing with his latest toy, a homemade stick and hoop, by his dad's bare and sooty feet; a clock, the only sound that can be heard (well, that and the rats in the walls) ticking. The clock just ticking and ticking the relentless march down to death.

Suddenly, Tindall Senior speaks. 'Michael,' he says, in a barely intelligible Yorkshire dialect, 'what do you want to be when you grow up?' Tins almost jumps out of his skin in shock because his dad never speaks to him, thinking it too affectionate. But Tins eventually plucks up the courage to reply, 'Well, father, one day I'm going to win the World Cup and marry a princess.' Mr Tindall turns puce with rage, whacks Tins round the back of the head and says, 'Not bloody likely! You're going down the coal mine, like your father, and your father's father, and your father's father's father. I still remember that Billy Elliot from two doors down and all the trouble he caused, and all the shame he brought on his poor father with that dancing bollocks ...'

But my favourite story that I made up about Tins is as follows. It's close to the bone, and would not get past most censors, and soppy people online who get offended on others' behalf would have a field day. But bear with me. What makes it is that my impression of the character in the story is remarkable, if I do say so myself. The question I pose is: how did a gnarly northern man with a nose that used to be able to smell around corners suddenly become part of the most famous family in the world? I mean it makes no sense, but does give credence to the cliché 'Dream big, anything can happen'. So, to explain this absurd happening, I concoct a story that when Tins was young he wrote to a certain television show which fixed it for kids to fulfil their dreams. 'Now then, now then,' I say, 'I have a letter here from a young boy called Michael Tindall. It says, "Dear Jim, could you fix it for me to win the World Cup and marry a princess." Well, Michael, funny you should ask, because I've been corresponding with members of the royal family for a number of years …'

It's all bollocks of course; well most of it is. The audiences love it but understand that it's all just a joke.

**AP:** I'm sometimes asked if Tins has to watch what he says because of his royal connections, but that's not really the case. I sometimes tease him about being royalty, and Hask obviously goes a bit further, but I don't think we've ever pushed him to give more than he was willing to give or put him in an uncomfortable place on air. And he knows perfectly well where the line is.

I imagine that when you marry into the royal family, you're given a list of dos and don'ts and tips and tricks, and one thing he does is simply not reply if you ask him the wrong kind of question. For example, I might send him three questions on WhatsApp, and he'll reply to the first two and ignore the third. I might ask that third question again, and if I don't hear back, I'll know the answer is no (then again, that might just be the Yorkshireman in him).

It's easy for people to forget that Tins is a bona fide sporting legend – a World Cup winner, no less – and being married to Zara is only one part of him. At the same time, the podcast is his vehicle to use as he wants, and it doesn't have to be all about rugby. And while revealing all is not an option for the royal family, Tins realises that showing a bit of leg can be beneficial.

Having had royal birth and wedding announcements on the podcast, we decided to dedicate an episode to the Queen following her passing.

Not many people knew the Queen personally, so listening to Tins' reminiscences on the podcast was both moving and fascinating. Unlike royal reporters, he was able to give us unfiltered insight from inside the gates, and it was only then that I became fully aware of the genuine awe he had for the family, what they represented and the good work they did. Tins described how the royal family had come together in the days after the Queen's death, how close Zara had been to her, and his regret at not asking her more. He also spoke about his relationship with King Charles, including a story about almost accidentally curtseying before him, which was a welcome bit of humour.

Before the 2023 World Cup, Tins asked Princess Anne and the Prince and Princess of Wales to appear on the podcast. I'd imagine that took a bit of gentle persuasion, but the fact they agreed to do it was a great example of why Tins is so good for the establishment he married into.

That day was a very special and surreal experience. For a start, we recorded the podcast in the room where the Queen filmed with Paddington Bear, and afterwards Tins gave us all a tour of Windsor Castle. Just watching Princess Anne meeting Hask was odd, because it's not really a classic combination, like ham and eggs. But Tins is the kind of open, down-to-earth bloke who gets on with everyone, and the royals clearly felt comfortable with him in charge. And because they trusted him, the interview showed them in a fun, relaxed light, which led to glowing media coverage.

The pod had three million views in 72 hours, which smashed the existing record to smithereens. Naturally the papers were most interested in what the Prince and Princess of Wales had to say, which included stories about intense tennis matches between the two of them, competing in mum and dad events at school sports days and Prince William's love of Aston Villa (of all the teams he could have chosen …). But the star of the show was actually Princess Anne, Tins' mother-in-law, who had Hask right where she wanted him.

The royals knew we were spending most of the World Cup on a cruise ship, so Prince William said to Hask, 'What on earth are you doing that for? Are you going to be the anchor?' Hask shot back, 'Well, it sounds a bit like anchor.' And Princess Anne chimed in, with perfect comic timing, 'Yes, I see that.' I wish we'd been able to keep that in. I think it would have done the royal family's reputation the world of good – down with the kids and all that – and I could have retired happy there and then.

**JH:** When we turned up at Windsor Castle, everyone was panicking, which put me on edge a bit. And when I find myself in an awkward situation, I tend to overperform, in an attempt to make people feel more comfortable.

Now it's a huge privilege to be invited into the inner sanctum of the royal family, and I don't want to sound ungrateful, but I have to say I thought it would be like Henry VIII's court, with long tables piled up with wild boar, swans and peacocks, plus great flagons of wine. But there wasn't even a tray of custard creams. Once I got over the grandeur of the place, I became acutely aware I was desperate for a drink, so I started coughing and saying out loud to anyone who would listen, 'Anyone else thirsty?' and 'Wow, it's a hot day today, must stay hydrated.' After about 15 minutes of this, as if by magic, this woman appeared out of nowhere. 'Hello,' she said, 'I'm Polly, would you like a tea or a coffee?' I asked if I could have some tea (if you are going to drink tea anywhere it would be in a castle; I imagined that every English castle had a dedicated tea wing, where the stuff was brewed around the clock in giant gurgling urns), and she served me up an absolute peach of a cuppa. When I asked for something to go with it, I expected Polly to return with a couple of big trays loaded with brightly coloured macaroons, scones with clotted cream and jam and exotic fruit tarts. But instead, I got a couple of broken rich teas and what appeared to be a half-eaten malted milk – I could see that it was a leftover from a box of Family Circle biscuits. So not even M&S, which took the shine off the day if I'm honest.

I found this little bell, and every time I rang it, Polly would come scurrying in. I said to her, 'I couldn't get a club sandwich or something, with a crescent of crisps?', but she couldn't, and eventually someone took the bell off me. Luckily, I'd brought along an M&S sandwich, but when I started eating it, someone else appeared and shooed me into a corridor. They'd been on red alert since our MD Nic spilt coffee on what was probably a priceless Chippendale cabinet, and I assume that members of the royal family don't eat sandwiches from a packet while standing over priceless Louis XIV tables.

I then had a wander around the place, but I was sure I was being followed. Every time I stuck my head around a door, someone would say, 'What are you doing in here?' I thought I'd at least walk away with a couple of souvenirs, but while I was eyeing up some wine glasses in the kitchen, someone said to me, 'We count them in and out again …' They didn't say, 'We know your sort', but they may as well have done.

We were briefed on how to address everyone when we met members of the royal family; what we should call them upon first meeting them and then what after. For example, Your Royal Highness and then Sir or Ma'am. When William finally turned up, I said, 'Aah, Your Royal Highness. You alright boss?' Some bloke who was hovering around, presumably his private secretary or some such, started coughing (he might have actually been choking on something, it was difficult to tell). I quickly realised that I hadn't left enough time between 'Your Royal Highness' and 'you alright boss', and that his private secretary, or whatever he was, thought I was the scum of the earth.

Then Princess Anne came into the room and said, 'How long are we recording for?' When she was told we'd planned to record for an hour, she replied, 'An hour? What have we possibly got to talk about for an hour?' I did think to myself, 'They must get constantly rushed around from place to place, I'm not sure if we'll get much out of them.' But once we'd sat the three of them down, they were great. You could tell their people were still in panic mode, because there was a lot of flapping going on off camera, but once we'd made them laugh and loosened them up a bit, everyone seemed to calm down.

Princess Anne burying me with her anchor gag certainly helped, which I thought was brilliant.

All three of those guys are great advocates for sport, not just at an elite level, but also in terms of how it can help improve people's everyday lives. When you tell a doctor you feel depressed, they're likely to tell you to get outdoors and exercise, whether it's going for a walk, a bike ride or a round of golf. Sport and exercise provide you with a purpose, expend energy, and make it easier to sleep at night, and William and Catherine were great on all that stuff.

I think the podcast humanised them a little bit, and I kind of wish they'd let us put the uncut version out, because it would have blown the public away. As it was, they came across as down-to-earth, fully engaged, funny and knowledgeable (Princess Anne knew more about sport than almost anyone I've ever met). It was a far more enlightening chat than I expected, not because I thought they'd be dull (I already knew that they weren't), but because I know how everything to do with the royal family is so carefully controlled.

**MT:** The tribute show we did after the Queen's passing was emotional. Obviously, the end was going to come at some point, but she was still working a few days before she passed away, so it was a bit of a shock.

She had one hell of a life, gave so much to the country and was always so kind. I loved the fact that she was like a grandmother to everyone in the UK, because of how long she'd been Queen. We'll never see her like again.

My relationship with the royal family began before I started dating Zara. William and Harry were keen rugby fans in the early 2000s and the England players met them numerous times, and through them I met Princesses Eugenie and Beatrice.

It helped that Zara's mum, the Princess Royal, had been a top rider (she won individual gold at the 1971 European Championship and competed at the 1976 Olympics), as had Zara's dad. The Princess Royal understood how hard I'd had to work and the sacrifices I'd had to make as a professional rugby player, and she just loved the game. The Duke of Edinburgh was a keen sportsperson as well, whether it was cricket, polo or carriage driving, so he knew the kind of people sportsmen were and enjoyed chatting to them. Meanwhile, the Queen was patron of lots of sporting charities and obviously mad about horseracing. She spoke to trainers, owners and jockeys all the time, so knew a great deal about what sportspeople had to go through, which is hell in the case of jockeys.

And because all of them understood where I came from, and accepted that completely, I never felt uneasy in their company. Believe it or not, marrying into the royal family was pretty easy for me. They were always nice to me, and I was always nice to them. Simple really.

I'm sometimes asked if the Queen did informality like 'normal' people, and the answer to that is yes. Her life wasn't like an episode of *Downton Abbey*, with meals on long tables and everyone dressed in their finery every night, and Zara and I would often watch the racing with her on TV, as I'm sure lots of people reading this have done with their gran. Lunches were also relaxed, especially up in Scotland, where lunch would often be heading out into the open space of the Scottish Highlands for a picnic. There's a great picture of my daughter Mia sitting with the Duke of Edinburgh that captures exactly what those afternoons were like: members of a very close family who loved each other dearly spending precious time together. Yes, there's a lot of drama surrounding the royal family, but they aren't much different to anyone else underneath it all.

The royal podcast made perfect sense because we had the biggest competition in rugby coming up, and the Princess Royal, William and Catherine are patrons of the three home nations, Scotland, England and Wales respectively.

The Princess Royal has been patron of Scottish rugby since 1986. She goes to most Scotland games at Murrayfield, her son Peter played for Scotland schools, and she keeps up to date with Gloucester's results. And because she's a real rugby fan, not just someone who was parachuted into a role against her will, she can have a proper informed conversation about it.

The podcast is all about supporting and elevating rugby, which we think is the best game in the world. A team can't rely on one very talented individual in rugby, as is the case with so many other team sports; you need at least 12 players to have a good day at the office. Even when Jonah Lomu was trampling all over everyone at the 1995 World Cup, he still needed the forwards to win the ball in the first place and his fellow backs to get it to him. Plus, they lost in the final. Then there's the fact that you have to put your body on the line for your mates either side of you. But some of that messaging has been lost. Instead, rugby is constantly being bashed in the media, which we'll return to later. That's why I thought it would be nice for the Princess Royal to come out and bat for the game.

The Princess Royal has made friends with lots of players down the years, including former captain Rob Wainwright, who she's particularly close with, and the sadly departed Doddie Weir. It's the characters she likes most about the game, and the reason there are so many big characters in rugby is because you've got to be a bit unusual to want to play such a dangerous game, in the same way that you've got to be a bit unusual to want to ride a horse over massive obstacles.

To be fair to football, I think it does still produce big personalities, it's just that they have to keep their characters hidden. Take Jack Grealish: he got drunk after Manchester City won the treble in 2023 and the papers made him out to be some mad, out of control alcoholic. Ridiculous. I'm all for Jack Grealish celebrating a treble in style, it's exactly what he should have done. He didn't get into football to be a role model, he just enjoyed kicking a ball around and happened to be very good at it, but suddenly he's meant to be one. And that means he can't even have a few drinks without people getting offended. That's the madness of the world we live in, and I'm just glad that rugby is at least partly immune to it.

William and Catherine aren't hugely knowledgeable about rugby, they're more occasional fans, but they do care about the power of sport, such as how it can bring people together and help with physical and mental health. So for them, the podcast was more about why they loved sport and why it's so important.

It was a great day, crowned by the Princess Royal's legendary putdown of Hask. She read him perfectly, and it's not often you see Hask speechless. I actually think she'd get on with him very well because there are always plenty of jokes when Hask is around, and she loves having a laugh.

# THE
# BAD

# 15

# IN THE DOCK

**MT:** The podcast was becoming more and more successful – it was certainly Joe Media's biggest show because it was sponsored by Guinness – and eventually we thought, 'We need to start figuring out what's going on.'

Along with our producer, we were booking guests and organising pretty much everything, and the moment that really made us think we could be doing things ourselves was a live show in a warehouse in Wales, which attracted 1,200 people. That was the night we had a competition to see who could get the most famous person on the phone, which resulted in Rebel Wilson making an appearance. We were starting to do various bits and pieces like that, and we realised that those ideas were coming from us, not from Joe Media. Looking back now and at what we do, there is a lot more production work than we ever thought, but still not enough to keep us in the dark about how the financial model worked.

Meanwhile Joe Media seemed to be doing whatever they wanted, which didn't amount to much. We had very limited knowledge of how much money was coming in and where it was all going and felt that we weren't getting a fair share, business-wise. But whenever we asked for more money, whether in the form of higher wages, shares or a cut of the profits, they told us no.

We should have seen the writing on the wall when they sent us to Japan for the 2019 World Cup and the producer and the rest of the crew had to sleep in a McDonald's in Hiroshima. Despite the success of the podcast, they were running things on a shoestring budget, and I couldn't help thinking, 'This is not how you run a business.' Then they started paying us late, which is when we started giving serious thought to setting up our own production company.

**JH:** *House of Rugby* got very popular very quickly, and you could tell that Joe Media's bosses were getting a bit giddy, because they'd turn up to recordings and be very pally and back-slappy around us.

Me, Payno and Tins were being paid okay money, but nothing to write home about, and we started to think that maybe we should have skin in the game. And after some business advisers showed us how much we could be making, relative to listening figures, Payno and Tins wanted us to leave and set up on our own. Payno particularly got very excited and 'blue sky' with his thinking, but I came along, flopped the old chap out and pissed all over his chips.

My concern was that between the three of us, we wouldn't have time to run our own business. This podcast had been purpose built for us, and it was easy. We turned up once a week, chatted for an hour, then went home. Also, I'd been offered the world a million times since becoming a professional rugby player at 17, and crashed and burned more times than was sensible. I was jaded, didn't believe what these business advisers were telling us. So I persuaded Payno and Tins to stay for another year and then think about doing something ourselves. Amazingly, I was the cautious one in the group.

The second season was flying. We'd had some amazing trips, like the World Cup in Japan, we were doing live shows, and the podcast's popularity was going through the roof. But we were coming up with lots of ideas that they weren't implementing, and we felt like we weren't really in control of things.

There was the time a load of Guinness people were invited to watch us record an episode of the podcast, and it just so happened that team socials were on the agenda. I told the story of the time I was on the King's Road in a pair of shoes that had been cut into sandals and with my testicles hanging out the bottom of a pair of jeans that had been cut into shorts, and apparently the Guinness people, who were watching on a screen next door, had a meltdown. A considerable chunk of that recording ended up on the cutting room floor.

Another time, I got buffaloed (caught drinking with my right hand when I should have been drinking with my left), so I posted a video on social media of me explaining what had happened and necking a pint of Guinness. Some bloke from Joe Media must have called me 20 times, plus sent me a load of text messages pleading with me to take the video down. When I finally replied to him and asked him why, he said, 'Because you're not drinking responsibly.'

This guy was almost in tears because he thought we were going to lose Guinness as a sponsor, but I told him to spend less time worrying about me necking pints and more time worrying about doing his actual job properly. Then the owner called and ordered me to take the video down, and while I did so, I couldn't get my head around their thinking. If I'd posted a video of me ploughing through 24 pints of Guinness, shitting myself and curling up into a ball on my can-strewn kitchen floor, fair enough. But it was just one pint!

The fact they hadn't been paying me was even more of a sore point. Then one day, straight after the recording of a podcast, and bang in the middle of the first Covid lockdown, they casually told us they were going into administration. There was no being pally or slapping our backs now.

I got straight on the phone to my management agency, who told me I was owed £50,000. I knew it was bad, but I didn't know it was that bad. In case you were wondering, I never worked with that agency again, and I never got paid a penny of that 50 grand. I felt like an inmate in prison who had just dropped the soap and realised he was going to get dry fucked into oblivion.

Without boring you with the details or naming names (it's all on the internet if you want an alternative to stabbing your eyeballs with a cocktail stick), the Irish side of the company had taken out a loan to develop the business and used the UK side of the company as a guarantor. But when the Irish side was unable to pay the interest on the loan, the UK side, which was also in a spot of financial bother, wasn't able to shore it up, which is when the administrators swept in. And the whole time this company was steaming towards the iceberg, no one bothered telling me, Payno or Tins. It turned out in the administration process that the business had more cowboys in the company than a spaghetti Western.

**AP:** We did a couple of years under the *House of Rugby* banner with Joe Media, who were making quite big waves. But it became apparent that while we had something pretty special on our hands, we weren't being very well looked after – and that somebody, somewhere, was.

Because of my background in media, I thought that not only should we be doing the podcast more for our benefit, but also that we could do it better.

I wanted to leave at the end of season one but soon realised we wouldn't be able to get set up and sponsored in time for the 2019 World Cup in Japan.

But Joe Media, having agreed to increase our wages, started paying us late, or not at all. And halfway through the second season, in May 2020, they went into administration, which caused a lot of friction, because Hask was owed a lot of money, while Tins and I were owed a fair amount.

Joe Media were bought out of administration a couple of months later, but we quickly realised that we didn't want to get into bed with the new owners. We made perfectly reasonable requests about equity and increased wages, but they turned them all down. So we decided to set up on our own. We had the fanbase, we were doing amazing things, it made perfect sense.

# 16

# GOING SOLO

**MT:** When Covid hit, it gave us more freedom as not being able to get into the studio meant we could get people like Dan Carter and Richie McCaw on via Zoom, mainly because they had nothing better to do than speak to people on podcasts.

We'd already started exploring whether we could go off and do our own thing when Joe Media went into administration. And while they owed us money, which wasn't ideal, we thought that their financial issues might be a blessing in disguise, because now we had no choice but to make other arrangements.

I was worried what would happen to all the podcasts we'd done with Joe Media if they went bust – who would own them? – and it just so happened that Payno's wife was an intellectual property lawyer. She had a poke around and discovered that no one owned the IP rights for *House of Rugby*, so we applied. It was really a back-up plan in case nobody bought Joe Media, but looking back, we probably made a mistake there, because instead of calling ourselves co-owners with Joe Media, we applied for the rights outright.

The administrator probably didn't help the situation, because he advised us to keep doing the podcast, to help sell the business. What we should have done was mothball the podcast because they owed us a lot of money and only Hask out of the three of us had ever signed a contract with Joe Media, and I think that had expired. But we decided to keep ploughing on until the administrator informed us they'd found a buyer, at which point we told the new owners that we were going to do our own thing unless they paid us the money we were owed, and would discuss having a stake in the pod. They did offer £250 an episode more but didn't agree to the other stuff we asked for, so we decided to look elsewhere.

After talking to four or five different companies, we went with Platform Media, who were mainly about written content but wanted to get into podcasting. A bit of quid pro quo went on: they offered us a good financial deal and wanted our podcast to be a YouTube channel as well, which meant raising the production standards. In return, we'd put them in touch with people we knew, so that they could expand their portfolio. It all sounded perfect.

**JH:** We thought *House of Rugby* was a good name; it certainly had a lot of recognition, which is why we went ahead and registered it ourselves. I mean the muppets hadn't even done that, so anyone could have had it. It was the smartest thing for us to do as the company no longer existed. We also spoke to an intellectual property lawyer (not Payno's wife, she had better things to be doing with her time), who assured us there would be no issues if, at the right time and the company was not resurrected, we wanted to use the name *House of Rugby* because people associated *House of Rugby* with me, Payno and Tins, and we had goodwill in the name.

In the end, we decided we didn't want anything to do with the name so went with an alternative that Payno came up with, *The Good, The Bad & The Rugby*, which was genius from him (even a clock is right twice a day). We went in all guns blazing down that path, with *House of Rugby* soon becoming a distant, if painful, memory.

But while we were preparing for the first season out on our own, we got a letter from the lawyers of the new owners, an outfit we won't name, saying they were suing us for something called 'passing off'. None of us had a clue what that meant, but we soon discovered that they were basically accusing us of nicking part of their business and show format and passing it off as our own.

We assumed that the new owners had looked into the business and realised they'd bought the square root of fuck all, because that was the reality. They got a domain name and social media handle. None of the other shows along with ours had any contracts or intention of staying with them. And because they had shareholders to answer to, and we were the most successful product they had, they came after me, Payno and Tins, despite the fact we weren't contracted to Joe Media.

**AP:** I vividly remember the day we got the papers. My wife, the kids and I were about to set off for some glamping site with some very good friends of ours, and it was my son's birthday, and I'm not sure I said a word all weekend.

**JH:** Our lawyers were very confident that there was no case to answer, especially as we agreed to move forward as *The Good, The Bad & The Rugby*. The basic case centred around the fact we had trademarked the name of the original show and they wanted the *House of Rugby* name back. They said we were thieves and bad people. We told them they could have it back if they paid us the money we were owed and discussed what happened to back catalogues of shows we had done. We decided to change the name of the podcast to *The Good, The*

*Bad & The Rugby* to be on the safe side and because we thought it sounded better (it also fitted nicely with our individual characters, Payno being 'the good', me being 'the bad' and Tins being 'the rugby'). But the lawyers just got more and more aggressive.

Then we discovered how much a sponsor had paid for *House of Rugby* over the first two seasons, which blew our minds. We knew Guinness were sponsoring the podcast, because we'd drink it during an episode, drink it on stage, and mention it on our social media channels. But we could only guess where all the sponsorship money went (me and Tins got a small raise for the second season).

We hoped Guinness would carry on sponsoring us as *The Good, The Bad & The Rugby*, which would have helped bail us out financially, but it wasn't to be.

The other side were clearly clutching at straws and looking for a smoking gun they never found. They kept getting our lawyers to ask us to do continuous keyword searches in our emails and WhatsApp messages – 'Guinness', 'branding', 'money-grabbing bastards'. This went on and on, and it was hell.

I got the feeling that the new owners who were suing us thought we were all loaded (especially Tins, because of his royal connections). But none of us had that kind of money sloshing around our bank accounts.

Elsewhere, things were getting very shady and surreal. Some character from the company who had bought Joe summoned our producer Simon for a meeting at his house and told him, 'Listen, I know some pretty powerful people. I can get Vladimir Putin on the phone …' Luckily for us, Vladimir had bigger fish to fry than a rugby podcast, such as finalising arrangements for a full-scale invasion of Ukraine (then again, he probably had Dr Evil on speed dial as well).

By this time, I was thinking, 'How the fuck did our nice little rugby podcast turn into a legal case and imaginary threats from wicked dictators?' But I never actually spoke to anyone from the other side, not one person, and I never met anyone. The only correspondence I had was a legal letter saying they were suing me as an individual, alongside Payno and Tins. To be fair, it was poor Payno who bore the brunt of it. He was the one who had to say, 'It's nice that you're excited to sign us up, but we're probably going to set up on our own', which obviously didn't go down very well. And he was the one who had to deal with the fallout when they found out about the trademark.

It's not that I wasn't interested, it's just that everyone on our side thought I'd go mad and start smashing things up. That's not how I conduct business, but my conversational style is, admittedly, very blunt. I won't bow down to these people. I'll tell them straight that I'm not going to do something, that they're talking shit, that they need to fuck off and think again. So poor Payno ended up taking the lead because he was the sensible, mature one. It also meant we were only getting charged once and not three times.

Handing over the reins to Payno in hindsight was something I regret doing. Not because he didn't do a good job, but because I'm not fazed by this stuff. I've had to deal with lots of legal problems in the past, been threatened numerous times, sued, cross-examined – all of this doesn't fluster me, whereas Payno was hammered every day and was not used to this level of aggression. It wore him down, the poor bloke, whereas this sort of thing is like a normal day in my life. I do know how to conduct myself and never blow up, but I will also not be intimated or threatened. One of my favourite things to do is when I get a super-aggressive letter from a lawyer, where they use verbose writing that basically calls you a moron and a dick without saying it directly, I always go online to their chambers' website and look at what they look like in real life, the person behind the big words. They always look like fucking virgins who used to work at Blockbuster or McDonald's. Which makes me smile and take the heat out of it for me. I did reply to one miserable cow lawyer who basically called me a knuckle-dragger, and said that I had no sense of reality. I replied using the sentence 'without prejudice' then followed it with 'Why you not smile, pussy cat?' (channelling my inner Borat again). She went fucking mental and said, 'Just because you said without prejudice doesn't mean we can't read it in court, blah, blah, blah.' I replied with a smiling emoji which made her go even more mental, then I just stopped responding, which really ruined her day. It was nice to rattle her cage. My lawyers did tell me not to respond like that again, which was the smart move.

**AP:** Tins was largely kept out of it for profile reasons, and while Hask has had more court cases than most of us have had hot dinners, and never seems too bothered about any of them, he was largely kept out of it for profile and volatility reasons. As such, I ended up running pretty much the whole case.

The pod was meant to be a hobby – natter for two hours about rugby every Monday, maybe have a pint and then head home. But because it was Covid time, no one was running events and my corporate hosting had dried up. I was also trying to run a small start-up through furlough and every brand had pulled their marketing budget. So while we were trying to paint a jolly picture on air as we launched *The Good, The Bad & The Rugby*, behind the jokes and the laughter I was very, very stressed.

But it's the process that grinds you down – the costs, the relentless communications, the endless hours spent working on it when you could be doing something more productive, enjoyable and necessary, like spending time with your family. I'd find myself writing notes on my phone at 2 a.m., about things I thought were relevant to the case. And whenever we walked together as a family, I'd be a couple of metres ahead, mumbling.

**JH:** Maybe I should have got involved earlier on, because I've had more legal issues than Donald Trump over the years, so lawyers don't really intimidate me. Then again, I'm not sure how much I could have helped, and my more aggressive, hard-line approach might have made things even worse. Plus, I was writing books, DJing, making music and speaking five times a week during that period. That meant Payno was the one being bombarded with phone calls, emails and letters, most of them from people asking for money, which made him extremely stressed. He's got a wife and kids, as well as a day job, so he'd have to give up nights and weekends to this absurd legal case we'd got ourselves involved in.

While all this was going on, we re-emerged as *The Good, The Bad & The Rugby*, which meant we were just about able to cover the legal fees. However, while we launched in a blaze of publicity (we managed to get Carole Baskin from Netflix's smash hit *Tiger King* to do the first episode trailer, along with Eddie Jones as the first guest) our relationship with Platform Media wasn't without its complications, because they got caught in the crossfire between us three and the wankers who were suing us (that's one of the reasons I'd wanted to make the podcast ourselves, but that wasn't an option given the situation we found ourselves in). And once again it was poor Payno who was doing the firefighting, patching up rows between me and various people, drafting witness statements for the legal case, and enquiring as to why everything was costing so much fucking money.

Then we found out that the opposition board of directors had form for buying companies, folding them, rolling into another company, then paying themselves off. So we decided to do something quite ballsy, which was apply for something called security for costs. That meant that the other company had to prove that they could pay for legal costs if we won. We knew that if we won, they were never going to pay us, they would just fold the company, which a lot of people do, but because we were three individuals we had no way of getting out of it if we lost. The judge ruled in our favour as their financial records were as transparent as Trump's. Of course, when it came to pay the first tranche of money in escrow, they missed the deadline for the payment, which I thought was a good sign.

Unfortunately, our lawyers were also chasing us for unpaid bills. By this stage, Payno was in pieces, struggling to sleep at night and wandering around like a zombie during the day. He hardly ever dressed for dinner and was off his snuff. Meanwhile, Tins was working flat out, mining his little black book and trying to come up with new ideas for the company.

As soon as we saw each other, everything seemed fine with the world. In fact, I don't think any of us had a cross word throughout the process. But as soon as the podcast recording was over, it would be back to the nightmare. There were a few teething problems with our new production company, I was rowing with people and storming off, and I quit twice. Meanwhile, Payno was on the verge of a nervous breakdown. He was terrified that I was going to blow up our new business partnership, none of us had earned any money from the podcast for 18 months and we still weren't certain we'd win the case. Plus, if it did make it to court, we knew there would be a media circus. I'd been red top fodder for years, while anything to do with royalty was tabloid catnip.

Then a QC we'd hired as a consultant suddenly told us he wouldn't be able to do the case if it went to court, so we were now trying to claw that money back as well.

I was all for continuing the case when they had asked to pull out, but our lawyers suddenly went from being very bullish to, 'Actually, maybe, you know, it might just be better to walk away ...' By this stage, I wanted to kill someone. I said to them, 'Last week you told us we were gonna win, now you're telling us we might lose. Make it make sense!' But when I learned just how heavily Payno was being hounded for unpaid legal bills, I came to my senses. I thought the money had been coming into *GBR* and going to the lawyers; it turns out for whatever reason there was a cashflow problem, and we actually owed our side £500,000. When you realise you owe that amount of money, it kind of puts you off pursuing a case that you should win, but if you know anything about litigation it's not certain, which kind of puts you off.

I told Alex I would handle our lawyers and for him to just divert everything to me. Which he did. I fired off an email to the billing department who were harassing Payno and sharpened them right up; they'd get the money as soon as we had it. They stopped.

We eventually agreed with the fuckers from the other side.

They launched *House of Rugby* and it was wank. It hobbled along for a couple more years before being wound up in the UK (some of the crew ended up joining us), before the enemy (the people suing us) collapsed at the start of 2024. Hardly surprising because they'd spent over £1 million fighting us.

I was surprised to learn what our final legal bill was. I thought, 'We didn't even go to fucking court, how the fuck is it that much?!'

Anyway, I had a mate called Ray who used to be a solicitor. Ray is a genius who loves a fight, and he'd got me off a big bill in the past. So I got Ray on board, he looked through the documents. Payno really didn't want to go to war with another group of lawyers, but I didn't think we had a choice. It was a matter of principle and we didn't have enough money in the business to cover the costs, which meant we would have to put our hands in our own pockets, and they wanted paying yesterday. So we went for a meeting at our lawyers' offices and Ray grilled them for a couple of hours. They were pulling out files left, right and centre; it was like Prime Minister's Questions with folders and little tabs. We could have fought them, but after two years of hell we decided that it was best just to move on. Fighting lawyers is never the smartest move. However, cooler heads prevailed, and we paid them.

**AP:** I wouldn't want to go through those 18 months again. It was the most extraordinary waste of everybody's time and money, and while it was incredibly stressful for me and pretty stressful for Tins (I'm not sure about Hask, that man seems bulletproof) it was really just a game for the other side. All they wanted to do was remove us from the market so that their product wouldn't be devalued. It was cockblocking, for want of a better expression.

I'll never forget the day it all came to an end. I was pretty emotional and incredibly relieved. But it's not as if we could claim victory because the case left everyone out of pocket (apart from the lawyers, who made a fortune).

But as crazy as it sounds, I'm glad I went through it. You learn so much about yourself in trying circumstances, and it was remarkably fulfilling to stand up to whatever was thrown at us. We were three individuals being sued by a wealthy company trying every trick in the book – David versus Goliath, if you like – but we refused to break. And while that kind of experience can leave permanent scars, even if you don't lose in the strictest sense, we drew a line underneath it and said, 'That's it, it's done, let's start looking forwards again.'

Now I think of that case as a sub-plot in the story of how we started again. It certainly brought the three of us closer together. Now we're doing things the way we want to do them, much more for our benefit. I sometimes wonder if we'd be flourishing as much had our journey been smoother.

**MT:** I felt sorry for Payno because he was the one sat in front of a computer all day, dealing with everything the lawyers were throwing at him while trying to run his new tech business. But taking nothing away from Payno's sterling efforts under fire, it was a stressful time for all three of us.

When we should have been making nice money from the podcast, we basically had to do it for free for two years, which meant Hask and I were having to do more and more to bring in money. That wasn't easy while the pandemic was in full swing. And while we ended up walking away with a win on paper, the whole process left massive holes in all of our pockets.

I have thought, 'Would we have invested the money we spent in the business if we'd known where it would be now?' Probably, but we should never have had to go through what we went through. At first, I agreed with Hask that we should countersue. But that would have meant more money, more wasted time, more stress, and we weren't guaranteed a win at the end of it.

We were all exhausted, so it was time to put that saga to bed, concentrate on the good things in life, including the podcast, and take grim satisfaction from the fact that the case was so bad, it set a new legal precedent, meaning what happened to us should never happen to anyone else. And while there are easier forms of teambuilding, such as jungle training with the SAS, it certainly strengthened the bonds between me, Payno and Hask.

# 17

# UPSETTING WOMEN

**JH:** I only recently learned about so-called microaggressions, I thought a microaggression was when a small person started giving you shit or a crap little dog yapped at you. It turns out it is when someone says something without meaning to cause any offence because they have always said it or used to say it in the past, and the other person who is sick of that kind of stuff starts berating them for being almost as bad as Hitler and it all blows up. I may be putting my own spin on it, but this is what it means in my book.

Microaggressions are common, everyday slights and comments that relate to various aspects of one's appearance or identity such as class, gender, sex, sexual orientation, race, ethnicity, mother tongue, age, body shape, disability, or religion, among others. Or so the *Oxford English Dictionary* says.

One young woman told me about the time some elderly bloke was doing a speech at her rugby club. When he started talking about a player who 'had played for every team, from the minis to the first XV', this young woman and her mates started screaming at him, 'No, he hasn't! He's never played for the women's team!' They wanted to storm the stage and stop the old bloke in his tracks.

As she was telling this story, I was thinking, 'This bloke was in his sixties. Women's rugby was barely even a thing when he was playing. Why couldn't these women cut him some slack?' Meanwhile, this young woman was going on about the fact that all these microaggressions add up and grind her down and that the poor bloke doing the speech really needed to 'do better'.

About the time I was being educated about microaggressions, we did a live show in Swansea. And when we came off stage at the interval, our two social media people, both women (which is an important detail), were really flustered. I asked them what was wrong, and they told me that just before we'd gone on stage, they'd posted on our social media channels. The post consisted of a picture of Dylan Hartley and Steve Thompson, a list of England's five most-capped front-row MEN (I'm not making the same fucking mistake again) and the title, 'MOST CAPPED ENGLAND FRONT-ROW FORWARDS'.

Now, if they'd told me they'd posted an article advocating the slapping of women, I'd have been upset. But I didn't think this was a particularly big deal. They'd posted on the podcast's channels, the podcast dealt with men's rugby, there were two men in the picture. I thought it was quite clear that this was a post about the men's game. 'Who,' I thought, 'could possibly get angry about it?' Then I looked at the comments under the post, which was a lot of people getting angry about it. Mainly it was people saying, 'DON'T YOU MEAN MEN?!' and banging on about former prop Rocky Clark, who played 137 times for England women, 23 times more than Jason Leonard.

I couldn't believe it. Not only did I think it was a strange battle to pick, but me, Payno and Tins had recently set up a women's rugby podcast, *The Good, The Scaz & The Rugby*

('Scaz' referring to England legend Emily Scarratt). We were on the side of women's rugby, we wanted it to grow, and now we were being attacked for a microaggression we hadn't even committed.

One of our social media people was crying, telling me she 'should have done better', and I was telling her not to worry about it, that it really didn't matter, that anybody who was upset about the post must be a complete idiot. Then I saw a comment from a female player, who had been a recent guest on *The Good, The Scaz & The Rugby*: 'I think you meant to say "most capped England MALE front-row forwards". Please stop disrespecting the women like this. Because the way you've named the list, we know Rocky Clark tops it. Please do better.'

To which I replied, 'Have a day off.'

My reply was only up for a few seconds before I deleted it and wrote something a bit more considered, along the lines of, 'Why are you attacking us when you must know we're on your side and gave you a platform to come on our podcast? It's obviously a men's rugby podcast, and all you're going to do is marginalise people who currently support you and make people who don't even more hardline. Don't attack the people on your side.' But social media being what it is, people were all over my original reply like seagulls on chips, screen-shotting the hell out of it, and by the time I came off at the end of the show, the situation had gone nuclear. People were avoiding me and giving me evils, and I was thinking, 'How the hell has this happened?' Then I drove back to the hotel and went to bed. Don't get me wrong, it wasn't weighing heavily on my mind and I slept like a baby, but there was definitely some drama. Little did I know what I was going to wake up to.

The following morning, the managing director of Platform called me to say how upset our social media people were with my attitude and that I needed to talk to them. I thought, 'They were the ones who got us into this mess!' Then when I looked at the social media comments, they weren't just from people who were slightly irritated by the omission of the word 'men's' in the original post, they were also from people who thought I was the second coming of Attila the Hun.

People were calling me every name under the sun, people were telling me how sorry they felt for my daughter (or that they hoped she grew up to be treated as badly by men as I'd treated women's rugby players), people were apoplectic that I'd told a female player, who also had a full-time job, to have a day off ('The patriarchy is real! Feminism doesn't have a day off!'), and there were even death threats. Plus, the whole shit-show was all over the papers already. I was being struck down with great vengeance and furious anger from all sides (although I don't think anybody called me a Nazi, which surprised me – in certain circles, telling a woman to have a day off is up there with genocide).

It was all very *Alice Through the Looking Glass*, to the extent that I started to get a bit paranoid. I thought, 'If these two social media women are upset with me for telling another woman to have a day off, what other complaints might people have?' I've never been a handsy person or inappropriate, but what stories or jokes might have been misconstrued?

I was really concerned that this was going to go downhill really quickly, So I had a chat with these two staff members, apologised to them and calmed them down. I shouldn't have responded and not in the way I had. I think they found that I had made light of a difficult situation that women faced. Frankly, I should have known better, having responded before and caused other shitstorms, but I did feel that the two women were being attacked and were upset, which was a slight on all of us and I wanted to defend them. I felt we were all getting attacked so that's why I reacted. Alas, I now found myself slap-bang in the middle of a whopping great minefield.

The podcast's sponsor had been on the phone to our production company, telling them I had to make a public apology and that they needed a seven-point plan of how we were going to deal with the situation. I told them quite forcefully, with a lot of swear words thrown in, that I was not going to apologise because I hadn't done anything wrong. I kept thinking, 'Why are these people so worried about what I'm up to? What are they doing to fight the patriarchy, apart from slagging me off on social media? And what are they doing for women's rugby?' Ironically, probably not as much as we as a company had been doing. It goes back to what I was saying earlier about people complaining and trying to burn people's careers, without actually making a change. They don't attack the problem, they just get rid of a person.

Sexism is alive and real, and of course prevalent everywhere to some degree, which of course includes rugby. For example, I'd introduce Chloe to a certain generation of rugby fans and they'd all just stare at her, like she was a piece of meat. And when she'd say something about rugby, they'd completely ignore her, because they assumed she knew nothing about it. Sometimes, one of them would repeat what she'd just said, and I'd say to them, 'She just fucking said that!' So I wanted to do what I could for women's rugby, and on top of setting up our women's rugby podcast, I'd started working on women's rugby broadcasts.

Two weeks before all this happened, I'd worked for TikTok at an England women's game against Ireland at Welford Road, when Scaz won her 100th cap. I loved it, it was such a refreshing experience. Unlike the men's game, it was fun and full of positivity, and I wasn't worried that some meathead in a Barbour coat was going to start berating me for something I did or said in the dim and distant past. I came away from that game thinking, 'Wow, I can see how people might prefer that to men's rugby.' I became a cheerleader for women's rugby, raved about it on social media, but now I had suddenly become Death, the destroyer of women's rugby. I could certainly never work in women's rugby again, and after all the abuse I wouldn't really want to.

The person who worked for Platform, who wanted me to apologise to calm the sponsors, kept phoning me all the way from Swansea to Devon where I was speaking at an event. I was being driven there, so I was in the back shouting and swearing my head off – 'Fuck off! I'm not apologising! I haven't done anything wrong! You tell me what I've done wrong!' – while the driver was laughing his head off. In the end, I said, 'Tell you what, if you want to be Billy Big Bollocks, fucking fire me! Stand me down from the podcast and put out a statement!' But, shock horror, he didn't want to put himself out there in the public domain, instead they wanted me to burn myself so they could keep earning. I said he could go fuck himself and the only way they were going to get an apology out of me is if they fired me. He hung up in a huff, then called back to tell me that if I didn't apologise, the main sponsor was going to withdraw sponsorship.

That call changed everything, because that wasn't just my money, it was also Tins' and Payno's. So I got on the phone to both of them and said, 'Listen guys, they've backed me into a corner. I don't want to apologise, and my apology won't really mean anything, but I'd rather be rich and wrong than poor and right.' So I ended up doing one of those social media apologies that looks like one of those hostage statements, when they're going on about how lovely and hospitable their captors are, when they're actually living off rice water and some bloke just off camera has a bazooka aimed at their head.

My first apology, such as it was, mentioned that the social media post that had caused the clusterfuck had been put together and published by two female members of staff who also played rugby, and that they hadn't seen a problem with it. But when I sent it to be cleared, I got a call from someone telling me I couldn't under any circumstances refer to them. I said, 'But it's the truth! They did it!' That didn't cut any ice, so I phoned one of the social media women and asked her what the problem was. She pleaded with me not to mention her and her mate, and I said, 'Right, so you just want me to get thrown under the bus, even though you know I had nothing to do with it and you posted it.' She said, 'Basically, yes …' To say I was incandescent is an understatement, and I honestly felt like quitting right then.

To be fair to Payno and Tins, they didn't think I had anything to apologise for either. But they hadn't told anybody to have a day off, so didn't want to get involved. So off I went and recorded a second apology, which was one of those non-apology apologies that didn't mention the word sorry once.

**AP:** Hask's comedy idol is Ricky Gervais, and at times he can be even more unfiltered than Ricky Gervais, which is obviously a recipe for controversy.

Hask has a very particular set of beliefs, and while he's very rational, he's also very rigid. If he believes something to be nonsense, he'll be tempted to make it known. I just haven't got the energy, the time or the interest to be fighting battles that aren't really mine to fight; Hask, however, has. He's prepared to die on hills for his beliefs, and he's almost perished a few times.

While we're incredibly comfortable with *The Good, The Bad & The Rugby* – who it's for and our roles on it – we decided we needed to build and fund a women's rugby podcast, partly because women's rugby is exploding, so it made sense from a business point of view, and partly because it was the right thing to do. I have a daughter who plays sport, Tins' daughter plays rugby (Hask's daughter has only just started walking but I'm sure she'll play sport one day), and we had a platform, so we were in a good position to help.

We could have started devoting episodes of *The Good, The Bad & The Rugby* to the women's game, but we thought that by creating a separate podcast, presented by women, it would be the show that they wanted it to be. That's why *The Good, The Scaz & The Rugby* has a distinct identity to our podcast, and a strong one, partly because it doesn't feel tokenistic in any way.

I thought the comment from the former England player was overly aggressive, especially coming from someone who had been on *The Good, The Scaz & The Rugby* and who I thought understood that we were trying to help. I thought it looked like posturing, because she could have just sent one of us a WhatsApp and said, 'Do you know that the post you've put up doesn't make clear that you're talking about men's rugby?' Had she done that, we'd have made the change in a flash and the controversy would have been avoided.

Hask isn't able to walk past a provocation, he has to bite. And when he bites, he and everyone around him gets sucked into this vortex of drama. So the day after doing a fun show in Swansea, he's all over the papers for 'disrespecting women', our production company and sponsors are wondering what they've got themselves into, and Tins and I are wondering if the podcast will survive.

Having said that, since I started working with Hask, I've learned to stop worrying so much about being liked; and that when you get sucked into one of Hask's vortexes of drama, which come along quite often, you'll be like a cork in a storm: yes, you'll disappear beneath the waves and feel like you might drown, but if you don't panic, you'll eventually bob back up again. Hask is pedal to the metal in everything he does: if he wants to have a fight, he'll have a fight, and if standing up for what he believes in means things getting broken, so be it. I much prefer the easy life, whereas Tins is somewhere in between. Like Hask, he has strong beliefs, but he chooses his battles more carefully.

MT: Payno, Hask and I knew what lane we operated best in, which was men's rugby. But we also knew how big women's rugby was going to get, because it was one of the fastest growing sports in the world. On top of that, our awesome producer, a decent rugby player in her own right, played professionally and was a big advocate of women's sport. So at some point, we all got together and decided we needed a women's rugby podcast, to stand alone from *The Good, The Bad & The Rugby*.

If we were going to do a women's rugby podcast, we wanted the biggest names involved. Emily 'Scaz' Scarratt, who had been playing for England for well over a decade and won the World Cup in 2014, was an obvious choice, as was South African journalist and presenter Elma Smit, who was a massive champion of women's rugby. And so *The Good, The Scaz & The Rugby* was born.

I was the third wheel in the first couple of series, but the plan was always for me to fade into the background at some point, because we wanted the show to be by women, for women. Payno, Hask and I would watch the Women's Six Nations, but none of us were watching much of the Allianz Women's Premiership, now PWR, so women's rugby was very far from being our area of expertise. So eventually, I was replaced by England scrum-half Natasha 'Mo' Hunt, and *The Good, The Scaz & The Rugby* had its own distinct identity.

So when everything kicked off with this social media post,

I couldn't help thinking, 'Okay, fair enough, maybe they should have been more careful. But we've got two separate podcasts now, and that was posted on *The Good, The Bad & The Rugby*'s social media feeds. Would anyone be moaning if a post about the most-capped female England front-rows appeared on *The Good, The Scaz & The Rugby's* social media feeds and didn't use the word women?'

When we came off for the interval in Swansea, I turned on my phone to find hundreds of notifications, including that comment from one of our guests. I was fuming because I'd been on *The Good, The Scaz & The Rugby* with her and really bigged her up. She was a prop but also an amazing athlete who had recently scored an unbelievable try for Bristol against Sale, which was why we invited her onto the show – the show Payno, Hask and I had set up and were funding for no profit at the time!!

I thought Hask would blow a gasket when he read it. As it was, he didn't say much when I showed it to him, just mumbled something about it being ridiculous. But after the show, I discovered that he'd said something along the lines of 'have a day off', which wasn't the wisest thing to do. I know Hask isn't a misogynist, he was just pissed off that somebody we'd promoted had attacked him. But I understood why his words were being interpreted in that way. They were advocating for greater acceptance of the women's game, and he was telling them to have a day off – at least that's how some people wanted to see it.

By the following day, the molehill had grown into a mountain. Hask was under attack in the comments sections, the papers were making out he was a misogynist, our production company was demanding he apologise, and an England player had pulled out of a scheduled appearance on *The Good, The Scaz & The Rugby*.

I was on Hask's side, in that I didn't think he had any reason to apologise. I'm all for apologising when you genuinely think you're in the wrong, but not simply because it seems like the right thing to do. Maybe he could have said he chose the wrong words, but nothing more than that.

In the end, I decided to phone her. After she'd got over the shock, I reminded her that we'd changed the social media post as soon as it was pointed out to us that it didn't contain the word 'men's'. I also suggested that instead of launching a personal attack, she could have just said, 'Guys, don't forget Rocky Clark', like most people managed to do. Or simply phone Scaz or our producer, whose numbers she had. She sounded quite sheepish on the phone but spent the next few days posting training pictures along with the words, 'I can't have a day off.'

The saddest part about the whole story is that women's rugby had lost somebody with a great reach (as well as the podcast, he's written books and has millions of followers on social media) who could have been a tremendous advocate for the women's game in the future. People in the women's game will forget about the controversy eventually and probably start inviting Hask back, but I'm not sure Hask would do it.

Two days after appearing in Swansea, we had a show in Dublin. We met our guest Rory Best in a pub beforehand and we were all so pissed off that we sank six pints of Guinness before we went on, before necking six more during the show. It was the loosest show we'd ever done, because we were all thinking, 'Fuck it, this could all collapse tomorrow.' Hask was told not to say anything and the first thing he does when he walked out was tell the audience to 'have a day off'.

# 18

# FLAK

**AP:** You probably won't be surprised to learn that a lot of people shout at us, usually via email and social media, but that's going to happen when you have two high-profile people with strong opinions. There are those who don't think a member of the royal family should be swearing and telling bawdy stories, and there are those who hate Hask with every fibre of their being simply because he's so loud and brash. There are also those who think a rugby podcast shouldn't be broadcasting from Ibiza, which we've done a few times.

Cruising is not really my bag (either kind, just to be clear), but we ended up spending a few nights on a cruise ship during the 2023 World Cup, partly because Marseille was all out of hotel rooms, partly because the company needed some on board entertainment (that's what I mean about the podcast taking me in bizarre new directions – if you'd told me five years ago that I'd end up being a cruise ship entertainer, I'd have scoffed, and it is somewhat emblematic of the decline of my reputation as a serious broadcaster).

Those were some of the most alcoholic days of my life, including a couple of overnight trips to Ibiza. Hask knows a lot of people on the White Island through his DJing, and we ended up doing a podcast on the roof of the ME Hotel. And while 50 per cent of our audience absolutely loved that we were living it up in Ibiza, drinking rosé and talking about rugby in the sunshine, the other 50 per cent absolutely hated it: 'Why are you in Ibiza? What's it got to do with rugby? Why are you drinking on air? This is not what rugby should be!' But you can't spend your life worrying that people will disapprove of your choices. If you try to appease middle-aged men in Barbour jackets, you'll never go anywhere.

Occasionally, I'll bite. The other day, somebody left a message on YouTube calling me an 'insufferable snob'. I'd had worse, but 'snob' is particularly cutting. So I clicked on his bio, which took me straight to his website. He was a wedding photographer, and there at the top of his homepage was his mobile number. I couldn't resist phoning him, and he made the mistake of picking up. I said to him, 'Hi, it's Alex Payne from *The Good, The Bad & The Rugby*, how are you? I thought I'd give you a call because I saw your feedback on this week's show and I was wondering what part of it upset you so much.'

'Well,' he replied, in a thick West Country accent, 'I just think you're an insufferable snob.'

'Right. Which part gave you that impression?'

'It's just what I think you are.'

'Listen, I'm very happy to receive constructive feedback, and if you don't like what I do, fair enough. But I think "snob" is inaccurate, because it implies that I look down on people, which I absolutely don't do. The podcast is a broad church, we have anyone on and celebrate who they are, whatever their background.'

'Yeah, no, you're probably right, "snob" probably isn't the right word.'

'Okay, what word is the right one?'

He tried to argue his way out of it, but after about 15 seconds he said, 'D'you know what, Alex? I'm so sorry. I've just had triple heart bypass surgery. I've been at home on my own for three weeks and I'm feeling very lonely. I don't know why I said what I did, it's not me and I feel really embarrassed.'

I told him I appreciated the apology, offered him tickets to a show next time we're in the West Country and we left it at that. You might think that story makes me sound a bit thin-skinned, but I don't make a habit of it, and the truth is it's a bit of sport and important to jab back every so often rather than covering up in the corner and soaking up blows. This guy deleted his comment and replaced it with a grovelling apology, and he's a reminder that people who send nasty messages often do so because they're unhappy with their lives.

After a recent show in London, our producer forwarded me an email he'd received from someone who was very upset by Hask's performance. It was a small venue that night, and Hask said a few things he probably wouldn't have said at the London Palladium. All the same, this email struck me as massively over the top. It went something along the lines of: 'I've heard him say things I didn't like on the podcast before, but having attended a live event, I never want to listen to *The Good, The Bad & The Rugby* again. James Haskell is an arrogant, elitist, misogynistic, homophobic arsehole.'

I wrote this woman a reply, before deciding not to send it. But what it said was, 'I'm really sorry to hear that you didn't enjoy the show, but I'm going to have to correct you on a few things. You have accused James of being misogynistic, homophobic and everything else, but he's demonstrably not. He has performed at Pride, he was the first rugby player to appear on the cover of *Attitude* magazine, his brother is gay. He has been instrumental in building the most successful women's rugby podcast in the world, which has an all-female staff, gives a platform to two female England players and has helped a female rugby presenter from South Africa relocate to and carve out a career in the UK. When you lazily accuse him of being these things, you're failing to recognise that he's not a man who just says stuff on social media and then leaves it to others to do the work, he is actively doing good things for minority causes.'

But that's the world we live in now: there are lots of people banging on about what they stand for on social media but not actually doing anything constructive, while simultaneously attacking people who are doing good things because their words occasionally fail the purity test. Hask makes life hard for himself at times, and I sometimes wish he wouldn't say some of the things he does, but he also doesn't get anything like the credit he deserves. I kind of wish I'd sent that email now!

I did get in touch with someone after a show with England number eight Billy Vunipola, when he reiterated his support for Australia's Israel Folau, who had recently said that gay people, atheists and a whole load of other people were going to Hell. This person was furious with our treatment of the issue and particularly critical of Hask for not challenging Billy (Hask did challenge Billy, but most of that got edited out, which Hask will expand on later). I said to this person, 'You're not seeing the whole picture. You'll struggle to find someone from the sporting world who has done more to support the LGBTQ+ community.' We ended up having a civilised conversation, and that incident reminded me that social media isn't a place for nuance, it's for people who aren't interested in the whole, people who would rather listen to a 90-second clip before spewing their preconceptions into our comments sections.

We recently did a show titled 'LIV Rugby', which was all about whether rugby should consider taking Saudi Arabian money, as LIV Golf and lots of other sports have done. We discussed if it was inevitable; we discussed what rugby would do with the money; we discussed the possible downsides, including Saudi Arabia's poor human rights record; but we were also up front about the fact that we weren't as educated as some on the subject. But despite trying to be balanced, the comments section was full of people calling us a disgrace, accusing us of glossing over atrocities, and threatening to cancel their subscriptions. However, when we posted a poll on Instagram, asking the question, 'Should rugby take Saudi Arabian money?', 75 per cent said yes! It demonstrated that the people who shout the loudest aren't necessarily in the majority, which is one of the reasons I usually shy away from the fight.

I've got a lot going on in my life. I spend my time babysitting Tins and Hask, running a tech business, building our Blackeye Gin business, attempting to keep my wife happy, watching my kids play sport. It's not that I don't care about what's going on in the world, it's just that I don't know enough to weigh in. Does that make me narrow-minded? Possibly. Do I want to be like Hask, who uses up an awful lot of energy fighting for his beliefs? No! If you want to rage about something, that's your right. I'd rather spend my time in the sunshine with a cup of coffee.

**MT:** I am very lucky, but there are a lot of assumptions made about Zara and me that simply aren't true. I have heard some people say I'm worth £25 million, but I wish they'd tell me where it is, because I'd love to have it.

People think that working members of the royal family get up every day, shake a few hands, cut the odd ribbon, and not much more than that. But now I've seen behind the curtain, I know there's a lot more to it than that. Being a working member of the royal family is all-consuming, you don't have your own time or your own space. With us sitting outside the working royals it allows us to do things our way, which works better for us.

It can be frustrating when you know the truth and other people simply aren't interested in it, but you just have to live with it. In fact, that's one of the royal family's mottos: 'Never explain, never complain.' I try not to think about it, although it took me a long time to get to that point. And I also try to be myself. Maybe that's why I reverse pothole so much, because I want people to know that I'm actually a decent bloke, which goes back to wanting to be liked.

When I was younger, I was obsessed with people liking me, and even now, if someone wants a selfie with me or whatever, I'll sometimes talk to them to the point where they'll want to get away. It's not quite as bad as Hask and Payno make out, but they must be onto something as my wife agrees with them. Every now and again, I'll get stuck with someone who's really drunk, but I still won't have the heart to cut them off, unless they're really rude. In stark contrast, if Hask gets cornered by someone for too long, he'll just tell them to back off.

Actually, I did refuse a selfie with someone following a live show, just after Wales had been knocked out of the World Cup. I came out of the club and walked straight into this Welsh guy who was hammered. His eyes widened and he roared, 'Tindall! Can I have a photo please?' I replied, 'Of course you can, but only if you promise to cheer for England in their semi-final next week.'

'Sorry, bud,' said the Welsh guy, 'I can't do that.'

'Why not? You're not even in it anymore.'

'I just can't do it.'

'Fair enough, but I can't do the photo then.'

'Are you serious?'

'Yeah. If you're not gonna cheer for England, it can't happen.'

He started to walk off, before turning round and saying, 'Are you having me on?'

'No!'

This guy just looked so confused, as was I to be fair. I thought, 'If he wanted a photo so much, why didn't he just lie to me?' Amazing. If Wales were playing a southern hemisphere team in a World Cup semi-final, I'd be cheering them to the rafters, but Celts will cheer for anyone else but England.

But spending too long talking to people isn't the worst trait in the world. And as long as your friends and family love you, that's all that counts. As for everyone else, you hope they'll like you, but if they don't, they don't. And if they don't like you, you can even use that as a self-improvement tool.

I try not to have rows on social media, like Hask, but I generally don't block people either, even if they abuse me. If you are asking why I'm on SM, I try to use it for my reasons, to say what I want to say as well as promote things if I need to. Instead, I have honest and frank conversations with myself: 'Is what they're saying about me true, even if they haven't expressed themselves in the right way? Even if they've called me a load of horrible names?' It almost never is.

JH: I wouldn't say I struggle with my mental health, but I do take care of it. And just because I don't have depression or anxiety doesn't mean I don't go through hard times. As I write this book, I'm being publicly shamed for my marriage break-up and followed around by journalists and cameramen.

A newspaper recently ran an article accompanied by a photo of me talking to Payno's sister with a misleading caption including the words 'mystery blonde'. My dad had actually been standing on the other side of me, but they cut him out to make the story sound more juicy. The other day I had been walking with one of my female mates to a different bar during the Glastonbury festival when the *Daily Mail* papped me with the caption 'Haskell with leggy blonde', which always goes down well at home. There was no substance to any of these stories. I mean, imagine how Payno would react if I had been getting it on with his married sister?

Before that show at the London Palladium, when I spoke about my separation from Chloe and all the grief the media were giving me, Payno said to me, 'Please, no 9/11 jokes tonight.' I got a bit humpy with him, because I'd told that 9/11 joke a million times before, and it's not a joke about the people who died on 9/11, I just talk about the time my old England teammate Tom Wood 'crumpled like the Twin Towers' when Andy Farrell asked us for some honest feedback (our contact at Continental Tyres was actually great in that situation – when she was made aware of my joke by a bunch of panicking underlings, her response was basically, 'James Haskell doesn't work for Continental Tyres and his opinions aren't ours', and that was the end of it).

I said to Payno, 'Don't tell me what I can and can't say', and when he asked me how I was at the start of the show, I replied, 'Not great. People are writing stories about me that aren't true. I've got carloads of press hanging out on my street and my neighbours, most of whom are Jewish, are freaking out because some of the cars are unmarked and Israel is currently at war with Gaza. The poor people think they're going to be shot or blown up. I'm still living at home with my ex and I've got to turn up and perform as if everything is fine.' I could have been speaking to a psychotherapist.

That show came hot on the heels of one we did in Guildford, when I'd gone a bit scattergun and made a load of jokes – JOKES! – about getting sued, losing half my money, not remembering where I'd put most of it anyway ('was it Switzerland or the Cayman Islands?') and not having a pot to piss in. (I also made a gag along the lines of, 'If you see anyone filming or writing, they work for a newspaper. And if they're writing in crayons, they work for the *Daily Mail*.') When Chloe read what I'd said in the papers, she freaked out. I had to tell her that while I didn't really have a secret bank account, I did actually have a pot to piss in, and that I'd just made it all up to get a few laughs on stage. I have no problem throwing myself and other people in my life under the bus for a laugh as it's clearly all a joke. I always become the most exaggerated version of myself when I perform. I become whatever I think will get the most laughs. However, I admit that when taken out of context or appearing in the papers you can sometimes look like a dick.

I've come to realise that it doesn't matter if the *Daily Mail* runs articles saying what an awful person I am. People who already hated me will continue to hate me, but people who appreciated me will continue to appreciate me. I might get more abuse than normal on social media, but who cares about them? In the real world, everything remains the same. I don't have people chastising me for my behaviour in the street, our podcast audience isn't going down, and as long as I don't do anything illegal and it doesn't cost us money, we'll just keep moving on. The bottom line is that the kind of people who hate me for the odd risqué joke are also the kind of people who when they see a nice field with a family having a picnic, they fill in the nice pond with concrete, they plough the family into the field, and they blow up the tree and use the leaves to make a dress for their wife who's also their brother.

# THE
# RUGBY

# 19

# TURNING GAMEKEEPER

**MT:** Hask's relationship with his dad was similar to mine in some ways, in that we both had to deal with plenty of fairly blunt criticism growing up.

My dad played a decent standard of rugby back in the 1970s and was always barking instructions at me and my brother, who was three years older than me, from the touchline. One day, I was in the kitchen when my brother and dad returned home after a game. My brother ran straight upstairs and my dad roared, 'I'm never watching that boy again!' It transpired that Dad had been shouting orders from behind the posts after the other team had scored a try and my brother had turned around and told him to fuck off. Having told Dad I'd never do anything like that, a couple of years later I was playing a game, Dad was shouting orders at me, and I told him to shut the fuck up.

Like Hask, that constant criticism made me quite chippy. But it also gave me a determination to prove people wrong and made me realise that criticism is an essential part of being a sportsperson. That might sound quite old-fashioned, but the ability to take criticism, process it, and work out if it's warranted, rather than get angry and fly off the handle, is a skill in itself.

I should make clear that most of Dad's criticism was of the constructive kind. If I had an average game, he'd take me aside afterwards and say, 'Right, you missed that tackle there, didn't make that pass there, this is what you need to do to improve …' But if I had a really good game, he'd happily tell me. I think that relationship with my dad informed how I doled out criticism on the podcast: I needed to be honest, but I also needed to be measured and fair.

Unlike a lot of pundits, we weren't in the business of calling players useless just because they'd had a bad game. Instead, we'd try to explain to our audience that professional rugby was a bit more nuanced than that. Nobody who plays for England is a bad rugby player. They might have flaws, but being negative about them on a public forum isn't going to help them get better.

I know what it's like to have people constantly saying and writing negative things about you. Former England fly-half and *Times* columnist Stuart Barnes was always giving me pelters, and I'd be lying if I said that didn't irritate me. Now, Stuart will rave about someone who plays the game similar to how I played it, which is odd, but I actually get on quite well with him. He loves his horseracing and is quite easy to talk to, and it helps that I understand the media a bit better nowadays. Columnists need to be provocative otherwise they won't get read. They also don't write headlines, which are often far more inflammatory than the words underneath.

Stuart has also spent the last decade or so swinging between lavish praise and harsh criticism of Owen Farrell, but we didn't want to be like that. Does Owen have bad days? Yes. But he's obviously a class player, that's why he's played over 100 games for England. And nobody who cares as much about England as he obviously does deserves the kind of treatment he gets. Never mind Owen Farrell, anybody who puts in the work to make it to international level deserves respect, even if they're playing for a development country. Look at how Portugal played in the 2023 World Cup, like absolute superstars despite quite a few of their team being amateurs. They've all sacrificed something along the way, so none of them are deserving of rough treatment.

Players wanted to come on the podcast because they knew we understood the game better than most people and weren't fickle, swaying this way and that with public opinion. Having said that, I soon learned that you'll upset some of your audience even if you try to be measured and fair.

Heading into the 2019 World Cup, everyone was raving about Ireland and saying they might even win it, but I'd sometimes say on the podcast, 'Look, this Ireland team isn't actually very good, someone's gonna figure out how to beat them in Japan.' I got pelters from Irish fans on social media, and it became this thing that I hated Ireland. What happened? Ireland got hammered by the All Blacks in the quarter-finals.

I honestly thought Ireland might win the 2023 World Cup, and I was rooting for them because they played entertaining rugby. But I still had people accusing me of hating them, based on the fact I thought they were beatable in 2019, even though that turned out to be true. I've also got South African fans on my case at the moment because I don't like how they choose to play rugby. And if there's one group of fans you don't want on your case, it's them.

Eddie Jones' England were a difficult team to appraise, especially for the last couple of years that he was in charge. It wasn't that I didn't like them or want them to do well, it was just that I was struggling to work out what Eddie was trying to do. I played in teams that kept picking up wins despite playing shit, and I was happy with that. But just because you keep picking up wins doesn't mean you should be immune from criticism, because as soon as you start losing big games, the fact that you were playing shit for ages suddenly becomes relevant. Should you have been playing a different style of rugby all along? Should you have been more expansive? Should you have been tighter? Should certain players have been involved and other players not?

A lot of people thought England were going to be a disaster at the 2023 World Cup, largely based on their build-up, which was, to be fair, pretty dismal. Head coach Steve Borthwick had a reputation as an analytical coach who was fixated on the set piece and unable to see beyond the stats, but there were mitigating factors for the team's poor performances. When Borthers was appointed at the end of 2022, he inherited Eddie's team, which wasn't a settled one, because Eddie had used so many players. And Borthers was still trying to work things out, make that team his own, get the players on board with what he was trying to do, and that takes time. So I wasn't surprised when England reached the semi-finals – I thought they should have done given the group of players they had – and they got into the position to beat South Africa but just couldn't finish it off.

I'll admit that I found the first couple of games of the 2024 Six Nations deflating. When he picked young lads like Tommy Freeman, Fraser Dingwall, Ethan Roots and Ollie Chessum for the first game against Italy, I thought Borthers was finally loosening the reins. But they were poor in that game, despite winning, and not much better in beating Wales. I was thinking, 'Jesus, we reached the last four of the World Cup a few months ago but we seem to have gone backwards.' And I remember getting a drunken text from my producer after the Wales game, saying he never wanted to watch Steve Borthwick's England again. I think a lot of England fans agreed with him.

The knives really came out for Borthers after the loss to Scotland, but Hask and I went on the podcast and said how happy we were with how they played. I hadn't seen us try to attack so much in years and we scored off a set piece strike. At least they had a go, and it was a style of rugby I'd pay to watch. Yes, we dropped the ball a ridiculous number of times, but that kind of stuff can become infectious. They hadn't become useless rugby players overnight, they could put that stuff right, and it certainly wasn't the coach's fault.

Given how we played against Scotland, I thought we'd cause Ireland problems, which is exactly what happened. For the second game in a row, England played an attacking brand of rugby, opened Ireland up repeatedly and pulled off a narrow victory, which I wasn't expecting. And even though France just pipped England in the final game, I thought afterwards, 'That was one hell of a Test match and I'm fully on board with watching this lot.'

Yes, we'd only finished third in the Championship, and we'd lost two of the three games I was so excited about, but the atmosphere at Twickenham during and after the Ireland game summed up my mood, which was one of relief and elation: 'At last! And thank God!' I know there are people who think winning is everything – and there's certainly nothing wrong with winning ugly every now and again – but sometimes playing great rugby in defeat goes down a treat. And I was chuffed for Borthers because we'd played together since we were 16 and I knew what a good person he was and how much he cared.

**JH:** I think I've changed quite a lot of people's opinions about me through the podcast, in a positive way, but I've also succeeded in making a mockery of my career, which is probably not a good thing.

When Gary Lineker suggests that he was a shit footballer, everyone knows he's joking, because it's well known that he was one of England's greatest strikers who won the Golden Boot at the 1986 World Cup. But when I suggest I was a shit rugby player, some people listening think it must be true. I've suggested it so often that even I've started thinking it must be true.

Apparently, that's a real psychological phenomenon – if you talk about yourself negatively often enough, the mind stops knowing if it's real or not. For me, it started when I was still playing. I'd make jokes about my handling ability, even though it was good, and people would repeat them back to me. I'd be thinking, 'Was I shit? Or have I made something half real that wasn't? Payno even said you have to stop talking yourself down, as you are damaging how you were known. I'm addressing people now who have never seen me play and all they know is what I say or what others joke about.

On tour, I used to make out that Tins had a drink problem. I'd make it a running joke throughout the show, so that whenever Tins said something daft, I'd just have to do a drinking gesture to get a laugh. Tins didn't really have a drink problem, it just fitted with the image (just like Dean Martin didn't really have a drink problem, but pretended to so that Frank Sinatra and Sammy Davis Junior could get a laugh out of it – yes, I did just compare Payno, Tins and myself to the Rat Pack), but you've got to be a bit careful with that kind of stuff because while we know we're just creating a bit of a fantasy world, some people think everything we say is 100 per cent true.

Similarly, when we started joking on the podcast that I don't watch rugby, I lost credibility in the eyes of some people. They'd write in the comments section, 'Haskell doesn't even know what he's talking about!' In the end, I said to Payno, 'We've got to stop saying I don't watch', and I felt the need to do a couple of shows where I went into granular detail about defensive systems. People were raving about it – 'More of that, please' – but I was thinking, 'Yes, I can do that kind of stuff, but it's not really what I enjoy doing.'

Do I watch rugby live every weekend? No, because I've got 101 other things to do, including spending time with my baby. But I do watch the big games and Premiership highlights, and I will do my research if I know we're going to be discussing certain games and certain players on the podcast. For example, before I interviewed Ellis Genge and Jonny May, I spent quite a long time watching highlights of their games and reading up on their careers. That was the right and respectful thing to do, for Ellis and Jonny and the audience.

**AP:** Some readers might be surprised to learn that we are contractually obliged to talk about rugby on the podcast. However, it's not always easy to keep Hask's mind on the game.

Hask can be a very insightful analyst when he wants to be – it's just that he doesn't usually want to be. We'll be watching a game at Twickenham and he'll be working on his laptop, whether it's to do with a new book or a new piece of music. Meanwhile, Tins will have eyes for nothing else than the rugby. He loves it, studies it, knows almost everything about it. You might call him a rugby nause, and he'd add a huge amount to anyone who wanted to work with him (he sometimes comes up with ideas on the podcast and they'll be taken up by some governing body or other four or five months later).

Hask does love the game and has very strong opinions on it (he often flips his lid about how rugby is run and reckons that if someone gave him a month to fix things, he'd do it in a week and then go off on a three-week holiday), but he doesn't love the game like Tins does. Hask can take it or leave it, and if he wasn't involved in the podcast, he'd probably leave it altogether.

The show with boxing promoter Eddie Hearn was a taster of where Hask might take the podcast. Hask hosted that episode, and it was an hour and 20 minutes of mutual appreciation, with Tins ostracised on the end of the sofa.

Eddie had a lot of interesting things to say about rugby – he reckoned the sport wasn't accessible enough and lacked personalities, and said he couldn't name more than half a dozen current players, which was quite frightening – but I was transfixed by the peacockery on display. The strutting was like nothing I'd ever seen before. And that kind of show is right in Hask's sweet spot, while Tins really likes getting into the nitty-gritty of the game.

# 20

# STATE OF THE GAME

**AP:** Rugby is going through a period of seismic change, and I think most supporters would agree with Tins and Hask, in that it's not the players who are letting down the sport right now, it's everything around it. Tins is going to love this – 'Here goes the catastrophiser again …' – but here's my take on the state of the game, and I'll be honest – it pains me to write this. Anyone who watches a lot of professional rugby will tell you that the product is often amazing. The quarter-final weekend at the 2023 World Cup delivered four sensational games: Argentina's thrilling late charge against Wales; New Zealand's nerve-shredding win over Ireland; England just managing to hold off a marauding Fiji; South Africa's controversial one-point victory over hosts and favourites France. The knock-out stages of Europe's Champions Cup were also magnificent, as were the Premiership play-offs. However, there were too few people watching or talking about these games.

There are still plenty of people who think that rugby union is the greatest game on earth, but they exist in a goldfish bowl. Outside of that goldfish bowl, press coverage of club rugby is shrinking and it rarely makes the news. Ask random people on the street to name a famous England rugby player and chances are they'll say Jonny Wilkinson, who's been retired for 10 years. People of an older vintage might even say Will Carling, who called it a day almost 25 years ago. Or maybe they'll say James Haskell or Mike Tindall, but not because of anything they achieved on the rugby field (sorry chaps), but because of their relationships and appearances on *I'm a Celebrity*.

It's a real sadness of mine that three decades after rugby union went professional, it's less popular than when it was an amateur game. How can that even be possible? It's possible because of the people who run it.

Rugby is suffering a slow death by committee. We're still having the same conversations about the game's problems that we were having 10 years ago. There's no getting away from the fact that English rugby cocked up professionalism, allowing it to develop in the wrong way for 30 years, and now people are trying to unpick and rebuild it in an era of empty bank balances.

Too many rugby authorities wanted the game to be all things to all people and it ended up being far less than it should have been to hardly anyone. In recent years, they've lost sight of the core appeal of rugby, namely that it's a brutal, gladiatorial sport played by incredible athletes. By tinkering with the laws to make it less physical, in order to make it more inclusive, it's succeeded in alienating people who loved and supported it for what it was.

Rugby has to get on top of the concussion situation, but you can do that without diluting the very essence of the sport and ending up with something wishy-washy. Former England lock Courtney Lawes said it brilliantly the other day: 'Rugby is a game for anyone, but not everyone.' In other words, most people who watch professional rugby wouldn't want to play it because of its brutality.

Compare rugby to MMA, UFC in particular. One of the reasons UFC grew so large so fast is because it was totally unapologetic about its appeal. On top of that, it was largely led by one man, Dana White, which meant it had a clarity of vision. Under his stewardship, UFC became a global multi-billion-dollar business, and White became crazy rich himself. And good luck to him.

The RFU should run the game in England from top to bottom. Instead, we have an unworkable situation whereby the RFU runs England rugby, the clubs run the Premiership, and amateur rugby is a mishmash. For years, the RFU and professional clubs have been fighting for control of the game and the players, and it's been hugely damaging. It's been wasted time and wasted energy when they could and should have been building something great.

In New Zealand and Ireland, club sides are connected to their respective unions, but in England, clubs spent the best part of 30 years trying to spend their way to success, without the revenue to make that spending sustainable. I recently saw a stat that said the cumulative losses of Premiership clubs in the first 25 years of the competition was more than half a billion pounds. When private investment company CVC got involved with rugby in 2020, they had big commercial plans for the game. But when Covid came along, most of their money went on keeping clubs afloat rather than growing the game. Both Wasps and Worcester went into administration in 2022, before London Irish were wound up the following year. All the remaining clubs remain in debt.

One of the biggest mistakes rugby ever made in the UK was walking away from Sky, and I'm not just saying that because I used to work there. Sky provided slick, extensive coverage. There would be billboards all over towns, Sky Sports News would relentlessly plug upcoming games and do features on players. Very importantly, they provided a connection with the football audience. For example, if Manchester United were playing Liverpool, a sizable proportion of viewers would leave the TV on and carry on watching when they switched to a Premiership rugby game. Some of those viewers would think, 'I quite liked that', and end up watching the Heineken Cup and autumn internationals as well. Now, because rugby coverage is so fragmented, rugby fans don't know where to watch it, let alone floating football fans.

The story goes that Premiership Rugby walked into a corner office at Sky HQ and said, 'We want you to cover three games a weekend', and Sky replied, 'The league isn't strong enough for that, but we'll show two, and we'll give you £60 million over three years.' The clubs said no, Sky said fair enough, and Premiership Rugby went off and did a deal with ESPN, which gave them two games a weekend and Sky one. Laughably, the total sum of money was £54 million, £6 million less than the original offer from Sky, despite an extra game being shown.

That was 15 years ago, and Sky eventually ended up walking away from club rugby altogether. One of the reasons they got fed up with it is because they were having to deal with so many different entities, whereas with cricket they'd just have one conversation with the England and Wales Cricket Board and get stacks of content in return. There's something sad about the fact that rugby just wasn't worth the effort, but that's the truth.

Now, Sky Sports News barely talks about rugby. And while losing the game has had no effect on Sky's bottom line, the finances of Premiership Rugby and European Professional Club Rugby (EPCR) have nosedived. They don't have the marketing engine that Sky, the premier sports broadcaster in the country, has, which makes it more difficult to attract commercial partners, means fewer people are watching, and fewer people can name you any players.

European rugby is a shadow of what it once was. I was very fortunate to be involved with some of the greatest days of what was then the Heineken Cup, at a time when Sky was paying £24 million to broadcast the tournament. But the EPCR, having made all sorts of outlandish promises about how they were going to make European rugby more successful than ever, with more big sponsors and a revolutionary new format, instead made a complete hash of things.

A wonderful competition which people used to cram into pubs all over the country to watch has become a sideshow. The format has been turned into an absolute clusterfuck, brands aren't interested in sponsoring it, players aren't as interested in playing it, and fans aren't as interested in watching it.

Meanwhile, down in the southern hemisphere, there are real concerns about Super Rugby. When I was a kid, I'd watch the likes of Jonah Lomu, Christian Cullen, Tana Umaga, Carlos Spencer and Justin Marshall on Sky every Saturday morning, and it was like rugby from another planet. But a once great competition has become a drifting ship. South Africa's teams have joined the Celtic and Italian sides in the United Rugby Championship (URC), Fijian and Pacific Island teams have been added, Melbourne Rebels have gone under. It's lost its magic. I couldn't even tell you when the competition starts and finishes, or when it's on television.

The whole structure is broken and it's going to take a huge effort to stop it from sinking further and further into quicksand. During Covid, Hask went as far as to say that he hoped the whole lot would collapse, so that the game could be rebuilt from the ground up in a more rational way. Lockdown was a gloomy time for a lot of people, admittedly, but I'm not sure Hask was wrong.

What would I do if I was in charge? Well, we wouldn't have club games on international weekends. We wouldn't have this ludicrous global season which means exhausted, broken northern hemisphere teams have to tour southern hemisphere countries during what is meant to be their summer break, and vice versa. Ireland's international players have just finished a 55-week season. It's insanity.

As it stands, we have World Rugby running the World Cup, the Six Nations running the Six Nations Championship, the RFU running the England team and second tier Championship, Premiership Rugby running the top division, EPRC running European competitions, plus all the other international unions, Super Rugby in the southern hemisphere, and they're all fighting each other. Instead, we need one centralised organisation that does the lot. Have different departments by all means, but they should all be under one roof, all working from the same blueprint, all drawing from one centralised pot of money, all sitting down together with the same potential sponsors. It sounds radical, but radical is what rugby needs to be to get out of the mess it currently finds itself in.

First on that central organisation's list of things to do would be to create a sensible international calendar, instead of the shambles it is now. In 2023, we had the Premiership starting during a World Cup, then breaking for a bit of European rugby, then restarting for six weeks, then stopping while the Six Nations was going on, meaning there was no Premiership rugby for two months.

Fans of any sport need clarity, but as it stands, rugby fans don't know if they're coming or going. What competition is on this week? What channel is it on? How much will I have to pay for it? As any keen reader of books will know, if a narrative isn't clear, people will give up trying to follow it, which is exactly what's happening with rugby.

There are some really good people working in the game, but they're usually beavering away in corner offices, far from where the big decisions are made. And effecting change is glacial, because there are too many competing opinions. The upshot, at least at the moment, is death by paralysis.

The NFL has it right. The 2023 regular season started on 7 September, finished exactly four months later, with each of the 32 teams playing only 17 games. After that, the four rounds of play-offs, including the Super Bowl, were condensed into a month. It was as easy as A, B, C for fans to follow. They knew what channels it would be on and when, they knew all the best players would be on display, and it was a top-quality product from beginning to end. But here's the real killer, as far as rugby is concerned: despite a smaller global audience and far fewer games (Tins has all the stats), the NFL generates far more money than rugby could ever dream of making. One thing's for sure, you won't see the Kansas City Chiefs in any financial peril any time soon.

Like American football, rugby needs fewer professionals, centrally contracted, playing fewer, bigger games; it needs those players and games to be marketed far better; and it needs to try harder to reach kids from less privileged backgrounds.

Rugby is far more ethnically diverse than it was 20 years ago. The England squad that won the 2003 World Cup contained one black player, Jason Robinson, and he'd come over from rugby league. But now there are plenty of ethnic minority players in and around the England set-up, which reflects wider society as well as rugby, and while the majority of England's 2023 World Cup squad attended selective schools (some of them lads from working-class backgrounds who won scholarships), quite a few didn't, including Joe Marler, Ellis Genge and Manu Tuilagi.

There's no doubt that the opportunities for kids to play rugby in state schools are far fewer than if they attended a public or grammar school, and that's largely down to the nature of the game. Whereas with football you just need some open space, two sets of goalposts (or jumpers), some cones and a few balls, coaching rugby is a far more complicated proposition. Coaches really need to know what they're doing, not least because rugby presents more risks, and you need kids of all shapes and sizes to form a team. If you're dealing with kids who have no real concept of rugby, that's likely to be a very difficult task.

Producing quality rugby players requires a very specialised environment, and you can't really have a go at public schools for providing that environment. There are lots of other ways for people to engage with the game, whether it's tag rugby, touch rugby, even walking rugby, which I'll probably be playing soon, but public schools will continue to be at the top of the spear because they have the money, the resources and the coaches.

Ideally, more kids would be learning how to play the game at clubs, but we lost a staggering number during and after Covid. That means from mini-rugby to adult rugby, we've shed thousands of players at grassroots level in recent years, and that was a trend that started before Covid. Nevertheless, when I take my son to play at Richmond every Sunday, they have a phenomenal set-up. And when they played in a cup competition against Battersea Ironsides, where Kyle Sinckler learned his rugby, there must have been 700 kids there. Maybe that's where grassroots rugby is heading – fewer clubs overall but the surviving clubs becoming bigger and bigger entities.

Part of the reason for fewer players is societal change. Trying to get 30-odd people together for a game of rugby is no simple task because there is so much else going on in people's lives, especially at weekends, even more especially if you have a family. People don't want to be training a couple of times a week; they can't spend a whole day on the weekend travelling to a game, playing it, having a few beers in the clubhouse afterwards, and travelling home again; they don't want to risk getting injured and being off work for weeks.

A couple of years back, Tins threw his weight behind the RFU's Back in the Game campaign, which emphasised the social benefits of playing rugby. At the time, Tins was still turning out occasionally for his local team Minchinhampton RFC, which is at the heart of the community. That ability to bring people together is what rugby has (or can have) over most other sports.

I've watched my boy go on a journey from mini-rugby, which he really didn't like, to contact rugby, which he absolutely loves. I'm not a pushy parent by any means, but I kept taking him back, gently persuading him that one day he'd start enjoying it, and eventually the wind picked up in his sails and he started tearing around the field with gusto.

There is a lot of scaremongering around rugby at the moment, regarding the physical toll it can take, and that is no doubt dissuading some parents from introducing their children to the game. But in general, rugby will give anyone who plays it far more than it will ever take away, and there is no more inclusive game in terms of the kinds of children who can play it. Yes, every team needs a glamour boy or girl who can run the 100 metres in double-quick time and score tries for fun, but it also needs big grunters up front who can win the ball in the first place, as well as smaller, quicker-witted kids who can link everything together.

Rugby has increased my son's confidence, made him more sociable, and provided him with friendships that will endure for the rest of his life. And while he might not even realise it, rugby is teaching him a lot about life and how it works. He is certainly now aware that when you get knocked down, you can still get up again and win. And while he hasn't reached the 'let's knock seven bells out of each other and all have a pint in the clubhouse afterwards' stage of his rugby career, he knows that when the final whistle goes, the right thing to do is shake hands with the opposition and clap them off the pitch.

I wish that broadcasters did more to make the game more appealing to youngsters. While my boy loves playing the game, he's not particularly enamoured of how it's presented on TV. Watch coverage of Six Nations games on the BBC and it's almost exactly the same as it was 25 years ago. There might be female presenters, pundits and pitch-side reporters, but the format remains very traditional.

I can't see why broadcasters can't tailor their coverage to different demographics, because the TikTok generation that my son is part of consumes media in a very different way to us oldies. We can grumble about the short attention spans of kids all we like, but it's not going to change. If they want rugby to be presented by Ant & Dec, or even a couple of glove puppets, so be it.

I've started playing touch rugby again, on Wednesday evenings down in Richmond, and it's one of the highlights of my week. I have a proper runaround with good friends and a few people I don't know, we have a couple of pints and a good chat in the clubhouse afterwards, and it's all great fun.

Rugby clubs, in all their forms, are sanctuaries for a lot of people, and I find taking my boy to rugby on a Sunday morning and playing midweek touch quite life-affirming. Rugby clubs are like ecosystems, in that they need the interaction of lots of good people to survive. That's a nice thing to be part of, certainly preferable to sitting at home watching TV or shopping in B&Q.

Having said all that, for rugby at the elite level to survive, there needs to be a complete separation between the amateur and professional games, which may well happen organically.

Hask and I recently worked on the Continental Tyres Schools Cup Final at Twickenham, between Harrow and Kirkham Grammar School, and the standard of rugby was out of this world. You could tell that these kids were professional athletes in all but name, training five times a week, besides regular gym sessions, and I wasn't surprised to hear that three of the lads picked up pro contracts a few weeks later. And it made me think that perhaps rugby is moving towards the NFL model, with fewer people playing it to a higher standard. If you show promise as a youngster, you'll be snapped up by a school that takes the sport very seriously (as is the case with high school sports in America), before joining an academy (the equivalent of university sports in America) and then a professional club. I'm not saying I'd like to see that happen, because I'm not sure where it would leave the grassroots game and smaller pro outfits, but it's certainly a possible scenario.

Of course, rugby would be on the minds of far more people in England if the national team was consistently successful, which it hasn't been since the 2003 World Cup. And that goes back to what I said at the beginning of this rant, about the game being led by people all pulling in different directions.

Because the New Zealand and Ireland rugby unions contract players, they can tell them when they can and can't play, how long they can play for and what position they can play in. If a player is looking a bit frazzled or carrying a knock, they can tell their club to give them a rest for a couple of weeks. If a player doesn't look fit, they can put them on a conditioning programme. And because the club sides are essentially seen as feeders to the national team, the national teams tend to be very cohesive units. Meanwhile, the England head coach is picking from 10 clubs, all of whom play the game a different way. I don't know if these hybrid contracts they're cooking up will make a big difference or not, but I assume they will make it harder for a head coach to chop and change personnel, which might lead to greater cohesion.

If I've made the state of rugby sound quite depressing, I think the comeback might be on. As I said at the beginning, the product is as good as it's ever been, at least in Europe and at international level. The Premiership is a better competition with 10 teams, even though they got there by accident. Some of the play over the last couple of seasons has been sensational, particularly by Harlequins. France's Top 14 illustrates that club rugby in Europe can be profitable, if marketed correctly. Every time Toulouse play there are 20,000 fans in the stadium and it's the cream of the crop, including some of England's best talent, performing in a Test match atmosphere.

Steve Borthwick's England are starting to play some expansive, exciting rugby, the sort of stuff the more casual fan can get on board with. I'm excited about the men's World Cup in the United States in 2031, that will be an amazing spectacle, and the women's World Cup in England in 2025 will take a fast-expanding game to a whole new level. Progress is being made on many fronts and I'm optimistic that the game will get to where it should be. It's more of a long, slow march than a blitzkrieg, but it's better than standing still.

JH: I know Tins calls Payno 'the catastrophiser', but he's right about the state of rugby – it is not in a good way. We've seen London Irish, Worcester and my old club Wasps go into administration in the last couple of years, while Melbourne Rebels were wound up at the end of the 2024 Super Rugby season. Meanwhile, there's a big governance row going on in New Zealand, while South African rugby doesn't seem to know whether it belongs in the southern or northern hemisphere.

A firm recently did a study on all the professional clubs in the world and they discovered that only seven of them were profitable, which is just absurd. The women's game is growing, but the men's game seems to be stagnant. Fans, or potential fans, can't find it on TV, either because it's on some subscription channel they've never heard of, or it's so badly marketed. And when they watch it, they don't have a clue what's going on because it's so complicated.

Rugby has never really stopped being an amateur sport at heart, even though it went professional almost 30 years ago. Part of me loves the grassroots mentality that pervades the sport – its community vibe, the fact it cherishes its values and traditions – but that kind of stuff can hold a sport back in what is supposed to be a professional environment. Elite sport is meant to be a business, and business is meant to be about making money. And to make money, the product has to remain at the cutting edge of society.

The English Premiership is basically lots of different self-interested entities all pulling in different directions, with no one in overall charge. Players are being told they can't ply their trade abroad if they want to be picked for England, but why would they want to play for an English club when they could get paid a lot more playing for a French one? Rugby players have short careers, and they play a game that wrecks their bodies – I've had spinal surgery, my back is fucked, I limp everywhere from arthritis in my ankle – so I'm all for them making as much money as possible before retiring. And if the England team is weaker as a result of the policy, it can't be a good thing.

Too many people making decisions in rugby have never played the game, which is why it's run so badly. Even people who did play the game morph into unimaginative, uninspiring, spineless politicians once they enter the world of administration. They're on a good wicket, staying in nice hotels, eating nice meals and drinking nice wine. Why would they change things?

I'm a fan of the old sitcom *Yes Minister*, and that's exactly what the world of sports administration is like. Every governing body has a Jim Hacker, someone who once had genuine dreams of making sweeping changes but has grown jaded over time. They become jaded because they come up against colleagues in the mould of Sir Humphrey Appleby, whose primary job was to thwart any change. Over time, the Hacker character becomes cynical and self-interested, mainly about clinging on to power rather than making a difference.

Almost nothing any rugby administrator has done in the last 10 years has made the game better. I honestly couldn't tell you what any of them do. When they do make a decision, it takes ages. People have been talking about changing contact rules in training for the best part of a decade and nothing has been done. People said the new eligibility rules, which World Rugby introduced in 2022 and allowed players to switch allegiance after a stand-down period of three years, were revolutionary, but they weren't revolutionary at all because it took them God knows how long to get them over the line. Their fear that it was going to ruin the game was disproved very quickly so all the panic was for no reason, and it will be the same if they let foreign players live abroad and play. The only thing that I think they did well was not letting transgender persons play women's rugby; it would have been insane to let that through. Luckily, they didn't.

I've asked World Rugby chairman Bill Beaumont to come on the podcast but he'd never do it. My opening question would be: 'So, Bill, what do you actually do, apart from collect honours from the monarch?' John Jeffrey, the guy who's tipped to take over from Bill, certainly won't be coming on either, not after the hammering he took from Tins in Hong Kong.

If I was put in charge (highly unlikely, I know), the season would be significantly shorter; there would be one entity in charge of all professional rugby; I'd get rid of all the irrelevant tournaments that nobody really wants to play in; I'd introduce a universal calendar and make rugby a summer sport in the southern hemisphere; I'd introduce a franchise model, like in American sports, and stick all those franchises in one world league that only lasted a few months; if they didn't let me do that, I'd make sure the Premiership served the England team better, because there's nothing like success on the international stage to drive interest. I'd let players play wherever they wanted to, without it affecting their eligibility for international rugby (as it stands, that rule is tantamount to restriction of trade); I'd make sure that all international teams had equal voting rights and that the smaller teams got the chance to play the biggest teams regularly (World Rugby is constantly banging on about wanting to expand the game, but we see the same old fixtures year after year); I'd ban almost all contact in training; any player who got concussed would be rested for a minimum of three weeks, no exceptions; the game would be marketed properly, so that people knew when and where big games were happening and who the best players were.

A good example of how bad rugby is at promoting itself is the Netflix documentary series *Full Contact*, which follows teams through the 2023 Six Nations. Netflix had already released the Formula 1 series *Drive to Survive*, which was massively successful, the golf series *Full Swing*, and the tennis series *Break Point*, but I have it on good authority that various rugby characters weren't really on board with *Full Contact*, and it showed. I only watched a couple of episodes and they didn't really show you anything compelling. Clearly the coaches didn't want cameras around and there was none of the intensity, the emotion, the rivalry, the drama, or the authenticity that *Drive to Survive* had in spades. It wasn't rugby as it really is, it was a sanitised version of the sport.

Perhaps F1 bosses were happy to let the cameras in because they knew it was such a well-run, successful sport. On the flip side, maybe the people in charge of rugby were reluctant to fling open the curtains because they didn't want the public to see what a shitshow it is, full of people talking nonsense and trying to justify their jobs.

If you want to create superstar players, people who are household names, you've got to give them a chance to be themselves and facilitate exposure. The fact that clubs are so reluctant to do so tells me that they don't understand marketing and have no confidence in their product. Rugby really needs to look at what other sports are doing – especially American sports – and try to emulate them, but that won't happen unless they bring marketing experts into the fold, people prepared to take chances, people with vision.

On top of everything else, rugby union has a major identity crisis. In trying to be all things to all people, it's lost sight of what made it great in the first place. Rugby is a violent, aggressive sport played by big, powerful men and women. I realise that rugby has to do whatever it can to make the game safer, in light of the hundreds of players currently suing the game over brain injuries, but while people love to see great footwork and silky handling skills, they'll never stop wanting to see huge collisions.

The people in charge need to stop freaking out and trying to turn rugby into a collision avoidance sport. The real problem isn't rugby, the real problem is that players aren't being looked after. Those in charge need to make sure players don't play as many games and have a decent off-season; they need to make sure players take plenty of time off if they get a whack on the head; they need to tell teams to reduce contact in training or remove it from training altogether; they need to tell clubs to employ proper neurologists. At the same time, they should just be up front and admit it's a bloody dangerous sport.

As it is, all these new tackle height tweaks, which mean players keep being sent off for getting things ever so slightly wrong, are just making the product worse. So many big games have been ruined because a tackler made an error of judgement and got sent off; so many people are losing interest in the game because of this obsession with high tackles; and so many people have told me they'd rather watch rugby league nowadays, because while they've tried to make the game safer, they understand that big collisions are an integral part of the game and defenders will sometimes get things wrong.

I was recently invited onto Jeremy Vine's Radio 2 show to debate an academic who had concluded that rugby was a form of child abuse and that it should be banned for under-18s. I was already irritated that this guy was resorting to hyperbole to get his point across – you can say rugby is dangerous without equating it to child abuse – and then he said that anything that caused the brain to move was problematic, which I couldn't understand at all.

Long-jumping and pole-vaulting will cause your brain to move, playing tennis or squash will cause your brain to move, but this guy was fixated on rugby and didn't seem to have anything to say about riding motorbikes or BMXs or horses, let alone boxing or MMA. I sort of pissed on his parade when I pointed out that he was saying that basically any sport could cause you a brain injury, so had he looked into the others? Which he admitted he hadn't. It was bizarre, yet typical of the panic running through rugby at the moment. It's part of a wider movement of safety-ism in society that I find quite worrying. I completely understand why people want to make all sports, including rugby, as safe as possible, but these campaigns often veer into scaremongering. People should be allowed to do whatever they want with their bodies, within reason, and I'm concerned that by trying to make certain sports safer, they'll end up killing them altogether.

The NFL has continued to embrace the violence despite all the brain injury lawsuits it's been hit with. If a player gets hit from multiple different directions, they'll show it from multiple different angles. Unlike rugby, the NFL isn't worried about what Little Timmy's mum thinks, because it understands that Little Timmy is highly unlikely to play American football. But who cares if Little Timmy doesn't end up playing rugby either? As long as people are told the truth – that it's a violent, aggressive, dangerous collision sport that can cause serious injuries – they can make an informed decision.

I should clarify that I still think rugby is a great game and the on-field product is often excellent. There's a lot of exciting talent around (including France's Antoine Dupont, who's a genuine all-time great), there are some great teams at club and international level, there are lots of exciting match-ups (including some bona fide classics during the 2023 World Cup), and there are plenty of people out there who are fanatical about the game. But the game is constantly being let down by the donkeys who run things.

You can be the best sport in the world on paper, but if hardly anyone's watching it, what's the point? And if the people who are watching don't have a clue what's going on, in terms of all the ever-changing laws, a fair few of them are going to stop watching eventually. The structure of the game needs to be completely rebuilt, and I don't think World Rugby or the RFU or Premiership Rugby or the EPCR have the ability or even the inclination to do so.

Even those interested enough to go to games often get a terrible matchday experience. A decent ticket to watch England play at Twickenham during the 2024 Six Nations cost well over £100. If someone wants to take a couple of kids along and have a couple of piss poor pints of Guinness and some food in the stadium, you're looking at a small fortune. On top of that, getting to and from Twickenham is a nightmare, as is trying to find a pub, taxi or just about anything else after the game. But prices are only going to rise, because the money generated by England home games props up the whole edifice, from the grassroots game through to the men's and women's England teams.

I was sad about the demise of my old team Wasps, but not as sad as you might think. I was obviously gutted for the players and rugby staff who lost their jobs, but that club treated me pretty badly at times. I had so many run-ins with the bosses and every new contract I signed involved an offer of a pay cut. And I got to see exactly how not to run a club. Years ago, I told my old teammate Lawrence Dallaglio, who was on the board of directors, exactly how things were going to end at Wasps. I could see it coming a mile off, but they managed to fuck it up anyway by trying to be greedy and set up a bond, which ultimately brought them down.

**MT:** The product itself is in great shape. Whether it's the Premiership, the URC, the Top 14, or European competitions, teams are playing the game to an exceptional level, especially in the latter stages of those competitions. International rugby is also in pretty good shape, as the quarter-finals of the 2023 World Cup demonstrated.

It's the people who are running rugby who are letting it down. There are too many governing bodies and too many people content with taking their little cut from the game, while players aren't making enough, clubs are losing money and fans are suffering. They've got the structure all wrong, the commercial side all wrong, the fan experience all wrong. They're terrible at marketing the best players, they're terrible at attracting money.

Most countries' unions are losing money hand over fist, as are an awful lot of clubs all over the globe. France's Top 14 recently struck a 140 million euros a season broadcasting deal, but that was very much an anomaly. The Premiership's most recent TV deal was nowhere near that and worse than the previous one, and there is still no TV deal for the Champions Cup. One of the problems is that they keep going to the same sponsors, who know the game inside-out and exactly how much they need to pay. And they're not going to pay a penny more than that because they understand no one is in the queue to replace them.

Changes need to be made, and they can't just be small changes, they need to be revolutionary, so that a whole new audience is generated.

I think we need to create a club league that is on a par with international rugby. It would be the cream of the crop in terms of players, the best pitted against the best every week, and you'd commercialise the hell out of it, like they do with cricket's Indian Premier League. The players would get paid a lot more to play a lot less, which in turn would enable them to play at full tilt every time they stepped onto a field while suffering fewer injuries. On top of that, the money generated would filter down to the grassroots game.

Rugby union is possibly too reliant on the international game. Look at US sports like American football, basketball and baseball, and Aussie sports like Australian Rules and rugby league – they either don't have international teams at all or they don't play as many internationals. They still have a World Cup but it is dominated by three or four teams. Instead, most fans are invested in their local team, whereas club sides in union really struggle to attract fans.

Hardly anyone gives a shit about rugby union in Australia – the Waratahs don't attract many more than 10,000 fans to home games at Sydney's Allianz Stadium and it can hold 42,000. In South Africa, supposedly a rugby hotbed, its teams pull in poor crowds for URC games (in October 2023, 6,000 people watched the Lions play fellow South African side the Stormers at the famous Ellis Park Stadium in Johannesburg, which has a capacity of 63,000, while barely 3,000 people turned up to watch the Bulls play Llanelli's Scarlets at Loftus Versfeld Stadium in Pretoria, which can hold 52,000). It's well-known that South African sponsors convince people not to attend games because they'll get a better experience watching on TV, but that kind of attitude has to change. You should only be watching on TV because you can't get a ticket.

I'd structure the season like the NFL, so that you had three or four months of high explosive action and then it disappeared, apart from international rugby. The temptation to make the NFL season longer must be huge, given the money involved, but the bosses understand that less is more. People are still talking about the NFL in those eight months when the games aren't happening, and the shortness of the season means that every stadium is full to the rafters for every game and almost all the best players are available.

Even though rugby has a global audience of 800 million, it generates between £2–3 billion annually. Meanwhile, the NFL has a global audience of 400 million and generates an estimated $167 billion (TV deals, sponsorship, advertising, ticket sales, streaming and gambling, merchandise). Has World Rugby ever approached anyone from the NFL and asked for advice on how to run the game? Has the RFU? Has anyone? If they have, they didn't take any notice.

I sometimes watch Women's Six Nations games and the atmosphere is completely different to the men's game and closer to the NFL experience. I saw France play England in Bordeaux and there were loads and loads of kids, there was lots of chanting and singing, there was a carnival right outside, and I thought, 'The men's game could learn a lot from this.'

The men's game is a commercial juggernaut for the RFU but you're getting the commercial side of things all wrong if you're charging £200 for a ticket. It doesn't matter if you only charge kids £30, they have to go with adults, and a family of four might end up paying as much as £800, including travel, food and drinks. That's an absurd amount of money to watch a game of rugby and rules out huge swathes of society.

If you're paying that much money, you want the game to be entertaining. But we do have to accept that some games of rugby simply aren't going to be like that. The way rugby union was designed, every facet of it is a contest: the set piece is a contest, the breakdown is a contest, the high ball is a contest. Whereas in rugby league you get to keep the ball for six tackles, unless you drop it, in rugby union the ball can get taken away from you at any moment. That means there are lots of different ways of playing the game – kick it all the time, rely on your physicality and keep it tight, play it fast and loose with lots of running and offloading. Look at South Africa – the most successful rugby nation, but can be boring to watch. Saying that, they know their DNA and it gets the job done, so who can blame them.

Payno is always saying that we should bring the two rugby codes back together, but that would never work. For a start, rugby league is massive in Australia, so why would they want to make changes? And you'd just end up with two entities arguing with each other about what the game should look like, which is exactly what we're trying to get away from.

Most of all, I wish the game's bosses would stop apologising for the game being what it is. It's a fast, physical, dangerous game, but they're constantly trying to sanitise it to make it more palatable. Yes, we've got to do everything we can to protect players – less contact in training, better treatment, including guaranteed healthcare for players once they've hung up their boots, all the other stuff that Hask has already mentioned.

For lads of my era, including many of those who are involved in the brain injuries lawsuit against rugby's governing bodies, the biggest problem was training, not matches. I'd make more tackles in a Tuesday session than I'd ever make in a game, and I'd be tackling or getting tackled by massive props, locks and back-rows. I'd sometimes think, 'This hardly ever happens in a game, I usually just have collisions with other backs'. Meanwhile, the amount of training collisions in NFL has been drastically reduced over the last two decades or so.

But while training is certainly an area that needs to be looked at, there should be an acceptance that games are going to be brutal affairs. The game's lawmakers shouldn't be ashamed of the game's physicality, they should embrace and celebrate it, like they do in the NFL. As it is, by pandering to people who *are* worried about the game's physicality, they risk watering it down and even ruining it completely, just as boxing would be ruined if you made the gloves bigger and banned head shots. Can you imagine Eddie Hearn apologising for a ding-dong battle on one of his shows? Of course not, because he understands that's exactly what the fans want to see.

Ireland versus South Africa in the 2023 World Cup was savage – and everyone absolutely loved it exactly for that reason. It was nasty, two teams of warriors standing toe-to-toe. That's why we call them 'Test' matches, because they're supposed to test a player's mind and body to the absolute limit.

I'm not against making tweaks to the game at grassroots level, and it's good that some of those dark arts, like whacking people off the ball and eye gouging, have almost been eradicated from professional rugby (it used to be almost impossible to get sent off unless you tried to murder somebody). But professional rugby should still look like a battle. Instead, players are being sent off for getting things slightly wrong, and in some cases not even doing any harm, and big games are being ruined as contests and spectacles as a result.

When I collared John Jeffrey (who is widely reported to be taking over World Rugby from Bill Beaumount), I questioned his qualifications to run World Rugby, but he didn't really say anything. John is a great man and a great former player, but has never experienced the professional game and what the players go through now. Most of the actions getting banned from the sport are exactly what John prided himself on as a player. Also, when John takes over from Bill Beaumont, it is reported that Bill will probably head back to the RFU – not sure how that is progression for the RFU. I don't want to diminish their achievements in the game, but they both retired long before the advent of professional rugby, which means they can't possibly understand it properly.

If I ever spoke to him, I'd tell him exactly what I thought, namely that the RFU aren't fit to run the game. I wanted Agustín Pichot to be chairman of World Rugby, but Bill was voted in ahead of him in 2020. I didn't agree with everything Pichot wanted to do, but at least he wanted to shake things up. World Rugby and the RFU are stuck in this 'you can't change that' loop, and I'm constantly saying, 'Why the fuck not?!' If you want more people investing in the sport, you have to be radical. You have to be willing to shrug off the investors you already have and find money from people who can imagine a bigger and better version of the game; proper businesspeople who can attract multi-national blue-chip sponsors.

Rugby's bosses seem most afraid of alienating the purists, but there aren't many purists in any sport. When Barry Hearn took over darts, people told him he was ruining it with all the razzmatazz. But Hearn understood that while the razzmatazz would piss a few people off, it would attract many more new fans. Look at darts now: it's one of sport's biggest success stories, the players perform in packed venues everywhere they go, some of them are household names, and they make very good money because it's so well run. Modern darts isn't everybody's cup of tea, but who cares?

I love Gloucester's Kingsholm Stadium, but if I had a blank sheet and a budget there is loads that I would want to do. It is hard with historic clubs, because there are so many traditions that the old guard love, but you also need to reach the younger fan who is not as integrated in the club. If you stuck a DJ in the Shed, that's not necessarily going to work. The Shed love a tug-of-war and a brass band! But if you want to attract more sponsors then the razzmatazz sells far better and makes it something special to bring clients to, and so on. I think outside of the ground is the biggest thing that could change; I would love to have Kingsholm Road to close down every home game to create fan zones and also use the car park to make what's going on outside of the ground just as fun as the event in itself. This is where people could watch on a big screen while interacting with sponsor activations, skill zones, etc. These are just a few ideas but you could go after mums and dads who aren't rugby fanatics but might take their kids along to a game if there are other things on offer.

Some readers might be thinking, 'But football doesn't really have much razzmatazz on game days,' which is true, but there is so much more going on on the whole. Transfers and deadline day, fantasy league teams, superstar recognition of individual players, TV hype, etc. Football is a truly global game, attractive to everyone from any background. It's a way of life and also a way out of your current situation if you work hard and dedicate yourself. Football is such a behemoth and there is so much demand to see the product that it doesn't need to change. What rugby already has, which football doesn't, is a tradition of tailgate parties and integrated seating for fans so you can have a beer in your seats as well as outside the stadiums, which is very similar to American football.

There is a history of picnics out of car boots at Twickenham's West Car Park, with the adults having a drink and the kids chucking balls about. That's the kind of tradition that can be built on to attract those fancy fans. This is done at Twickenham, but you can't use it unless you have a ticket, which I think could change to engage fans that can't get or afford one.

# 21

# THE FUTURE

**JH:** I'm always wary when people try to explain how they achieved success, especially when they make out they had some kind of grand plan to begin with.

It happens a lot with American sports coaches. They'll win a few championships and go on to write books about how they did it, when the truth is often that they were able to draft a couple of outstanding players who made the team great. I only mention this because when we were setting up our podcast, it was never meant to be anything other than me getting paid a regular wage and a bit of fun, while setting me up for other things when I retired from rugby. Things just happened over the next six years, nobody designed anything. And the secret of its success isn't a secret at all: we're unashamedly ourselves, we're not scared to say what we think, we talk common sense, we get great things from our guests without fucking them over.

Let's face it, we'd never have got the podcast off the ground nowadays because we're three white, middle-aged, middle-class blokes (well, I'm not quite middle-aged, but the other two are). But back in 2018, I didn't give our supposed lack of diversity a single thought, maybe because rugby isn't the most diverse game anyway. All I was concerned about was being authentically us and the fact that we dovetailed neatly. Payno was in the driving seat, Tins was in the passenger seat, mostly being fun but occasionally turning into a bit of a rugby nause, and I was in the backseat playing up on every journey.

We laughed a lot, which is usually a good gauge of how well something is going; we were able to do it while drinking Guinness; it was well produced; and the figures showed that people liked it. Our listenership was massive compared to other sports podcasts, not just rugby ones, which made it feel even more worthwhile, as did the early live shows we did in pubs and Flat Iron Square in London, which were always busy. But mostly we just turned up every week and had fun, without thinking about why it had become successful.

I don't remember ever looking at the briefing documents, Tins and I would turn up on a Monday and all the stories would just come tumbling out. And over time, the focus switched from rugby to personalities and fun.

I suppose we had all bases covered without even knowing at the beginning. Tins had been out of the game for a few years before the podcast started but was a World Cup winner who had played with lots of guys from the amateur era. Being six years younger than Tins, I played in a slightly different era and was still playing when the podcast got underway, which meant I knew pretty much everyone in the England set-up, including the head coach. Plus, I'd played for the Lions and in leagues all over the world (apart from the Celtic league, because it always fucking rains). Payno had covered pretty much every game that Tins and I had played and was just a brilliant broadcaster. But more than any of that, we were three intelligent men with lots of life experience outside of rugby, so we could take the podcast wherever we wanted to. Whatever we offered an opinion on, they were informed opinions.

From a personal point of view, I enjoyed having some semblance of control. I'd been in a teacher-pupil relationship with rugby my whole life and had controlling parents (which was a good and a bad thing), but now I was free to say whatever I wanted. However, I'm not Katie Hopkins, spouting controversial shit just to get attention, I mean what I say, which is why I get irritated when I see someone from the production team sighing or shaking their head. Just the other day, I had it out with our producer because I could see him rolling his eyes and looking freaked out. I said to him, 'Just because you don't think like I think, that doesn't mean I'm not allowed to say it or that I'm wrong.' I wouldn't shout what I said from the rooftops, not because I don't believe it, but because feelings are more important than facts and you can't say what you think anymore, or you can but you just have to stay away from the isms. When I say stuff in the show, I say it to drive the conversation, even if I expect it to be edited out. I don't like people making me feel mental, when I know they feel the same way as me but they just don't say it.

It's reached the stage where we have non-rugby people trying to get on, usually when they have something to promote. But if they don't have much connection to rugby, we don't invite them on. However, while we'll carry on with *The Good, The Bad & The Rugby* in its pure, rugby form, the three of us will spin off in other directions. That's inevitable, because our audience is just as much about the chemistry as it is about the rugby, and my connection to the game is growing more and more tenuous.

Even now, I sometimes feel that I don't know enough about the current game to be giving an opinion on it. I still know enough people playing the game to feel connected to it, guys like Ellis Genge and Jonny May, but the current England squad doesn't contain many people I played with, and most of those I did play with are on the verge of retirement. I'm almost 40 now, and some of the lads in the England set-up weren't even a glint in the milkman's eye when I made my debut for Wasps. And I never wanted to be one of those pundits still banging on about the game long after the players are young enough to be their children. Who wants to listen to three lads who know somebody who knows somebody who now plays rugby for England? Certainly not me, so I'd be a hypocrite if I carried on doing a rugby podcast for too long.

Another issue is the sheer number of podcasts on offer nowadays. I'm not saying we invented the podcast, like Jake Humphrey once did (next he'll be claiming his father invented the question mark), but the landscape was nowhere near as crowded when we started out. We're still leading the pack, but guests tend to do the rounds, which I get a bit funny about. I feel like saying to them, 'Mate, by going on that podcast, you've diluted ours, because you're going to be regurgitating stories.' Plus, while a few players have slipped through the net so far, we've talked to almost everybody it's worth talking to.

I'd love to get Antoine Dupont on – what a player he is – but he hasn't fancied it so far. Another top target is Ardie Savea because he's one of the few All Blacks who seem happy to reveal his true personality. I've watched him and his brother doing dances on TikTok, which is almost sacrilegious in the staid world of New Zealand rugby, the equivalent of an England player coming out as a drag queen. In fact, a few years ago Savea's doctor told him to stop dancing on TikTok in case it tired him out, which just about sums it up. Having a bit of fun doesn't fit in with the famous All Blacks 'no dickhead' rule, but I bet when most of his teammates are scratching around for coaching jobs after they hang their boots up while 'staying humble', Savea will be cleaning up in the media. His recent move from the Hurricanes to Moana Pasifika is testament to how he wants to do things differently and is his own man. I think it's an amazing move for all the reasons you could think.

I'd love to do a show that showcases our personalities and friendships, something like what *Top Gear* became, before morphing into *The Grand Tour*. *The Grand Tour* is still meant to be about cars, in the same way *The Good, The Bad & The Rugby* is still meant to be about rugby, but it's more about Jeremy Clarkson, James May and Richard Hammond and the fun they have together.

Whether we'd be allowed on mainstream/legacy media, or whatever you want to call it, is open to question. We've got the biggest rugby podcast in the world but none of us has worked in TV or radio for ages. Maybe we've moved so far beyond the city walls that we're seen as loose cannons, or our demographics just aren't right. Not that it bothers me. I wouldn't be able to joke about Bill Beaumont being given another fucking knighthood on TV; I wouldn't be able to say that I think rugby is a shambles run by out of touch old-school men, or that World Rugby has a lot of work to do to turn things around. In short, I wouldn't be able to be myself, which means I wouldn't be able to tell the truth.

I've always said that we cannot, under any circumstance, let commercial partners dictate the tone of the podcast. Having said that, there have been times when I've had to toe the line, and maybe it's best that we have some constraints on us. If we ever got to the point where we were sponsoring our own pod, maybe with our own Blackeye Gin, that could spell disaster. They'd have to brand us with one of those parental advisory stickers, like they did with 2 Live Crew albums in the 1990s. That being said, podcaster Joe Rogan is himself and he gets away with it, but Payno says there is only room in the world for one Joe Rogan. I think there is space for more perhaps, or at least one James Haskell-shaped Joe Rogan.

I honestly don't want to drive things off a cliff, like that Thelma and Louise scenario that Payno is always going on about, with me at the wheel and him and Tins in the back, but I also think it's bound to happen because of the censorious world we live in. But until that time, I'm going to carry on saying exactly what I want, because that's a big part of what makes the podcast a success. Strong views divide opinion and lead to a lot of abuse – 'This podcast would be great if James Haskell shut up and fucked off' – but better to divide opinions and piss some people off than to pootle along harmlessly in the middle lane being watched by hardly anyone.

**MT:** Payno and I have a running joke that while Zara and I go everywhere together, whenever I invite him somewhere, he never brings his wife Corks.

I recently invited Payno and his family to the Badminton Horse Trials, with the offer of staying at ours, and he said he'd pop along but leave everyone else at home. I understood it – his kids had loads of stuff on – but we're rarely able to make things work.

Zara and I have known Hask and Chloe for longer – Chloe and I were on the Channel 4 show *The Jump* in 2015 and got on great. She's basically a female version of Hask, which made for an interesting relationship. Hask doesn't moderate his behaviour for Zara – he acts the same around her as he does around everyone else. But that's the beauty of the man. What you see is what you get, he hides nothing from anyone.

I speak to Payno on the phone most days, just to see how things are going, and he speaks to Hask more than I do. He's almost an uncle figure for him, in that he'll often phone him up just to ask him how he is. I'm shit at that kind of stuff, which I suppose makes me quite old-fashioned. I'm not even great on the phone with my parents, let alone Hask, and he'd probably say the same. Like a lot of men, we phone friends only if we have a good reason to phone them, while Payno being a beta or even delta male, he actively cares about people. Luckily, Zara is amazing at that kind of stuff, so I don't have to be.

The podcast has been a rocky journey at times, but I wouldn't change a thing. Actually, I might make the court case shorter and cheaper, but it's those tough times that have made the podcast what it is by bringing us closer together.

We created a lot of issues for ourselves by setting things up in a slightly weird way. Our first production company thought we were relying on them far too much, while we resented them telling us what to do and trying to get Hask to apologise all the time. As far as we were concerned, it was *our* podcast and they were just producing it. But those early issues led to us having a better understanding of how to run a business to benefit us and got us to the amazing place we are at now. We bicker at times, and I might stab the table with a steak knife when Payno starts catastrophising, but mostly we can have honest conversations without getting too cross, and the podcast is flying.

I can't see us driving over a cliff edge any time soon, but we might have to start planning a different route. It's almost reached the point where I've never played with anyone in the England squad, and I've only played against three or four at club level. Some of the Saracens boys, like Elliot Daly and Ben Earl, visit us in the green room quite a bit, so they keep me connected with what's going on and make me feel slightly less old, but I'm acutely aware of how far the game has moved on since I last laced up the boots in 2014.

At some point, we're going to have to start fading into the background and putting new people who know more about the current game front and centre. But we're also discussing whether the podcast should evolve into something else completely or become just one strand of a bigger brand.

The three of us are already doing live shows, tours and adverts; we've launched a women's rugby podcast and an Australian version of *The Good, The Bad & The Rugby*; we hope to get a Kiwi and South African version off the ground soon; and we'd like to get an American version up and running well before the 2031 World Cup over there. The idea is for *The Good, The Bad & The Rugby* to own a big chunk of the rugby landscape, so that potential commercial partners wanting to break into the rugby market see us as the first point of contact.

It's becoming increasingly obvious that we need to find other things for Hask to do. He's still far more knowledgeable than most people about rugby, and very good at explaining what's gone on, but he's got to be comfortable doing it, and he often doesn't have time to watch any rugby. That can be a bit of a nightmare, because he'll just give stock answers or go quiet and look like he doesn't really want to be there. The audience notices that because it's such a contrast with the ranting, raving, laughing, joking, bombastic Hask that appears when we're speaking about something that tickles his fancy.

We need to find ways of re-energising him, which might mean him interviewing more non-rugby people on his own, or more rugby people about non-rugby stuff, like when he chatted to Joe Marler about mental health. That would be perfect for him because he is genuinely intrigued by people, loves finding out what makes them tick. It might also mean binning Hask off for Six Nations reviews and replacing him with Jonny May, Ben Kayser, Shane Horgan, Wales's Jonathan Davies or Scotland's Rory Lawson. That would allow Hask to freshen up and return with greater vigour. Whatever happens, it will certainly mean Payno and me having to diversify around Planet Hask.

**AP:** We have a husbands and wives WhatsApp group, and while that's less active than it used to be, for obvious reasons, we are all still very close.

I get accused of never bringing my wife to anything, although there is some truth to that. Tins is always trying to get the families together and wanted to organise a house for everyone at the 2023 World Cup in France, but that never happened for various reasons. But I don't have Corks hidden in the attic, it's just that my children are of an age that makes logistics a complete nightmare. Meanwhile, Hask is going to do his thing whatever – Planet Hask rolls on, whatever happens in his private life – while Tins has more hired help than any man on earth, so can zip off to Australia, for example, at the drop of a hat.

My wife and I have been to Zara and Tins' house in Cheltenham a few times, which is always great fun. But mostly it's Hask, Tins and me, usually drinking together on the go, whether it's in Hong Kong, Japan, France or a cruise ship moored in Ibiza. And I've loved (almost) every minute of it so far. My wife often says, 'I can't believe I haven't spent more time with them', but that's mainly down to the fact that we're three very busy people, always spinning off in different directions. Any time together as families has to be planned meticulously, but that just makes it more valuable when it comes off.

My kids know who Tins and Hask are and what they're famous for, but I think they've probably found out too much about them from listening to the podcast, which sometimes should get an 18 rating. They're both brilliant with my kids in person, and my son Harry is in absolute awe of Hask in particular. He's never met anyone as big and noisy as Hask, and Hask is probably better with kids than with people his own age. Meanwhile, I think both Hask and Tins have more of an affinity with Corks than with me, but I don't mind that.

We've been through a lot together since sparking up the podcast all those years ago. Hask has retired, been married, had a baby and separated. Tins has had his third child, lost a very famous grandma-in-law and continued to support a father with Parkinson's (a few years ago, Tins posted an emotional tribute to his dad on World Parkinson's Day and has raised a lot of money for Parkinson's charities). Covid was rough for all of us, workwise (my day job has also been hit by recession and war in recent years), and we went through hell and high water together with that ridiculous court case. But that's real life, and we're all quite stoic people really. We'd certainly never claim we were having a worse time than anyone else, but we do think sharing can help.

Our spin-off show, *The Lock-In*, is for our superfans who pay a few quid a month, and we never talk about rugby on that, it's all about our lives. And I sometimes think I like doing that show more than *The Good, The Bad & The Rugby* because it is just a case of picking up the mic and nattering. And the people who listen to that show probably notice the changes in us more.

I'm a different animal now. Having spent 20 years never feeling comfortable about my personality in a public space, I finally have my own identity. My wife tells me I've become much more of a performer, instead of the nodding dog I was at Sky, probably because I'm less worried about what people think about me. I'm my own man, rather than 'Sky Sports' Alex Payne'.

When you work for an organisation, especially one as big as Sky, you have to conform to what the team wants you to be. I couldn't have much of an ego because it was my job to get the best out of everyone around me. But even though Hask and Tins played a team sport, they had to be selfish, like any other professional sportsperson. The routine that was foisted on them and their dedication to their craft meant family and friends had to come second, and they couldn't be caring about what anyone else thought about that. And some of that insouciance has certainly rubbed off on me.

I really went through the depths before finding Tins and Hask and seeing the light. I suddenly realised that I hadn't had the dream job after all. Actually, towards the end of my time at Sky, my soul had been disappearing. That's why I tell my kids now, 'Everything happens for a reason.'

I wouldn't change a thing, and I'm very grateful for what Sky Sports gave me, but it's hugely satisfying to have built something that's mine. And my life is far richer, more dramatic and more fun since I started doing the podcast. I've interviewed members of the royal family, Hollywood stars, greats from other sports. The podcast has generated great friendships and people love it in a way that nobody really *loved* Sky Sports' rugby coverage. When I see messages from people saying they've been struggling mentally but they'd get some relief from listening to our podcast every week, which was particularly the case during Covid lockdowns, that means a huge amount to me.

Since going into business with Hask and Tins, I've become a tougher person, in that I'm not prepared to put up with the sort of nonsense I would have done before. Paradoxically, I've come to crave drama in my life. I'll often get up in the morning and think, 'Right, what am I dealing with today? Oh, God, what's happened now …' But I enjoy riding along in what I like to call the sidecar of doom, holding on for dear life, with Hask at the wheel.

In fact, we have an unwritten agreement that we're all in it together, no matter what, and that it's all going to end one day in very dramatic and spectacular fashion, like Thelma and Louise driving over the edge of a cliff. That's possibly part of the appeal of the podcast, in that you never know which show will be the last.

While it's true that Hask has become slightly more sensitive and sensible, he hasn't changed much. He is, and always will be, Planet Hask. He's a DJ, a public speaker, he writes books (or gets other people to write them for him), he's a fitness guru, he's a podcaster, and he's a dad. I sometimes wish he stopped to admire his work every now and again, and took Tins' advice to do less for more, but it's impossible not to admire his work ethic. When we were doing the live tour, we'd finish a show in Oxford at 11.30 p.m. and he'd drive straight to Cardiff for a DJ set that started at 2 a.m. I'd think, 'Why doesn't he want to go home? Why doesn't he want to sleep?' If anything, his life is faster than it's ever been, and he's getting even tougher. But if he ever was to slow down, people would think there was something horribly wrong with him.

As for Tins, I don't think he'll ever change much either. In fact, he's probably hardly changed since he was two or three. He's just a happy-go-lucky northerner, very loyal and very easy-going. Except when he's had a couple of bottles of wine and he turns into Annoyingly Honest Mike.

I'm aware that we're more successful than other rugby podcasts, but I'm not particularly bothered about the competition. The author and motivational speaker Simon Sinek tells a story about attending a Microsoft conference and an Apple conference within a few days of each other. The Microsoft conference was all about doing battle with Apple and how they were going to overtake them as the world's biggest tech company. An executive even gave Sinek one of their new smartphones and said it was going to blow the iPhone out of the water. When Sinek turned up to the Apple conference, he showed one of their execs this new Microsoft smartphone and told him what the Microsoft exec had said, and the Apple exec replied, 'I'm sure they think that.' That was it, end of conversation. Microsoft wasn't mentioned at the Apple conference. Instead, it was all about how Apple could be better, end of story. And just as there is a smartphone for everybody, there is a rugby podcast for everybody. If someone wants to watch a different one to ours, I completely understand.

We have no qualms about flexing our muscles occasionally, whether it's recording a podcast with members of the royal family or visiting the White House. Does that make us tall poppies, whose heads people would like to see lopped off? Of course. That's why we need to keep reinventing ourselves and finding ways to keep the audience and ourselves entertained, surprised and challenged (especially Hask, who has the attention span of a toddler and won't want to be talking about just rugby for the rest of his days).

If Annoyingly Honest Mike had been a permanent fixture, we'd have gone over that cliff edge years ago. As it is, we've got a lot of road left. Where it will lead us, who knows.

# ACKNOWLEDGEMENTS

Thank you from Alex, James and Mike.

To the team behind the team, who were there at the start, and who are with us today – sincere thanks for hanging in there when all around you is melting. Whether it's Hask ranting, Payno demanding edits at midnight or Mike never turning up, how you keep the boat afloat is incredible and never gets taken for granted. JP, Teeps, Josh, Rob, Noz, Shira, Cath, Jaz, Tilly, Tommy No Chat, One Puss, Vape Dragon, Xander, Ant, Alpha, Tacko (that went well …), Sadie, Olly, Ollie, Ali, Craig, Sam, Darragh and Producer Tom. Plus the others whose numbers we've now blocked.

To Nic, for your steady hand at the helm, day in day out, as our MD. You must wonder how your vast experience with agencies, brands and governing bodies could possibly be of any use when it comes to dealing with what we throw at you. The fact you smile through it all is greatly appreciated.

To all the brands who've backed us – wow, we'd love to have been in some of your internal meetings along the way: Royal births announced in Umbro jumpers, Domino's pizzas thrown from helicopters, kids in tears on Vodafone shoots (thanks, Hask), broken Honda bonnets, sinking cruise ships and the longest contract foreplay with Continental that man has ever known. We love you all, thank you for hanging in there. And being brave enough to let us do what we do.

To the regulars – Jonny, Ellis, Fox, Ben and Shaggy – you polish our turd with your deep understanding of the game. Thank you for bailing us out with your intelligence.

To Elma, Scaz and Mo and the *GSR* squad – thanks for bringing the class to counterbalance our farce.

To all the players, past and present, who've been on *GBR* – thank you for allowing us to tell your story. For some, we've saved you from yourselves, for others we've opened new doors, for others we've closed them forever. Rugby needs more of the good guys, and hopefully we've helped you where we can.

To Rick, Sherry and Sayward – for believing in, backing and persevering at times with all things *GBR*. It's never a dull ride, thankfully. Hopefully in years to come you'll smile about it. Rather than weeping quietly.

To Ben, Ajda and the team at HarperCollins – thank you for taking our collection of words and crafting a book. Feel free to reach out to our production team if you need a good reference for a therapist.

To various lawyers up and down the land – you're welcome. Enjoy your new speed boats.

To our listeners, viewers, social media followers, tour audiences and trolls – thank you too. If a tree falls in a forest, and no one is around to hear it – does it make any noise? Profound. We think we'd still chat away even if no one listened – but thankfully you do. Which makes it a lot more fun. So thank you to all who tune in, download, buy tickets, leave comments, like, share and subscribe. You've made the last five years more fun than we could ever have imagined, and we are truly grateful. Here's to the next chapter.

Finally, Producer Si, who launched this shambles in the first place. Fuck you, Si. X